Mastering Infrastructure as Code with AWS CloudFormation

A comprehensive guide to
AWS Cloud Automation and Orchestration

Anchal Gupta

www.bpbonline.com

First Edition 2025

Copyright © BPB Publications, India

ISBN: 978-93-65891-553

To View Complete
BPB Publications Catalogue
Scan the QR Code:

Dedicated to

My beloved parents
Shri Naval Kishor Gupta *and* **Smt Anjali Gupta**

My parents-in-law
Late Shri Bhagwan Goel *and* **Smt Kamla Goel**

My loving wife
Aakarshi

My precious daughter
Idhika

My adored sister and brother-in-law
Neeti *and* **Siddharth**

and

My cherished nephew
Avyukt

About the Author

Anchal Gupta is a seasoned expert in Cloud Solutioning and DevOps ecosystem design, with over 14 years of hands-on experience in the IT industry. Throughout his career, he has consistently delivered innovative and effective solutions to complex technological challenges, earning recognition for his forward-thinking approach and problem-solving skills.

Anchal's expertise spans a diverse range of technologies, including Cloud Architecture, DevOps, Kubernetes, Docker, Jenkins, CloudFormation, Terraform, Cloud Security, RedHat OpenShift, and Linux systems. His journey has seen him rise from a System Engineer to a Cloud Solution Leader, where he excels in modernizing cloud infrastructures, optimizing operations, and driving cost efficiency.

A passionate advocate for knowledge sharing, Anchal actively contributes to the tech community as a member of the AWS Community Builder program. He is also an accomplished writer and speaker, sharing insights on DevOps strategies and cloud best practices through blogs, technical talks, and various public forums. Based in Noida, India, Anchal holds a B.Tech degree from Bharati Vidyapeeth's College of Engineering, New Delhi, and is regarded as an invaluable resource in the fields of DevOps and Cloud Architecture.

About the Reviewers

❖ **Pradeep A. Atkari** is a skilled cloud professional with extensive experience in both AWS and Azure cloud platforms, supported by an AWS certification and hands-on expertise in cloud infrastructure. With over a decade of experience in the tech industry, Pradeep has developed and reviewed a range of software solutions, from small-scale applications to enterprise-level systems, and is recognized for his background in Object-Oriented Programming. Holding a degree in Information Technology, Pradeep is dedicated to making complex cloud and infrastructure concepts accessible, providing valuable insights that resonate with developers at all skill levels.

❖ **Varsha Verma** is a highly skilled Cloud Infrastructure Specialist with extensive experience in Infrastructure Management, Cloud Cost Optimization, Cloud Assessment, and Governance. She has developed deep expertise across a broad range of cloud technologies.

She holds multiple industry certifications in leading cloud platforms, including Azure, AWS, GCP, and ITIL. Varsha is committed to helping organizations maximize the value of their cloud investments. Her work focuses on optimizing cloud infrastructure and cost management to ensure clients achieve peak efficiency and effectiveness in their cloud environments.

Currently, Varsha is an integral member of the Infrastructure and Cloud Specialist team at Accenture Technologies, where she partners with clients to design and implement robust cloud strategies that drive transformative business outcomes.

Acknowledgement

I am deeply grateful to my parents for their unwavering belief in me, which has always been a source of strength. Their love, sacrifices, and constant encouragement have shaped my journey and given me the courage to pursue my dreams. From instilling strong values to supporting my aspirations, they have laid the foundation for every step I have taken. I owe much of who I am today to their endless support and guidance. You are my first teachers, my guiding stars, and the bedrock of all that I have achieved.

I also extend my sincere appreciation to my parents-in-law for their blessings and inspiration, which continue to guide me. I am deeply thankful for their presence in my life.

A heartfelt thank you to my wife, who has been a pillar of strength throughout this entire process. Her unwavering support, encouragement, and patience made the completion of this book possible. She has stood by my side during challenging moments, always believing in my potential, and her love has been my anchor through it all. I am forever grateful for her role, not just as a life partner but as a constant source of motivation.

To my dearest daughter, I hope this book becomes a beacon of inspiration for you. May it remind you to pursue your dreams with passion and determination. Your cheerful spirit has been a bright light throughout this endeavor. You are my greatest blessing, and my love for you knows no bounds. Always remember how precious you are to me.

I am also deeply grateful to my sister and brother-in-law for their steadfast support. Their positive spirit and encouragement have been a constant uplift, infusing this journey with added warmth and motivation. I am truly fortunate to have you both by my side.

To my nephew, whose boundless energy and laughter added joy along the way, thank you for reminding me to find delight in the little moments.

A special note of appreciation to BPB Publications for this opportunity to share my knowledge.

Lastly, I want to express my deepest gratitude to the readers. Your interest in this book and encouragement are the driving force behind its realization.

Preface

This book **Mastering Infrastructure as Code with AWS CloudFormation,** is designed to help you automate and streamline the provisioning and management of AWS resources. As cloud adoption grows, understanding infrastructure as code becomes essential, and CloudFormation offers a powerful way to manage infrastructure efficiently on Amazon Web Services cloud.

Through step-by-step guidance, hands-on exercises, and real-world examples, the book covers both the fundamentals and advanced techniques of AWS CloudFormation. Each chapter builds upon the previous one, offering insights and best practices for creating scalable, resilient cloud architectures. Whether you are a seasoned DevOps engineer, Cloud Architect, Developer, or an AWS enthusiast, this book will help you unlock the full potential of CloudFormation and transform your approach to cloud infrastructure.

The book is divided into four main sections: Foundations of AWS CloudFormation, Template Deep Dive, Stack Management and Continuous delivery and Best Practices. Each section builds upon the previous one, offering a step-by-step progression from basic concepts to advanced techniques, ensuring a comprehensive learning experience.

Here is a brief description of what each chapter covers:

Section I: Foundations of AWS CloudFormation

- **Chapter 1: Getting Started with AWS CloudFormation** - This chapter introduces AWS CloudFormation, explaining its purpose, benefits, and use cases. It covers the core components like templates, stack creation, validation, and rollback mechanisms. It also introduces YAML and JSON as data formats for templates, with examples to illustrate key concepts.

- **Chapter 2: CloudFormation Template Fundamentals** - This chapter dives into the basics of Infrastructure as Code and the anatomy of CloudFormation templates. It explains how to use IAM policies in CloudFormation and guides readers through creating and deploying their first template. Emphasis is placed on understanding the structural elements of templates.

Section II: Template Deep Dive

- **Chapter 3: Version, Description and Resources** - This chapter explains about essential components of a CloudFormation template, including specifying the template version, adding descriptions, and defining resources. The chapter explores resource properties, dependencies, updates, and deletion strategies, along with techniques to manage multi-resource templates efficiently.

- **Chapter 4: Parameters, Metadata, Mappings and Conditions** - This chapter explains how to use parameters to customize templates and metadata to provide additional information. It covers mapping data for dynamic configurations and using conditions to control resource deployment based on specific criteria, enabling flexible multi-environment deployments.

- **Chapter 5: Macros, Transform and Outputs** - This chapter introduces advanced template customization techniques, including the use of macros for dynamic processing and the Transform function for template pre-processing. It covers some pre-defined macros along with the AWS Serverless Application Model (SAM), which simplifies building serverless applications by extending CloudFormation with SAM-specific resources and syntax.

- **Chapter 6: Pseudo Parameters and Intrinsic Functions** - This chapter covers the use of intrinsic functions and pseudo parameters to add dynamic content to templates. It explains how these features can customize CloudFormation templates, making them more versatile for various deployment scenarios.

- **Chapter 7: Enhancing Amazon Web Services CloudFormation** - This chapter covers integrating AWS Secrets Manager for securely managing sensitive information within CloudFormation stacks. It discusses the use of creation policies, helper scripts, and wait conditions to enhance deployment processes. Additionally, the chapter explains EC2 bootstrapping techniques for customizing server configurations and explores various strategies to automate and optimize stack management.

- **Chapter 8: Advanced CloudFormation, Custom Deployment and VPC Endpoint** - This chapter explores advanced deployment techniques, including importing stack values, resolving circular dependencies, and using custom resources. It also provides a guide to deploying stacks via the AWS Command Line Interface (CLI) and setting up VPC endpoints for CloudFormation.

- **Chapter 9: Harnessing the Power of CloudFormation Designer** - The chapter introduces the CloudFormation Designer, a visual tool for designing and managing CloudFormation stacks. It covers the tool's features, such as visual modeling, importing/exporting templates, and best practices for efficient stack lifecycle management.

Section III: Stack Management

- **Chapter 10: Understanding Stacks and Management** - This chapter focuses on managing CloudFormation stacks, including key strategies, protecting stacks, and handling stack drift. It provides insights on rollback triggers, drift detection, and CloudFormation notifications to ensure stack integrity.

- **Chapter 11: Nested Stacks** - This chapter covers the use of nested stacks to modularize and organize resources within a CloudFormation environment, enabling hierarchical management and reusability of infrastructure components. It discusses managing parameters, outputs, and updates in nested stacks, as well as practical considerations for deletion. The chapter also compares nested stacks with cross-stack resource sharing, highlighting their respective benefits and use cases.

- **Chapter 12: Understanding StackSets and Change Sets** - This chapter introduces StackSets for managing stacks across multiple accounts and regions, including drift detection and parameter overrides. It also covers Change sets, allowing users to preview changes before applying them, ensuring safe updates to stacks.

Section IV: Continuous delivery and Best Practices

- **Chapter 13: CloudFormation Continuous delivery** - The chapter explains the principles of Continuous delivery and how to implement them with AWS CodePipeline. It provides a guide for setting up a CloudFormation deployment pipeline, including a use case deployment to demonstrate the steps.

- **Chapter 14: Best Practices and Sample Templates** - This final chapter provides a comprehensive overview of CloudFormation's best practices, disaster recovery strategies, and tested template samples for various use cases.

Code Bundle and Coloured Images

Please follow the link to download the
Code Bundle and the *Coloured Images* of the book:

https://rebrand.ly/8c0bbf

The code bundle for the book is also hosted on GitHub at
https://github.com/bpbpublications/Mastering-Infrastructure-as-Code-with-AWS-CloudFormation.
In case there's an update to the code, it will be updated on the existing GitHub repository.

We have code bundles from our rich catalogue of books and videos available at
https://github.com/bpbpublications. Check them out!

Errata

We take immense pride in our work at BPB Publications and follow best practices to ensure the accuracy of our content to provide with an indulging reading experience to our subscribers. Our readers are our mirrors, and we use their inputs to reflect and improve upon human errors, if any, that may have occurred during the publishing processes involved. To let us maintain the quality and help us reach out to any readers who might be having difficulties due to any unforeseen errors, please write to us at :

errata@bpbonline.com

Your support, suggestions and feedbacks are highly appreciated by the BPB Publications' Family.

Did you know that BPB offers eBook versions of every book published, with PDF and ePub files available? You can upgrade to the eBook version at www.bpbonline. com and as a print book customer, you are entitled to a discount on the eBook copy. Get in touch with us at :

business@bpbonline.com for more details.

At **www.bpbonline.com**, you can also read a collection of free technical articles, sign up for a range of free newsletters, and receive exclusive discounts and offers on BPB books and eBooks.

Piracy

If you come across any illegal copies of our works in any form on the internet, we would be grateful if you would provide us with the location address or website name. Please contact us at **business@bpbonline.com** with a link to the material.

If you are interested in becoming an author

If there is a topic that you have expertise in, and you are interested in either writing or contributing to a book, please visit **www.bpbonline.com**. We have worked with thousands of developers and tech professionals, just like you, to help them share their insights with the global tech community. You can make a general application, apply for a specific hot topic that we are recruiting an author for, or submit your own idea.

Reviews

Please leave a review. Once you have read and used this book, why not leave a review on the site that you purchased it from? Potential readers can then see and use your unbiased opinion to make purchase decisions. We at BPB can understand what you think about our products, and our authors can see your feedback on their book. Thank you!

For more information about BPB, please visit **www.bpbonline.com**.

Join our book's Discord space

Join the book's Discord Workspace for Latest updates, Offers, Tech happenings around the world, New Release and Sessions with the Authors:

https://discord.bpbonline.com

Table of Contents

Section I
Foundations of AWS CloudFormation

CHAPTER 1

Getting Started with AWS CloudFormation

Introduction

In today's rapidly evolving tech landscape, managing infrastructure efficiently has become more critical than ever. Whether you are building scalable applications or maintaining complex systems, the ability to automate and control infrastructure plays a crucial role in ensuring smooth operations. This is where **Amazon Web Services (AWS)** CloudFormation steps in—a service designed to help you define and provision your AWS resources effortlessly.

In this inaugural chapter, we begin by exploring the foundational concepts of AWS CloudFormation and why it is essential for anyone looking to automate and simplify their cloud infrastructure management. With CloudFormation, you can transform manual, time-consuming provisioning tasks into streamlined processes, allowing you to focus more on innovation and less on repetitive setup work.

We will walk through the CloudFormation template, which is the cornerstone of **infrastructure as code (IaC)** and explain how it enables you to describe and automate the creation of AWS resources in a consistent, reliable way. Throughout this journey, you will discover how CloudFormation's declarative approach, using YAML or JSON, not only simplifies infrastructure management but also opens the door to more efficient, repeatable deployments.

Structure

The chapter covers the following topics:

- Knowing CloudFormation template
- Use cases
- Workings of CloudFormation
- Introducing the YAML data format
- Introducing JSON data format

Objectives

By the time we conclude this chapter, you will have gained a comprehensive understanding of the fundamental concepts of the AWS CloudFormation service and templates. This knowledge will extend to recognizing the inherent advantages of utilizing these templates, emphasizing their capacity to save time and effort in constructing your AWS cloud infrastructure. Additionally, you will appreciate the pivotal role played by these templates in automating the provisioning of AWS resources and facilitating the seamless deployment of intricate architectures. A nuanced comprehension of various use cases and scenarios for implementing AWS CloudFormation will further enhance your proficiency. Finally, you will acquire an insight into declarative language models such as YAML and JSON, recognizing them as foundational elements for crafting CloudFormation templates. This chapter aims to provide you with a solid foundation, enabling you to harness the efficiency and flexibility offered by AWS CloudFormation.

Knowing CloudFormation template

Before diving into the intricacies of CloudFormation templates, let us begin by defining the key concepts of IaC and the AWS CloudFormation service. This foundation will set the stage for understanding how CloudFormation simplifies infrastructure management.

In the dynamic landscape of cloud computing, IaC revolutionizes the way we conceive and manage digital infrastructure. Essentially, IaC treats infrastructure configurations, provisioning, and management as code, borrowing principles from software development to introduce efficiency and agility.

Conceptually, IaC transforms traditional, manual infrastructure management into a code driven, automated model. Its declarative nature allows practitioners to articulate the desired state of their infrastructure, enhancing clarity, version control, auditability, and collaborative development.

AWS CloudFormation is the IaC service offered by AWS, designed for orchestrating cloud infrastructure. This service enables you to define and provision AWS resources systematically, reproducibly, and in an automated fashion, simplifying the complexity of resource management. To make this process feasible, the service utilizes what we call a **CloudFormation template**.

In the realm of AWS CloudFormation, a CloudFormation template serves as the architectural blueprint—a virtual map guiding the deployment of your AWS infrastructure. Picture it as a recipe orchestrating the creation and configuration of various resources, whether computing power, storage, or network components, all in a seamlessly synchronized manner.

At its core, a CloudFormation template is a declarative script, typically crafted in either YAML or JSON format. It provides a clear and structured representation of your desired AWS environment, outlining the relationships, dependencies, and configurations of the resources, thus encapsulating the entire infrastructure setup. Further insights into the YAML/JSON declarative model will be explored later in this chapter.

Benefits

In the landscape of cloud infrastructure management, AWS CloudFormation emerges as a pivotal tool, offering a plethora of benefits and versatile use cases that streamline the deployment and management of AWS resources. Let us have a detailed look at a few of them:

- **IaC paradigm**: AWS CloudFormation epitomizes the IaC philosophy, enabling users to represent and manage their infrastructure in a code based, version controlled manner. This brings unprecedented advantages such as repeatability, consistency, and collaboration as infrastructure configurations become shareable, reproducible, and adaptable.

- **Automation and time efficiency**: One of the primary benefits of AWS CloudFormation is its capacity to automate the provisioning and updating of AWS resources. This automation drastically reduces the time and effort required for infrastructure deployment. By utilizing pre-defined templates, users can reliably and swiftly create complex environments, eliminating the manual configuration steps.

- **Consistency across environments**: AWS CloudFormation ensures consistency across different environments, whether it is development, testing, or production. The declarative nature of CloudFormation templates guarantees that the same set of resources is created every time, reducing the risk of configuration drift and enhancing reliability.

- **Scalability and elasticity**: With AWS CloudFormation, scaling your infrastructure becomes an effortless task. Whether you are provisioning resources for a small application or a large scale enterprise solution, CloudFormation allows you to scale up or down as needed, ensuring your infrastructure is elastic and adaptable to varying workloads.

- **Cost management**: By providing a comprehensive view of the resources and their interdependencies, AWS CloudFormation assists in effective cost management. Users can evaluate the cost implications of different configurations before deployment, making informed decisions to optimize resource utilization and minimize expenses.

- **CI/CD pipelines integration**: CloudFormation integrates seamlessly into **continuous integration and continuous deployment (CI/CD)** pipelines, supporting tools like Jenkins, GitLab CI/CD, and AWS CodePipeline. This enables the DevOps engineer to push changes through the pipelines and have CloudFormation update the infrastructure accordingly.

- **Integration with third party tools**: AWS CloudFormation extends its integration capabilities to seamlessly collaborate with third party tools, providing enhanced flexibility and interoperability within your infrastructure management and deployment workflows. Its versatility is not confined to overseeing components solely within the AWS cloud; rather, CloudFormation can also be harnessed to effortlessly integrate components supported by third party providers. This broadens the scope of your infrastructure orchestration, allowing you to leverage the strengths of external tools while maintaining a unified and streamlined deployment process.

- **Quick rollback and rollback triggers**: CloudFormation swiftly enable rollbacks in the event of failures during stack creation, preserving the integrity of the system. This ensures the safety and stability of the infrastructure.

Use cases

Let us explore some typical use cases for how AWS CloudFormation can be of significant assistance across various scenarios:

- **Application stacks for development, testing, and production**: AWS CloudFormation enables the creation of consistent application stacks across different environments, streamlining the development, testing, and production phases. This ensures uniformity and minimizes potential issues arising from environmental discrepancies. This minimizes the risk of deployment issues caused by variations in the infrastructure between different environments. For instance, imagine a development team working on a critical application. With AWS CloudFormation, they can create identical application stacks for development, testing, and production environments. This ensures consistency across all environments, eliminating issues caused by discrepancies between them. What works in one environment will work seamlessly in the others. By minimizing inconsistencies between environments, the team can focus on building great features instead of troubleshooting infrastructure differences.

- **Multi-tier web application deployment**: Deploying a multi-tier web application with AWS CloudFormation ensures the orchestrated creation of resources such as EC2 instances, load balancers, and databases. This simplifies the process, reduces manual errors, and enhances the scalability of the application. Consider a team building an e-commerce platform: using AWS CloudFormation, they can effortlessly deploy EC2 instances, databases, and load balancers in one go. The entire infrastructure comes together like pieces of a puzzle, reducing errors and making scaling as simple as running a script. This orchestration ensures the application can handle growing user demand without hiccups.

- **Cross-region and cross-account deployment**: AWS CloudFormation allows for the creation of stacks across different AWS Regions and accounts. This facilitates global deployments, disaster recovery setups, and resource sharing securely between distinct AWS environments. For instance, picture a company expanding into new markets for which they need their application to be available in different parts of the world. AWS CloudFormation allows them to replicate their infrastructure across regions with ease, ensuring a global presence and minimizing downtime. Furthermore, disaster recovery becomes more straightforward as they can quickly spin up resources in another region when needed.

- **Network infrastructure with Amazon Virtual Private Cloud (VPC)**: Imagine you are tasked with building a secure and scalable network for a new application. By leveraging AWS CloudFormation with Amazon VPC, you can design an intricate network architecture, defining subnets, security groups, and routing policies all in a template. With the click of a button, your network infrastructure is provisioned and ready to handle any scale, providing a robust backbone for your application's needs, without the hassle of manual configurations.

- **Security policy enforcement**: Implement security best practices by defining AWS Identity and Access Management policies and security groups within CloudFormation templates. This ensures consistent application of security policies across your cloud infrastructure. Visualize a financial institution needing to apply strict security policies across multiple AWS accounts. AWS CloudFormation enables them to define and enforce security rules consistently, from **identity and access management (IAM)** roles to security groups. This ensures compliance with security standards across the entire organization, reducing the risk of human error and maintaining the integrity of sensitive data.

- **Centralized logging and monitoring**: Consider a scenario where an organization needs visibility into its application's performance across multiple environments. With AWS CloudFormation, they can set up centralized logging and monitoring solutions like AWS CloudWatch. Now, the team can easily track logs and metrics from a single dashboard, gaining insights into the health of their applications. This unified approach to logging helps in identifying issues faster and ensures consistency in monitoring across all platforms.

- **Instant deployment of cloud based desktops with AWS CloudFormation**: AWS CloudFormation provides an efficient way to configure cloud based desktops rapidly, utilizing services like Amazon WorkSpaces. Imagine a fast growing startup that needs to supply cloud desktops to new team members on demand. Using AWS CloudFormation, they can swiftly set up standardized desktops with Amazon WorkSpaces, ensuring rapid and consistent deployment across the team. This approach guarantees that all team members have uniform configurations, leading to optimal resource utilization and cost savings, particularly in environments where desktop requirements fluctuate over time.

- **Custom machine learning (ML) model deployment**: Imagine a data science team preparing to deploy their latest machine learning model. Using AWS CloudFormation, they can automate the provisioning of the infrastructure needed for training, inference, and managing the model lifecycle.

- **Edge computing infrastructure**: Consider an augmented reality gaming company that requires low latency processing at the network edge. Using AWS CloudFormation, they deploy edge computing infrastructure with AWS Wavelength, ensuring the game runs smoothly with minimal delays. This setup allows players to experience real-time interactions without any lag, a critical component for gaming and other latency-sensitive applications like real-time analytics or Augmented Reality experiences.

- **Interactive data visualization platform**: Picture an analytics team that needs to present data in a visually engaging way. Using AWS CloudFormation, they deploy an interactive data visualization platform by integrating Amazon QuickSight with backend databases and scalable compute resources. With a few clicks, they create dynamic dashboards that provide real-time insights to decision makers, enhancing the organization's overall analytics capabilities.

- **User identity management with Amazon Cognito**: Imagine a development team working on a mobile app that requires secure user authentication for both Android and iOS. With AWS CloudFormation, they easily set up Amazon Cognito user pools, ensuring standardized, scalable user identity management. This approach allows for secure, seamless authentication, providing a unified experience for users and reducing the complexity of managing identities across platforms.

Workings of CloudFormation

AWS CloudFormation operates as an orchestration engine for the provisioning and configuration of AWS resources. To further illustrate the practical functionality of AWS CloudFormation, let us delve into a specific example that involves the creation of an Amazon **Relational Database Service (RDS)** instance.

For this example, the focus is on Amazon RDS, a fully managed relational database service by AWS. Users articulate their infrastructure requirements through a CloudFormation template, expressing the desired properties of an RDS instance, such as database engine, instance type, storage, security settings, and more.

Let us take a closer look at each step to understand exactly how AWS CloudFormation works for provisioning RDS instance.

Template

Users define their infrastructure requirements using a CloudFormation template written in either YAML or JSON. For instance, consider the following YAML template that specifies the creation of an Amazon RDS instance:

```
1.  AWSTemplateFormatVersion: 2010-09-09
2.  Description: Amazon RDS Example
3.  Resources:
4.    MyRDSInstance:
5.      Type: 'AWS::RDS::DBInstance'
6.      Properties:
7.        DBInstanceIdentifier: my-rds-instance
8.        AllocatedStorage: 20
9.        Engine: mysql
10.       MasterUsername: admin
11.       MasterUserPassword: admin123
12.       DBInstanceClass: db.t2.micro
13.       PubliclyAccessible: false
```

This simple template describes the desired properties of an Amazon RDS instance, including its identifier, storage allocation, database engine, master username, password, instance class, and whether it should be publicly accessible. Save the template locally or in an S3 bucket. For this specific demonstration, we will save it locally on our desktop as **rds_cft.yaml**.

> **Note: We will explore in greater detail the diverse components utilized in the template which is also discussed in the upcoming chapters.**

Create the stack

Now, we will create the stack using our template. The stack can be generated through either the CloudFormation console or AWS CLI. To initiate the creation process, we will specify the location of our template, depending on whether it is stored locally or in the S3 bucket. Let us explore the CloudFormation console for this setup.

After logging into our AWS account, we will navigate to the search panel at the top of the page. Subsequently, we will search for the **CloudFormation** service to access the **Console** page, as shown in *Figures 1.1* and *1.2*:

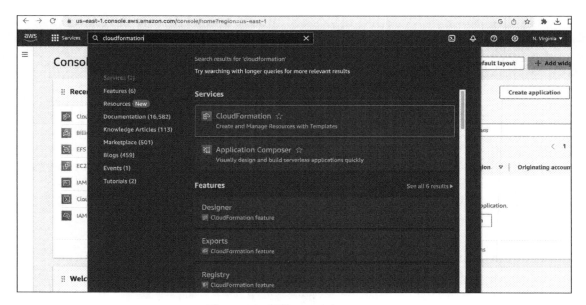

Figure 1.1: AWS console home page

The AWS **CloudFormation** console page is shown in the following figure:

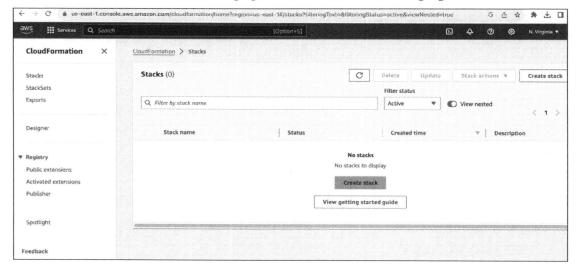

Figure 1.2: AWS CloudFormation console

Now, let us proceed by clicking on the **Create stack** button, which will open a new page where we can select the necessary options for specifying our template. For more details, please refer to *Figure 1.3*:

In our scenario, we will upload the template directly from our local system to the console. We will choose the **Upload a template file** option for this purpose. Once we select the template from our drive, AWS will store the uploaded template in its own S3 bucket. This bucket will then be used to provision the necessary resource in the next step. The details of the S3 bucket will also be populated on the page:

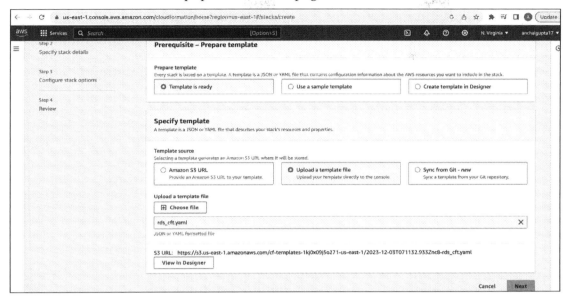

Figure 1.3: AWS CloudFormation create stack

Following this, we need to click the **Next** button. The page will redirect to a new page where it will prompt us to specify the **Stack name**. Here, we will enter a suitable name for our stack.

Please refer to *Figure 1.4* for the same:

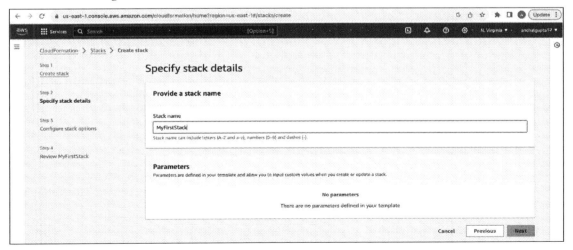

Figure 1.4: AWS CloudFormation stack name

The next page involves configuring the stack options, which we will discuss in detail in later chapters. For now, we will opt for the default options and then proceed by clicking the **Next** button.

Subsequently, the next page will appear for reviewing the stack, displaying all the necessary options we provided in the earlier steps. Please refer to *Figure 1.5* for illustrative purposes:

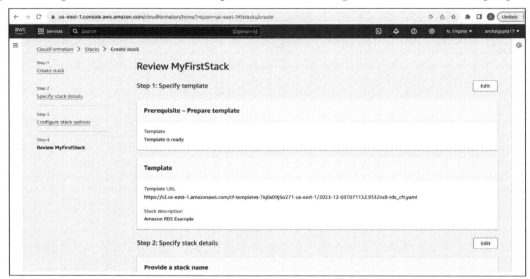

Figure 1.5: AWS CloudFormation review stack

Finally, we will click on the **Submit** button, which will then redirect us to the page where we can monitor the status of our stack creation.

Now, let us dive into the detailed backend operations that the AWS CloudFormation service executes after we click on the **Submit** button. The following are the steps and their order of execution:

- **Template processing**: CloudFormation processes the template, ensuring its syntax and structure comply with AWS standards. It then parses the template to extract resource definitions and resolves any dependencies.

- **Dependency analysis**: CloudFormation performs a dependency analysis based on the resource definitions. In this Amazon RDS example, dependencies might include the need for a security group, parameter group, or subnet group.

- **Execution plan generation**: An execution plan is generated based on the processed template and resolved dependencies. This plan outlines the sequence of actions required to create or update the Amazon RDS instance.

- **Resource orchestration**: CloudFormation orchestrates the creation or update of the Amazon RDS instance by making API calls to the AWS services responsible for managing RDS resources.

- **Stateful resource management**: Throughout the process, CloudFormation maintains a stateful record of the Amazon RDS instance's current state, tracking details such as endpoint information, status, and configuration settings.

- **Outputs and completion**: Once the Amazon RDS instance is successfully provisioned, CloudFormation provides Outputs specified in the template, such as the RDS endpoint. Currently, we have not included any Output information in our template for the sake of clarity and ease of understanding.

Refer to *Figure 1.6* for details:

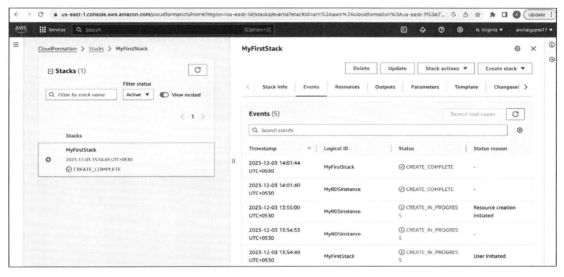

Figure 1.6: *Final stack creation events*

You can refer to *Figure 1.7* for more detail:

Figure 1.7: *Provisioned resource information*

Resource validation

Once all the above steps are successfully executed, users can then commence using the provisioned resource. To validate this, we can visit the resource console page (in our scenario, it is RDS). There, we can observe that the specified RDS has been provisioned with all the necessary configurations as outlined in our template.

Please refer to *Figure 1.8* for the same:

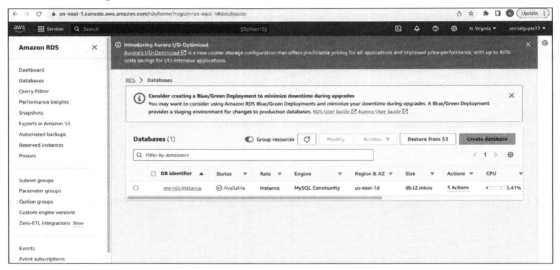

Figure 1.8: RDS console page

Rollback mechanism

If any part of the deployment encounters an error, CloudFormation initiates a rollback, reverting the stack to its previous state and ensuring the integrity of the infrastructure. In our scenario, since we did not encounter any issues with our template, no rollback was triggered from the AWS CloudFormation end.

> **Note: This example demonstrates how AWS CloudFormation streamlines the creation and management of AWS resources. Whether it is databases, networking components, or other AWS services, CloudFormation provides a consistent and scalable approach to infrastructure as code.**

Introducing the YAML data format

YAML, which stands for **Yet Another Markup Language**, is a human-readable data serialization format that has become a fundamental part of CloudFormation templates. YAML is often preferred for its simplicity, readability, and conciseness, making it an excellent choice for defining infrastructure as code in CloudFormation.

YAML basics

At its core, YAML is a straightforward and intuitive language that uses indentation to represent data hierarchy, eliminating the need for explicit markers such as braces or brackets. This simplicity makes YAML easy to understand for both beginners and experienced developers alike. Let us explore some basic YAML examples to help you understand its syntax and structure. These examples will showcase YAML's simplicity and readability:

- **Scalar values and indentation**: This YAML example defines personal information (**name**, **age**, **city**) and a nested **address** (**street**, **city**, **zip**) using key-value pairs with indentation to represent the hierarchical structure:

```
1.  # Simple key-value pairs
2.  name: John Tailor
3.  age: 30
4.  city: Chicago
5.
6.  # Nested structure using indentation
7.  address:
8.    street: 123 Main St
9.    city: Chicago
10.   zip: '1234567'
```

- **Lists**: This YAML document defines two types of lists. The first list, consisting of fruits (**apple**, **banana**), is defined under the key **fruits**. Another list is defined under the key **employees**, where each element is a key-value pair representing an employee's **name** and **role** (**Developer**, **Tester**):

```
1.  # List of fruits
2.  fruits:
3.    - apple
4.    - banana
5.
6.  # List of employees with key-value pairs
7.  employees:
8.    - name: Alice
9.      role: Developer
10.   - name: Bob
11.     role: Tester
```

- **Multiline strings and comments**: This YAML document showcases the use of multiline strings for detailed **description** and the inclusion of comments for additional context:

```
1.  # Multiline string
2.  description: |
3.     This is a multiline
4.     description in YAML.
5.     It allows for easy formatting.
6.
7.  # Comments
8.  # The following block represents a person
9.  person:
10.    name: John
11.    age: 25   # Age of the person
```

o The **description** key holds a multiline string denoted by the | symbol, allowing for the creation of a string that spans multiple lines.

The string under **description** is:

```
1.     This is a multiline
2.     description in YAML.
3.     It allows for easy formatting.
```

Note: Multiline strings are useful for preserving line breaks and formatting details.

o Also, the **# Age of the person** comment explains the purpose of the **age** key in the **person** block:

```
1.  # Comments
2.  # The following block represents a person
3.  person:
4.     name: John
5.     age: 25   # Age of the person
```

- **Mapping**: This YAML document explains the usage of Mappings in a template. Mappings provide a structured way to organize data, using key-value pairs to represent relationships and hierarchies within a document:

```
1.  # Mapping
2.  user:
3.     details:
4.        name: Jil
5.        age: 28
6.     preferences:
7.        colour: blue
8.        language: English
```

Let us understand the example structure in detail:

- o **Top-level key**: **user** is the top-level key in the Mapping. It represents a grouping or category if information related to a user.

- o **Nested Mappings**: Within the **user** Mapping, there are two nested Mappings: **details** and **preferences**.

- o Within the **details** Mapping, we have key-value pairs for **name** and **age**, representing the user's details for name and age.

- o Within the **preferences** Mapping, we have key-value pairs for **colour** and **language**, representing the user's preferences for color and language.

- **Complex structure**: This YAML structure represents a combination of various elements within a single template, showcasing a typical format frequently encountered during the design of CloudFormation templates:

```
1.  # Complex structure with lists and nested Mappings
2.  app:
3.    name: MyApp
4.    version: 1.0
5.    developers:
6.      - name: Ajay
7.        role: Developer
8.      - name: Dev
9.        role: Tester
10.   dependencies:
11.     - library1
12.     - library2
13.   settings:
14.     debug: true
15.     log_level: info
```

Let us explore this template in detail:

- o The **app** key serves as a container for multiple pieces of information related to an application, such as its **name**, **version**, **developers**, **dependencies**, and **settings**. This reflects a common pattern in CloudFormation templates where various resources and configurations are grouped under a single logical entity.

- o The hierarchical structure of the YAML mirrors the nested nature of CloudFormation templates. Resources, properties, and configurations are often organized in a hierarchical manner to maintain clarity and organization.

- o The use of lists, such as **developers** and **dependencies**, aligns with CloudFormation's ability to define multiple resources or **dependencies** under a single key.

- o The **settings** Mapping captures configuration details, similar to how CloudFormation templates include Parameters, Mappings, and other settings.

- o The structure is designed for readability and maintainability, essential aspects of CloudFormation templates. It makes it easier for developers and administrators to understand, modify, and extend the template.

Sample CloudFormation templates in YAML

Let us look at a few CloudFormation templates examples written in YAML:

- **CloudFormation template to build S3 bucket:**

```
1.  AWSTemplateFormatVersion: '2010-09-09'
2.  Resources:
3.    MyS3Bucket:
4.      Type: 'AWS::S3::Bucket'
5.      Properties:
6.        BucketName: my-unique-bucket-name
```

- **CloudFormation template to build EC2 instance:**

```
1.  AWSTemplateFormatVersion: '2010-09-09'
2.  Resources:
3.    MyEC2Instance:
4.      Type: 'AWS::EC2::Instance'
5.      Properties:
6.        InstanceType: t2.micro
7.        ImageId: ami-12345678
```

- **CloudFormation template to build IAM role**:

```
1.   AWSTemplateFormatVersion: '2010-09-09'
2.   Resources:
3.     MyIAMRole:
4.       Type: 'AWS::IAM::Role'
5.       Properties:
6.         RoleName: my-iam-role
7.         AssumeRolePolicyDocument:
8.           Version: '2012-10-17'
9.           Statement:
10.            - Effect: Allow
11.              Principal:
12.                Service: ec2.amazonaws.com
13.              Action: sts:AssumeRole
```

Introducing JSON data format

JSON, or **JavaScript Object Notation**, is a lightweight data-interchange format that is easy for humans to read and write and easy for machines to parse and generate. It is a common data format with diverse uses in electronic data interchange, including web applications and, relevant to our discussion, infrastructure as code tools such as AWS CloudFormation.

JSON basics

This section delves into the fundamental concepts and structures that constitute JSON, providing a comprehensive understanding of how to use it while designing the templates.

At its core, JSON is formed by combining the following two fundamental structures:

- **Objects**: Represented by key/value pairs enclosed in curly braces **{}**, objects can encapsulate various data types, fostering the creation of hierarchical structures:

```
1. {
2. "name": "Ram Sharma",
3. "age": 30,
4. "city": "New Delhi"
5. }
```

  Let us delve into another example to further illustrate JSON's versatility and object structure:

```
1. {
2. "person": {
3. "name": "Rohan",
4. "age": 22,
5. "isEmployee": true,
6. "isPermanent": true,
7. "address": {
8. "city": "Kolkata",
9. "zipCode": "700001"
10. }
11. }
12. }
```

- **Arrays**: Enclosed in square brackets **[]**, arrays provide an ordered list of values, allowing for the representation of collections or sequences:

```
1. ["apple", "banana", "orange"]
```

  Now, let us enhance the previous example, which focused on illustrating objects, by incorporating an array:

```
1. {
2. "person": {
3. "name": "Rohan",
```

```
4.  "age": 22,
5.  "isEmployee": true,
6.  "hobbies": ["reading", "biking"],
7.  "address": {
8.  "city": "Kolkata",
9.  "zipCode": "700001"
10. }
11. }
12. }
```

In the preceding example, an array is defined at *line 6*. This showcases a typical representation of a JSON template where both objects and arrays are defined within a single structure.

Key concepts

Now, let us unpack some key concepts that we will consider while designing a typical JSON template.

- **Strings**: Strings are sequences of characters enclosed in double quotation mark *""*. They are used to represent textual data.

  Example:

  ```
  1.  {
  2.  "message": "Hello, JSON!"
  3.  }
  ```

- **Numbers**: Numeric values in JSON can be either integers or floating-point numbers. JSON does not distinguish between them; it treats both as numbers.

  Example:

  ```
  1.  {
  2.     "quantity": 10,
  3.     "price": 3.99
  4.  }
  ```

- **Booleans**: Boolean values in JSON can be either **true** or **false**. They are useful for representing binary choices.

  Example:

  ```
  1.  {
  2.     "isAvailable": true,
  3.     "isExpired": false
  4.  }
  ```

- **Null**: The **null** value in JSON represents the absence of a value or a null value.

  Example:

```
1.  {
2.     "middleName": null
3.  }
```

Nesting and composition

JSON also allows for the composition of complex structures through nesting. Objects can contain arrays, and arrays can contain objects, enabling the representation of hierarchical and multidimensional data.

Let us explore an example to understand the same:

```
1.  {
2.     "bookstore": {
3.       "name": "Tech Books",
4.       "books": [
5.         {"title": "AWS Essentials", "author": "John Smith"},
6.         {"title": "JavaScript Mastery", "author": "Alice Doe"}
7.       ]
8.     }
9.  }
```

This JSON structure represents information about a **bookstore**. The **bookstore** has a name (**Tech Books**) and a collection of **books**, each represented as an object within an array. Each book object has attributes like **title** and **author**. This example illustrates the power of JSON in expressing nested and composed structures, making it easy to represent hierarchical and complex data relationships.

Sample CloudFormation templates in JSON

Now, let us examine the sample CloudFormation template samples that were used in the YAML section. We will convert them into JSON to facilitate a clear understanding of the structural differences between YAML and JSON formats:

- **CloudFormation template to build S3 bucket**:

```
1.  {
2.     "AWSTemplateFormatVersion": "2010-09-09",
3.     "Resources": {
4.       "MyS3Bucket": {
5.         "Type": "AWS::S3::Bucket",
6.         "Properties": {
7.           "BucketName": "my-unique-bucket-name"
8.         }
```

```
9.        }
10.  }
11. }
```

- **CloudFormation template to build EC2 instance**:

```
1.  {
2.      "AWSTemplateFormatVersion": "2010-09-09",
3.      "Resources": {
4.          "MyEC2Instance": {
5.            "Type": "AWS::EC2::Instance",
6.            "Properties": {
7.              "InstanceType": "t2.micro",
8.              "ImageId": "ami-12345678"
9.          }
10.       }
11.     }
12. }
```

- **CloudFormation template to build IAM role**:

```
1.  {
2.      "AWSTemplateFormatVersion": "2010-09-09",
3.      "Resources": {
4.          "MyIAMRole": {
5.            "Type": "AWS::IAM::Role",
6.            "Properties": {
7.              "RoleName": "my-iam-role",
8.              "AssumeRolePolicyDocument": {
9.                "Version": "2012-10-17",
10.               "Statement": [
11.                 {
12.                   "Effect": "Allow",
13.                   "Principal": {
14.                     "Service": "ec2.amazonaws.com"
15.                   },
16.                   "Action": "sts:AssumeRole"
17.                 }
18.               ]
19.             }
20.         }
21.       }
22.     }
23. }
```

In the preceding examples provided, we have presented the equivalent CloudFormation templates in JSON format alongside their original YAML counterparts. JSON, with its widespread compatibility and structured syntax, serves as the underlying format for many configuration settings, including CloudFormation Parameters.

YAML versus JSON

In our exploration of CloudFormation templates, it becomes evident that designing templates in YAML offers a more comfortable and human-readable experience compared to JSON. The concise and expressive syntax of YAML allows for a streamlined representation of complex structures, making it an ideal choice for crafting CloudFormation templates. Recognizing the importance of simplicity in understanding, we will predominantly use YAML for designing CloudFormation templates throughout this book. However, it is essential to note that CloudFormation Parameters files, a crucial aspect of template customization, are often expressed in JSON. Later in the book, we will delve into the use of JSON for designing Parameters file, ensuring a comprehensive understanding of both formats for effective CloudFormation development.

Conclusion

In wrapping up this chapter, we have covered crucial aspects of AWS CloudFormation. We explored the basics of CloudFormation templates, understanding their advantages, use cases, and the underlying workings that drive the orchestration of AWS resources. Additionally, we also learned about the YAML and JSON formats, essential languages for expressing CloudFormation templates. This foundational knowledge equips us with the necessary tools to build scalable and dynamic infrastructure within the AWS cloud. With these fundamental concepts in place, we are well-positioned for deeper exploration into advanced CloudFormation features and their practical applications in the upcoming chapters.

In the next chapter, we will investigate the important topics, like understanding IaC, checking out how CloudFormation and IAM work together, learning about cloud resource design principles, understanding how templates are structured, and trying our hand at creating and executing our first template.

Multiple choice questions

1. **What is AWS CloudFormation?**

    a. Cloud based storage service by AWS

    b. Email service by AWS

    c. Infrastructure as code Service by AWS

    d. Machine learning platform by AWS

2. **What does YAML stand for?**

   a. Yet Another Markup Language

   b. Yearly Analysis and Management Language

   c. Your Application Markup Language

   d. None

3. **Which data format is commonly used for defining CloudFormation templates?**

   a. XLSX

   b. XML

   c. CSV

   d. YAML

4. **What is the initial step in the backend operations of AWS CloudFormation after clicking the Submit button?**

   a. Dependency analysis

   b. Template processing

   c. Execution plan generation

   d. Resource orchestration

5. **What does CloudFormation do during the dependency analysis phase?**

   a. Creates a sequence of actions

   b. Processes the template syntax

   c. Resolves dependencies among resources

   d. Makes API calls to AWS services

Answers

1. c.

2. a.

3. d.

4. b.

5. c.

CHAPTER 2

CloudFormation Template Fundamentals

Introduction

In this chapter, we will navigate the fundamental concepts driving the seamless orchestration of AWS resources through code.

Beginning with an essential grasp of IaC role in automating infrastructure management, our journey into CloudFormation unveils its crucial functions and its interplay with IAM for secure resource provisioning. A significant addition to our exploration is the introduction of cloud resource design principles, underscoring the importance of effective templates for crafting robust and scalable cloud environments.

Central to our understanding is the dissection of CloudFormation templates, where we explore effective structuring techniques. At last, we will culminate our exploration with hands-on activities, specifically by crafting our inaugural template.

Structure

The chapter covers the following topics:

- Understanding infrastructure as code
- CloudFormation and identity and access management service
- Cloud resource design principles

- Understanding template anatomy
- Creating your first template

Objectives

By the end of this chapter, you will have gained a thorough understanding of AWS CloudFormation, its role in IaC, and its significance in modern cloud computing. You will explore core concepts, grasp the essential functions of CloudFormation, and understand its interaction with IAM for secure resource provisioning. You will also gain an understanding of principles that need to be taken care of while designing the template. Through practical exercises, including crafting your first template, you will demystify the process of translating code into tangible AWS infrastructure. Ultimately, this chapter aims to provide us with a solid foundation in CloudFormation, setting the stage for hands-on experience and deeper exploration in subsequent chapters.

Understanding infrastructure as code

Up to this point, we have acquired a preliminary understanding of the term IaC. However, let us delve into the reasons behind the introduction of IaC and how it has revolutionized the landscape of software engineering. In the past, the process primarily involved the manual setup of the entire development infrastructure. We will explore the motivations behind embracing IaC and examine its transformative impact on the traditional methods of software engineering.

IaC stands as a revolutionary approach to managing and provisioning computing infrastructure through machine-readable scripts rather than relying on manual processes or interactive tools. At its core, IaC treats infrastructure configurations as code, leveraging the principles and practices inherent in software development to streamline and automate the deployment and management of cloud resources. This paradigm shift is deeply rooted in the recognition that the traditional methods of configuring and maintaining infrastructure were prone to inefficiencies, errors, and scalability challenges. In the earlier days of software engineering, the manual setup of infrastructure was often a time-consuming and error-prone task, leading to inconsistencies across environments and hindering the pace of development.

IaC addresses these challenges by encapsulating infrastructure configurations into code scripts, which can be version-controlled, tested, and deployed with the same rigor applied to software applications. This not only ensures consistency across different environments but also facilitates collaboration between development and operations teams, breaking down traditional silos and fostering a more agile and iterative approach.

Let us explore some practical benefits of IaC:

- **Scalability**: Scalability is enhanced through the ability to easily replicate and scale infrastructure resources as needed.

- **Version control**: Version control mechanisms bring stability and traceability to infrastructure changes.

- **Reduced efforts**: Deployment times are significantly reduced, allowing for more frequent releases and faster response to changing business requirements.

- **No/minimal manual intervention**: The elimination of manual intervention ensures automated and consistent provisioning of cloud resources with no/minimal error.

- **Uniformity**: IaC fosters uniformity across cloud environments by codifying infrastructure configurations, ensuring consistent and reproducible setups across development, testing, and production.

- **Collaboration**: Promotes the development and operations teams to work collaboratively through IaC, fostering a shared, code-based language for configuring and managing cloud resources.

Numerous IaC tools are accessible in today's market. Some are open source, while others are proprietary offerings from leading cloud providers. The following enumerates a selection of well-known tools:

- **AWS CloudFormation**: Specifically designed for AWS, CloudFormation allows users to define and provision AWS IaC.

- **Terraform**: It is an open source tool by *HashiCorp*, Terraform supports multiple cloud providers and on-premises infrastructure. It uses a declarative configuration language.

- **Azure Resource Manager (ARM)**: Microsoft Azure's native IaC solution, ARM templates, allows users to define and deploy Azure infrastructure resources.

- **Google Cloud Deployment Manager**: This is **Google Cloud Platform**'s **(GCP)** IaC tool, enabling users to describe and deploy GCP resources using YAML or Python templates.

- **Ansible**: Ansible, an open source automation tool, includes IaC capabilities. It uses a simple YAML syntax and is agentless, making it versatile for various environments.

Understanding the mechanics of infrastructure as code

In a nutshell, IaC tools, including AWS CloudFormation, utilize API calls to interact with and manipulate cloud resources. Instead of manually configuring resources through a graphical interface, IaC tools rely on programmatic interactions facilitated by APIs. These tools send requests and commands using APIs to create, update, delete, or manage various cloud components. This approach enhances automation, scalability, and repeatability in cloud infrastructure management. By leveraging APIs, IaC tools ensure a consistent and efficient way to provision and configure resources in alignment with the desired infrastructure specifications defined in the code. This API-driven methodology lies at the core of IaC, enabling seamless communication between the code and the cloud environment.

CloudFormation and identity and access management service

In the realm of AWS CloudFormation, the seamless integration with AWS IAM holds paramount importance. IAM, a robust service providing secure access control to AWS resources, has become a critical companion to CloudFormation templates for several compelling reasons.

Before we begin with our infrastructure build up, we need to understand that managing access to AWS CloudFormation and the resources it creates is crucial for maintaining a secure and well-controlled environment. This involves granting permissions at two different scopes:

- **Granting permissions to AWS CloudFormation**: To execute stack operations, CloudFormation relies on an IAM role known as the CloudFormation service role. This role should be meticulously configured to grant the necessary permissions, including:

    o **Creation and deletion of resources**: Authorizing CloudFormation to create, update, and delete AWS resources on your behalf.

    o **Access to S3 buckets**: Permissions for CloudFormation to read templates and other artifacts stored in S3 buckets.

    o **Invocation of other AWS services**: Permissions to invoke other AWS services, such as Lambda functions, during stack operations.

- **Granting permissions to users**: Before users can engage in any AWS CloudFormation operations, it is imperative to meticulously craft IAM policies that precisely delineate the actions they are authorized to undertake. This involves specifying CloudFormation actions, resources, and the Conditionss under which these actions are permitted. Here are key considerations for designing such policies:

    o **Follow the principle of least privilege**: Adhere to the principle of least privilege, granting users only the permissions necessary for their specific tasks. Avoid unnecessary permissions to mitigate the risk of accidental or intentional misuse.

    o **Granular permissions**: Design IAM policies with granularity, specifying exact actions and resources that users are allowed to access. This approach provides fine-tuned control and closely aligns permissions with users' responsibilities.

o **Regular policy review**: Conduct regular reviews of IAM policies to ensure they remain aligned with the evolving needs of the organization. Remove any unnecessary permissions and update policies as roles or responsibilities change.

o **Proper naming convention**: Implement a proper naming convention for policies to define their purpose clearly. Using descriptive names enhances manageability and ensures clarity in understanding the intent of each policy.

o **Policy versioning**: Take advantage of policy versioning to track changes over time. This allows for a comprehensive audit trail and facilitates the ability to roll back to previous versions if needed.

o **Test permissions**: Prior to deploying policies in a production environment, conduct thorough testing of permissions in a controlled setting. This proactive approach helps identify and address issues before users interact with live resources.

Types of policies

Let us examine various types of policies that can be incorporated into our CloudFormation template:

- **Custom policies**: For the CloudFormation service role, these policies are instrumental in specifying the precise permissions required by AWS CloudFormation for creating and managing specific resources only. Through these policies, we can articulate the exact set of permissions granted to CloudFormation, ensuring a tailored and secure configuration as per our needs.

  Similarly, for user level access, these policies can restrict or extend permissions based on factors such as resource tags, stack names, or CloudFormation actions, providing flexibility in aligning permissions with organizational policies.

  Let us explore an example for a custom IAM policy that will allow CloudFormation to create an EC2 instance but will not allow it to be deleted:

```json
{
    "Version": "2012-10-17",
    "Statement": [
        {
            "Effect": "Allow",
            "Action": [
                "cloudformation:CreateStack",
                "cloudformation:UpdateStack",
                "cloudformation:DescribeStacks",
                "cloudformation:DescribeChangeSet",
```

```
        "cloudformation:ExecuteChangeSet",
        "ec2:RunInstances",
        "ec2:DescribeInstances",
        "ec2:DescribeInstanceStatus"
      ],
      "Resource": "*"
    },
    {
      "Effect": "Deny",
      "Action": [
        "cloudformation:DeleteStack",
        "ec2:TerminateInstances"
      ],
      "Resource": "*"
    }
  ]
}
```

Let us understand Allow Action items defined in this policy:

Allow Actions:

o **cloudformation:CreateStack**: Allows CloudFormation to create stacks.

o **cloudformation:UpdateStack**: Allows CloudFormation to update existing stacks.

o **cloudformation:DescribeStacks**: Allows CloudFormation to describe stacks.

o **cloudformation:DescribeChangeSet**: Allows CloudFormation to describe Change sets.

o **cloudformation:ExecuteChangeSet**: Allows CloudFormation to execute Change sets.

o **ec2:RunInstances**: Allows CloudFormation to launch EC2 instances.

o **ec2:DescribeInstances**: Allows CloudFormation to describe EC2 instances.

o **ec2:DescribeInstanceStatus**: Allows CloudFormation to describe the status of EC2 instances.

Note: Further elaboration on the tasks associated with Change sets will be provided in upcoming chapters.

Let us now understand the Deny Action items defined in this policy.

Deny Actions:

- o **cloudformation:DeleteStack**: Denies CloudFormation from deleting stacks.

- o **ec2:TerminateInstances**: Denies CloudFormation from terminating EC2 instances.

- **AWS managed policies**: We also have the option to utilize AWS managed policies that can be linked to the CloudFormation service role or user access role. This approach guarantees that CloudFormation service or users gains access to the specified services and resources outlined in the policy, streamlining the process of ensuring comprehensive and predefined permissions.

  Let us explore some pre-defined AWS managed policies tailored specifically for the CloudFormation service. These policies are conveniently accessible through the **IAM Policies** section on the AWS Management Console. Please refer to *Figure 2.1* for further illustration:

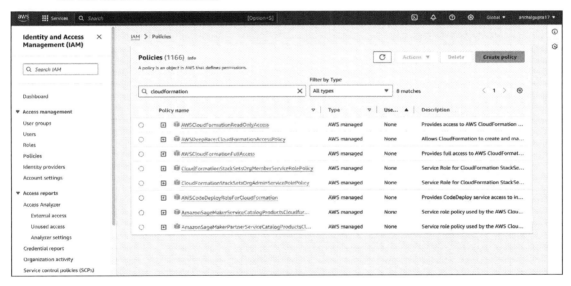

Figure 2.1: *AWS IAM Management Console*

We can type **cloudformation** in the search box. This will provide us the list of all CloudFormation based AWS managed policies.

Let us explore two of the frequently utilized AWS managed policies for CloudFormation:

- o **AWSCloudFormationReadOnlyAccess**: It is a predefined AWS managed policy designed to provide read-only access to AWS CloudFormation resources. This policy grants the necessary permissions for users or roles to view and describe CloudFormation stacks, resources, and changesets, allowing them to gather information about the existing infrastructure and configurations without the ability to make changes. Following is the policy snippet for more understanding:

```
{
    "Version": "2012-10-17",
    "Statement": [
        {
            "Effect": "Allow",
            "Action": [
                "cloudformation:Describe*",
                "cloudformation:EstimateTemplateCost",
                "cloudformation:Get*",
                "cloudformation:List*",
                "cloudformation:ValidateTemplate",
                "cloudformation:Detect*"
            ],
            "Resource": "*"
        }
    ]
}
```

This policy grants comprehensive read-only access to AWS CloudFormation resources. Users or service roles with this policy can describe, estimate costs, get details, list, validate templates, and detect stack drift across all CloudFormation resources in the account. The **Effect** is set to **Allow**, and the specified actions cover various CloudFormation operations, making it suitable for users who need to inspect and analyze stack configurations without the ability to modify them. The wildcard (*****) in the **Resource** field indicates access to all CloudFormation resources.

o **AWSCloudFormationFullAccess**: This policy is an AWS managed policy that provides comprehensive and unrestricted access to AWS CloudFormation resources and actions. This policy is designed for users or roles that require full administrative capabilities over CloudFormation stacks and related resources. Here is an overview of its components:

```
{
    "Version": "2012-10-17",
    "Statement": [
        {
            "Effect": "Allow",
            "Action": [
                "cloudformation:*"
            ],
            "Resource": "*"
```

```
■        }
■     ]
■  }
```

In the policy, the **Allow** effect is used to grant permissions for specified actions. The wildcard (*****) in the **Action** field signifies permission for all possible CloudFormation actions, encompassing activities such as creating, updating, deleting, describing, listing, and other actions available within CloudFormation. Furthermore, the wildcard (*****) in the **Resource** field indicates that the permissions bestowed by this policy are applicable to all CloudFormation resources present in the AWS account, without any restrictions. This broad scope ensures that the policy provides unrestricted access to perform a wide range of CloudFormation operations on any resource within the account.

In summary, this policy provides complete and unrestricted access to all CloudFormation actions and resources. While such policies might be suitable for certain use cases, it's crucial to implement the principle of least privilege to enhance security by only granting permissions that are necessary for specific tasks. Applying such broad permissions should be done cautiously and only when absolutely required for specific administrative roles.

> Note: If you do not specifically choose a role (a service role) when running a task with AWS CloudFormation, it will automatically use the credentials and permissions of the person or system that requested the task through the API. In simpler terms, CloudFormation acts as if it is that person or system, taking on their role to carry out the tasks outlined in the template.

Cloud resource design principles

When crafting CloudFormation templates for AWS infrastructure, adhering to sound design principles is paramount to building scalable, resilient, and efficient systems. These principles serve as the guiding pillars, ensuring that the resulting infrastructure not only meets immediate needs but is also well-positioned for future growth and adaptability. Let us explore each of these principles to begin our cloud resource designing journey:

- **Modularity and reusability**: Design templates with modularity in mind. Break down complex systems into smaller, reusable components, making it easier to manage and update specific parts of your infrastructure independently. Modular templates bring consistency not only within a project but also across different projects within your organization. When well-designed modules are shared and reused, you establish a standard set of practices and configurations.

- **Parameterization**: Leverage Parameters to make your templates dynamic and adaptable. Parameters allow users to customize the deployment based on their requirements, promoting flexibility and reusability. This prevents the need for template duplication with hardcoded values, promoting a cleaner and more maintainable codebase. Additionally, standardizing parameter names and descriptions enhances template readability and encourages best practices within your team.

- **Resource tagging**: Implement consistent and meaningful resource tagging. Tags are invaluable for managing and organizing resources, providing clarity on ownership, purpose, and other Metadata. By adhering to a consistent tagging strategy, you establish accountability for each component, making it clear who owns, manages, and is responsible for specific resources.

- **Dependency management**: Clearly define dependencies between resources to ensure they are created or updated in the correct order. Well-defined dependencies streamline stack operations, reducing the likelihood of provisioning errors. By expressing relationships in your template, CloudFormation orchestrates the provisioning process methodically. This not only enhances the reliability of your deployments but also simplifies troubleshooting by narrowing down the root cause of any issues.

- **Resource naming conventions**: Establish clear and consistent naming conventions for resources. Well-named resources enhance readability, simplify management, and contribute to a more organized AWS environment. This is particularly valuable for large scale deployments with numerous resources, where clear names act as beacons guiding administrators, developers, and other stakeholders.

- **Parameter constraints and validation**: Apply parameter constraints and validation to ensure that the values provided during stack creation meet specific criteria. This helps prevent errors and ensures the integrity of your infrastructure.

- **Resource deletion policies**: Set deletion policies for resources to control their lifecycle. Consider carefully whether a resource should be retained or deleted when the associated CloudFormation stack is deleted. Setting deletion policies is akin to providing an instruction manual for each resource's retirement process. It allows you to specify whether the resource should be retained, deleted, or follow a custom defined logic during stack removal. This granularity ensures that your CloudFormation stacks do not leave lingering artifacts or inadvertently purge critical data.

- **Security best practices**: Incorporate AWS security best practices into your design, such as employing the principle of least privilege, securing sensitive data, and implementing encryption where applicable. This proactive approach ensures that your cloud infrastructure remains in line with industry best practices and legal obligations.

- **Resource sizing and scaling**: Design resources with scalability in mind. Consider the potential growth of your application and configure resources to handle varying workloads efficiently. When crafting CloudFormation templates, assess the scalability requirements of each resource, be it compute instances, databases, or storage. Configure resources to scale horizontally or vertically based on the workload, enabling your infrastructure to seamlessly accommodate changes in demand.

- **Centralized logging**: Implement centralized logging mechanisms to capture and analyze logs from different resources. Integration with AWS CloudWatch Logs enables comprehensive monitoring and troubleshooting. This fosters a proactive and efficient operational environment.

- **Compliance and governance**: CloudFormation allows users to define and enforce compliance policies within templates. AWS Config can be integrated to monitor and assess compliance, while AWS Organizations assist in managing governance policies across accounts. The integration with these services ensures that your infrastructure adheres to regulatory standards and organizational policies.

- **Cost visibility and allocation**: CloudFormation templates can be tagged with Metadata that helps attribute costs to specific projects, teams, or departments. This ensures clear financial visibility and accountability through AWS Cost Explorer. This level of financial visibility aids in making informed decisions about resource scaling, right-sizing, and budgeting, ultimately contributing to efficient cost management within your AWS environment.

- **Optimization strategies**: Optimization strategy in the context of CloudFormation involves refining and enhancing cloud resource configurations to improve performance, reduce costs, and ensure efficient resource utilization. This includes fine-tuning Parameters such as instance types, storage, and network configurations, as well as implementing auto-scaling and load-balancing mechanisms.

Understanding template anatomy

CloudFormation templates serve as the blueprints for defining and provisioning AWS resources in an IaC approach. To effectively harness the power of CloudFormation, it is crucial to comprehend the anatomy of these templates. In this exploration, we will take a quick look at the different parts of CloudFormation templates. We will uncover the details that help users easily organize AWS infrastructure. More details about each part will be explained in the following chapters. For now, let us get a basic understanding of the template sections.

Structure of a template

A CloudFormation template is organized into several sections, each serving a distinct purpose in defining the desired AWS infrastructure. The primary sections include:

- **AWSTemplateFormatVersion**: This section specifies the CloudFormation template version. It ensures compatibility with the CloudFormation service and dictates the structure and syntax of the template. This is an optional section. For example:

```
AWSTemplateFormatVersion: "2010-09-09"
```

- **Description**: A human-readable description of the template, providing context and insights into its purpose. This section is optional but highly recommended for documentation purposes. For example:

```
Description: "A simple CloudFormation template for
creating an EC2 instance."
```

- **Metadata**: This optional section allows you to include additional information, comments, or instructions related to the template. It does not affect the AWS resources' creation but serves as supplementary documentation. For example:

```
Metadata:
  Author: "Ram"
  Version: "1.0"
```

- **Parameters**: In this section, you define input Parameters that users can customize during stack creation. **Parameters** enhance the flexibility and reusability of templates. Their presence in the template hinges on whether we are creating a versatile template with customizable options or a one-time-use template with fixed values for distinct configurations. This section is also optional. For example:

```
Parameters:
  InstanceType:
    Type: String
    Default: t3.small
    AllowedValues:
      - t3.micro
      - t3.large
    Description: Enter t3.micro or t3.large. The default is t3.
small.
```

- **Mappings**: **Mappings** provide a way to create conditional Mappings between a key and a corresponding set of named values. They are often used for regional or environment-specific configurations. This is an optional section:

```
Mappings:
  RegionMap:
    us-east-1:
      AMI: "ami-0456c3dd2da7fb87d"
    us-west-2:
      AMI: "ami-0a7345hgjae9a3dc2"
```

- **Rules**: This segment is essential for validating Parameters or combinations of Parameters passed to the stack. It involves the utilization of predefined intrinsic functions (covered in subsequent chapters) to establish **RuleConditions** and **Assertions**. While this section is optional, it plays a crucial role in ensuring the integrity and correctness of the input Parameters during stack creation. For example:

```
Rules:
  EnforceSecurityGroup:
    RuleCondition: !Equals
      - !Ref Environment
      - sandbox
    Assertions:
      - Assert:
          'Fn::Equals':
            - !Ref SecurityGroup
            - 'sg-test123'
        AssertDescription: 'For a sandbox environment,
the security group must be sg-test123'
```

- **Conditions**: **Conditions** define conditional statements that control the creation of resources, or their properties based on evaluated expressions. This is an optional section. For example:

```
Conditions:
  CreateProdResources: !Equals [ !Ref EnvType, prod ]
```

- **Transform**: This section allows you to invoke a macro or template transformation during the stack creation or update process. A **transform** is a set of custom processing rules that can modify the template's syntax or expand its functionality. It enables reuse of template components. This is an optional section. For example:

```
Transform: AWS::Serverless-2016-10-31
```

- **Resources**: This section is the heart of the CloudFormation template. It declares the AWS resources to be created or modified. Each resource has a unique logical ID and is defined based on AWS resource types. This is the mandatory section for the template. For example:

```
Resources:
  MyS3Bucket:
    Type: "AWS::S3::Bucket"
    Properties:
      BucketName: MyTestBucket
```

- **Outputs**: This section defines the values to be exported by the template, allowing them to be easily consumed by other stacks or external applications. This is also an optional section. For example:

```
Outputs:
  BucketArn:
    Description: "The Amazon Resource Name (ARN) of
the created bucket"
    Value: !GetAtt MyS3Bucket.Arn
```

> Note: While designing the template, it might seem fine to skip or breeze through some sections of your CloudFormation template. However, each segment serves a specific and vital purpose, contributing to the overall manageability and meaning of your IaC blueprint. Integrating these sections thoughtfully aligns your template's structure with its intended purpose, promoting clarity, flexibility, and maintainability.

Creating your first template

Now that we have grasped the fundamental anatomy of CloudFormation templates, it is time to apply this knowledge and embark on the exciting journey of crafting our own template. For the sake of clarity and comprehension, we will only use basic sections in our template as we attempt to set up an EC2 instance using the CloudFormation template. We will use YAML syntax to define our template.

We will use following basic sections for our template:

- `AWSTemplateFormatVersion`
- `Description`
- `Resources`

> Note: You can use any text editors like Notepad++, Visual Studio Code, Sublime Text etc. for writing these templates. These editors often have plugins or extensions that provide syntax highlighting and autocompletion for JSON/YAML.

Template

We will setup a basic EC2 instance in us-east-1 region of AWS. Following is the basic template which will help us in achieving the same. We will save the template on our local system as **Template_EC2.yaml**:

```
1. AWSTemplateFormatVersion: '2010-09-09'
2. Description: 'CloudFormation Template for EC2 Instance - t2.micro'
3. Resources:
4.   MyEC2Instance:
5.     Type: 'AWS::EC2::Instance'
6.     Properties:
7.       InstanceType: 't2.micro'
8.       ImageId: 'ami-079db87dc4c10ac91'
```

Here, we have used three main sections in our template, **AWSTemplateFormatVersion**, **Description**, and **Resources**. In the **Resources** section, we included fixed Parameters for **InstanceType** and **ImageId**. **InstanceType** configures compute and memory, while **ImageId** is the AMI id for EC2, region-dependent based on the AWS Region. These Parameters are specific to EC2 instance only.

Deployment

Now, let us attempt to deploy our initial template using the AWS Management Console. Since we have already addressed the backend operations of how CloudFormation works in *Chapter 1: Getting Started with AWS CloudFormation*, we will not delve into a detailed exploration here.

The necessary procedure is outlined in the following steps:

1. Login to the AWS Console as given in the following image:

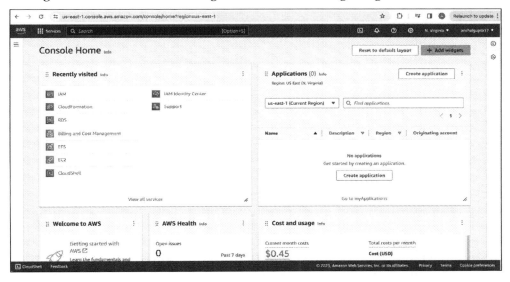

Figure 2.2: AWS Management Console

2. Navigate to the AWS **CloudFormation** service by using the search box on this page. Please refer to *Figure 2.3*:

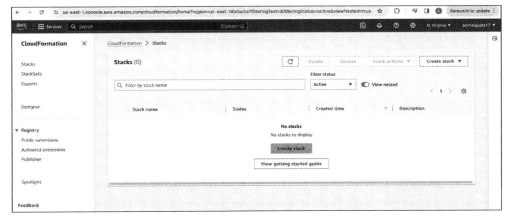

Figure 2.3: AWS CloudFormation console

3. Click on the **Create stack** option. This action will navigate to the next page, where we will be prompted to specify the template. Refer to *Figure 2.4:*

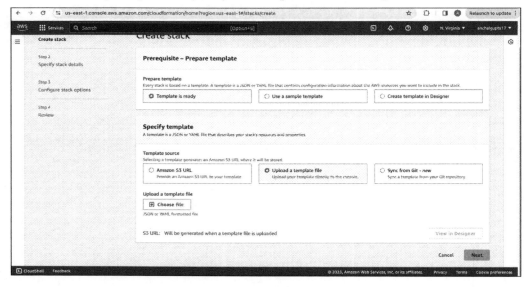

Figure 2.4: *Specify template*

On this page, we will choose the option **Upload a template file** and proceed to upload the template from our local system.

4. Once the template gets uploaded into the AWS S3 bucket, we will see the detail over the console page. Refer to *Figure 2.5:*

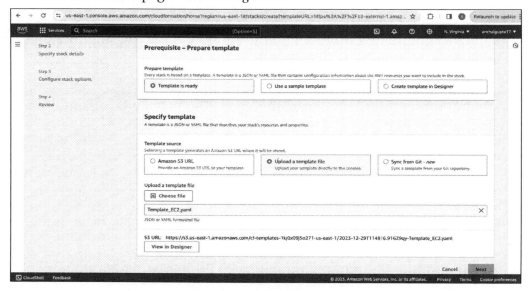

Figure 2.5: *Template uploaded*

Note: The other option, Create template in Designer, will be covered in upcoming chapters.

5. On the next page, we will provide the name of our stack. We will specify the name as **Stack-EC2**, representing that the stack creation is being done for an EC2 instance. Kindly refer to *Figure 2.6* for visual guidance:

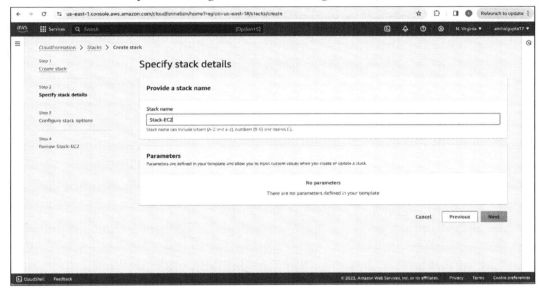

Figure 2.6: Stack details

Then we will click on the **Next** button. This will navigate us to next page where we will select the other options related to our stack's configuration. Refer to *Figure 2.7*. On this page, we will get the following options:

a. Tags

b. Permissions

c. Stack failure options

d. Stack policy

e. Rollback configurations

f. Notification options

g. Stack creation options

Note: For now, within the scope of this chapter, we will focus on the Tags and Permission sections on this page. We will discuss the other available sections later in the upcoming chapters, leaving them with their default configurations for now.

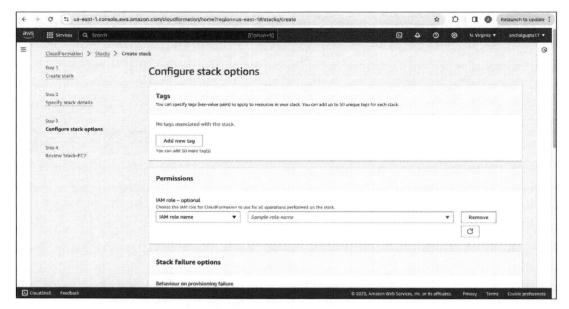

Figure 2.7: Stack permissions

6. Now, let us apply the IAM concepts covered at the beginning of this chapter. Currently, the user with which we have logged in is a root user, having full access to AWS services. For our easy understanding, we are not defining a separate policy for the CloudFormation service and will let it assume the role of the user. Refer to *Figure 2.8* for a visual representation:

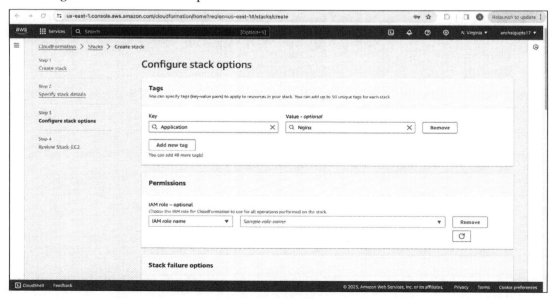

Figure 2.8: Tags and permissions

7. Let us assume that this EC2 instance will be used to host the nginx application. Therefore, we will define the tag accordingly. In the key tab, we will type **Application**, and in the value tab, we will type **Nginx**. Under the **Permissions** section, we will not define or select any role. This ensures that our CloudFormation service will assume the role of the user, which, in this case, is a root user.

> **Note: For real-time or production environments, it is not recommended to let the CloudFormation service assume the root user role. The best practice is always to have a dedicated role with a defined set of permissions as per the project's needs.**

8. We will then click on the **Next** button. This will navigate us to the next page where we will get the option to review our stack configuration which we have set in previous steps. Refer to *Figure 2.9*:

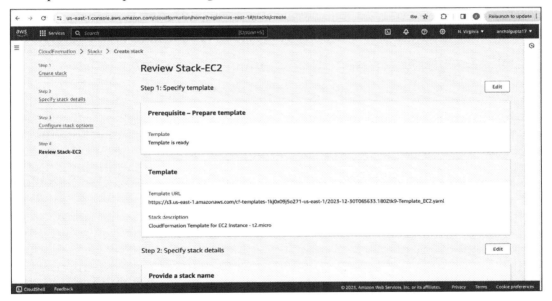

Figure 2.9: Review stack

9. Next, on the **Review Stack** page, we will validate the information and, upon verification, click on the **Submit** button. Refer to *Figure 2.10* for details:

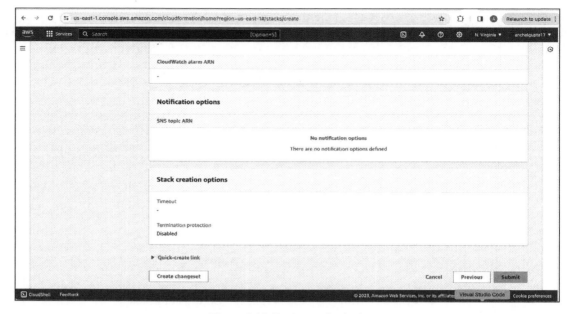

Figure 2.10: Review and submit

10. After clicking the **Submit** button, the page will take us to the final page where we can view the stack creation status. Please refer to *Figure 2.11* for more details:

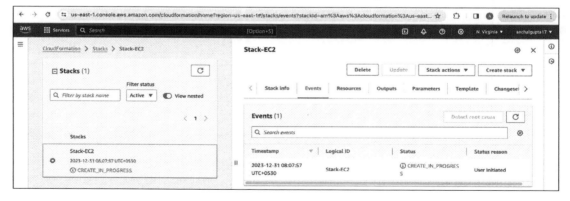

Figure 2.11: Stack creation in progress

In the preceding figure, we observe that our stack creation is in progress, indicated by the status **CREATE_IN_PROGRESS**. As the stack proceeds to create the defined resources, the status will dynamically change with the latest updates. This provides us with real-time visibility into the status of our stack.

11. Our stack has now completed and transitioned into the **CREATE_COMPLETE** state. This signifies the successful creation of all defined resources and configurations without any issues. Refer to *Figure 2.12* for more details:

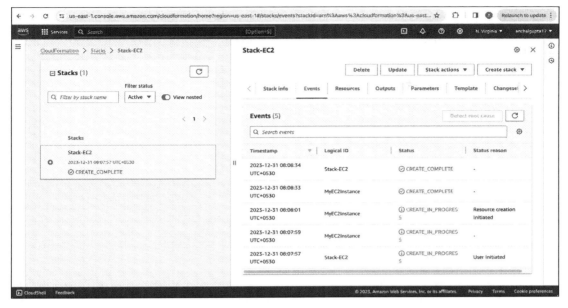

Figure 2.12: Stack completion

12. Now, to inspect the resources created by our stack, we will navigate to the **Resources** tab on the same page. Here, you will find the **Logical ID** and **Physical ID** of the newly created resource. Please refer to *Figure 2.13*:

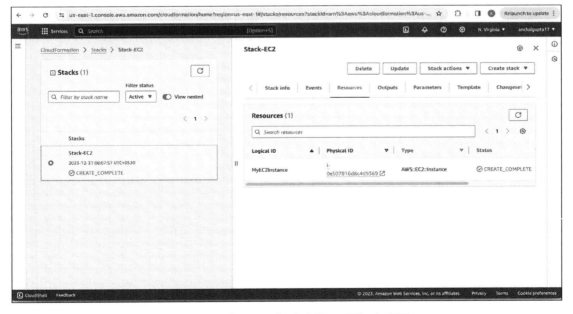

Figure 2.13: Resource Logical ID and Physical ID

13. The **Logical ID** is something we provide in our template when defining the resource. Please refer to the following code snippet:

```
1.  Resources:
2.    MyEC2Instance:
3.      Type: 'AWS::EC2::Instance'
4.      Properties:
```

So, the **Logical ID** for our EC2 instance is **MyEC2Instance**, as shown in *Figure 2.12*. The **Physical ID** is generated by AWS once the resource is created. Clicking on this ID will automatically navigate us to the EC2 console page.

In summary, **Logical ID** is a human-readable identifier defined in the CloudFormation template, while **Physical ID** is an AWS-assigned identifier for the instantiated resource. The **Logical ID** is useful within the template for references and updates, while the **Physical ID** is useful for identifying and interacting with the created resource in the AWS environment.

14. Now, we can check the status of the EC2 instance on the EC2 console page to ensure it is up and running. This marks the completion of our stack deployment. Please refer to *Figure 2.14*:

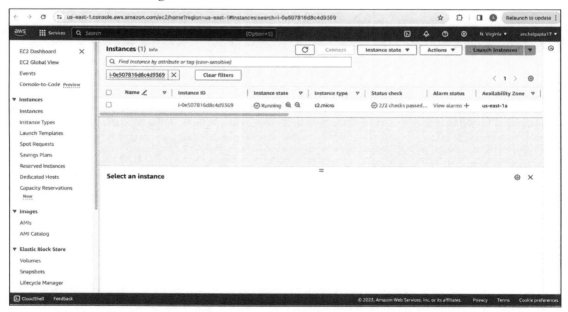

Figure 2.14: EC2 validation

Conclusion

In conclusion, this chapter provided a comprehensive understanding of key aspects of AWS CloudFormation, emphasizing its pivotal role in managing cloud resources through the concepts of IaC. We explored the integration of CloudFormation with the IAM service, emphasizing the importance of secure access control in cloud environments. The chapter also elucidated *Cloud resource design principles* to optimize the design and management of cloud resources. *Understanding the template anatomy* was a fundamental step, unraveling the essential components that constitute a CloudFormation template. We took a hands-on approach, which guided through the process of creating and deploying the inaugural CloudFormation template.

As we navigated through the chapter, the goal was to establish a robust foundation for harnessing the potential of AWS CloudFormation in automating and orchestrating infrastructure deployment.

In the upcoming chapter, we will dive into the intricacies of essential CloudFormation template sections, providing detailed insights into the AWSTemplateFormatVersion declaration, description section, resources, and Parameters. By exploring each of these components, our aim is to equip ourselves with a comprehensive understanding of how to structure and define CloudFormation templates effectively, ensuring clarity and precision in AWS infrastructure deployment.

Multiple choice questions

1. **What does IaC stand for?**

    a. Internet and Cloud

    b. Infrastructure as Code

    c. Intranet and Communication

    d. Information and Configuration

2. **Why is IaC considered beneficial for managing cloud resources?**

    a. It automates infrastructure provisioning

    b. It enhances security

    c. It increases manual processes

    d. It reduces cloud costs

3. **What is IAM used for in the context of AWS CloudFormation?**

    a. Infrastructure Monitoring

    b. Internet Access Module

    c. Infrastructure Automation Module

    d. Identity and Access Management

4. **Which section of the CloudFormation template is optional but recommended for documentation purposes?**

    a. Mappings

    b. Outputs

    c. Parameters

    d. Description

5. **What is the main purpose of the Resources section in a CloudFormation template?**

    a. Define input Parameters

    b. Specify Metadata for the template

    c. Define AWS resources to be created or modified

    d. Declare conditional statements

Answers

1. b

2. a

3. d

4. d

5. c

Join our book's Discord space

Join the book's Discord Workspace for Latest updates, Offers, Tech happenings around the world, New Release and Sessions with the Authors:

https://discord.bpbonline.com

Section II
Template Deep Dive

CHAPTER 3
Version, Description and Resources

Introduction

In this chapter, we will dive deep into the fundamental components that shape the structure of AWS CloudFormation templates. We will understand the intricacies of key elements, beginning with the `AWSTemplateFormatVersion` declaration and the essential Description section. Moving forward, we will embark on a journey to understand the significance of Resources, exploring various AWS resource types, and delving into the nuanced world of Resource properties and attributes.

Our expedition does not stop there; we will navigate through the lifecycle of Resources, covering their creation, management, dependencies, and the crucial aspects of updating and deleting resources.

Structure

The chapter covers the following topics:

- AWSTemplateFormatVersion
- Description
- Introduction to Resources
- Amazon Web Services Resource types
- Resource properties

- Resource creation and management
- Resource dependencies
- Resource deletion and update

Objectives

By the end of this chapter, you will gain a comprehensive understanding of AWS CloudFormation's foundational components, starting with the **AWSTemplateFormat Version** declaration. You will recognize its crucial role in defining the CloudFormation template version, ensuring compatibility and adherence to syntax standards. Additionally, you will appreciate the significance of the Description section and understand its role in documenting templates for clarity and future reference. This knowledge will help you to create well-documented templates that enhance collaboration and maintainability.

Moving on, you will acquire an in-depth knowledge of Resources, including an introduction to various AWS Resource types. A detailed exploration of Resource properties and attributes will follow, providing you with the insights needed to effectively define and configure AWS resources within your templates. As you navigate through the lifecycle of Resources, mastering the creation, management, deletion, and understanding dependencies, you will gain essential skills for designing efficient CloudFormation templates.

AWSTemplateFormatVersion

At the core of every CloudFormation template lies the **AWSTemplateFormatVersion** declaration, a fundamental element shaping the blueprint for AWS infrastructure. This version declaration acts as the cornerstone, defining the syntax and structure adhered to by the template. In essence, it determines the template's compatibility with the CloudFormation service. Let us have a look at the key functions of this section:

- **Syntax definition**: The declaration specifies the version of the CloudFormation template language. This is vital for maintaining consistency and ensuring that the template aligns with the expected structure. For example, a template using an outdated or incompatible version might face issues during execution.

- **Compatibility assurance**: As AWS evolves, so does CloudFormation. New features and enhancements are introduced, and the template version helps ensure that the template can leverage these updates without compatibility issues. It acts as a marker for CloudFormation to interpret and execute the template accurately.

- **Template evolution**: Over time, AWS introduces improvements and additions to the CloudFormation language. The **AWSTemplateFormatVersion** provides a means to indicate which version of the language the template follows. This is crucial when dealing with templates created at different times, allowing CloudFormation to interpret them correctly.

Structure

The **AWSTemplateFormatVersion** declaration is typically placed at the beginning of the template, serving as an initial marker for both the CloudFormation service and users reviewing the template. It follows a simple structure:

```
1. AWSTemplateFormatVersion: "version_date"
```

Here, the **version_date** is replaced with the specific date format associated with the desired CloudFormation template version. As of the writing of this book, the employed version provided by AWS is **2010-09-09**. An example of the same is as follows:

```
1. AWSTemplateFormatVersion: "2010-09-09"
2.
3. Resources:
4.   MyEC2Instance:
5.     Type: "AWS::EC2::Instance"
6.     Properties:
7.       InstanceType: "t2.micro"
8.       ImageId: "ami-12345678"
9.       KeyName: "my-key-pair"
```

In this simple example, the **AWSTemplateFormatVersion** declares the template's language version, ensuring compatibility with the CloudFormation service. The template then defines an AWS EC2 instance (**MyEC2Instance**). The **Properties** section provides details such as the instance type, **Amazon Machine Image (AMI)**, and a key pair for secure access. This compact template demonstrates the role of **AWSTemplateFormatVersion** in setting the language version and facilitating the creation of AWS resources.

> Note: As we discussed in Chapter 2, CloudFormation Template Fundamentals, the **AWSTemplateFormatVersion** declaration is technically optional in a CloudFormation template. If it is not provided, AWS CloudFormation assumes the default version, which is 2010-09-09. However, explicitly specifying the version is recommended to ensure compatibility and adherence to the desired template structure and syntax.

Description

The Description section in a CloudFormation template serves as a human-readable and informative text, providing context and insights into the purpose and functionality of the template. While technically optional, including a meaningful Description is highly recommended for documentation and clarity. This section adds a layer of documentation to your CloudFormation template. Its primary purpose is to offer a clear and concise explanation of the template's intent and functionality. Here are some key aspects to consider:

- **Human-readable information**: The Description is a free form text field that allows you to provide a plain language explanation of what the CloudFormation template is designed to achieve. It should easily be understood by anyone reading the template, including team members, collaborators, or individuals new to the project.

- **Template purpose**: Clearly state the purpose of the template. What kind of AWS resources will it create? What is the overarching goal or use case?

- **Documentation aid**: The Description acts as living documentation. It helps in understanding the template's structure and purpose over time, especially as projects evolve and different team members collaborate on the infrastructure.

- **Versioning and change log**: You may include versioning information or a change log in the Description, providing a quick reference for users to track modifications and updates.

While we have previously examined sample templates in earlier chapters that included the **Description** section, let us take a closer look at this specific aspect in a dedicated example. The following example illustrates the usage of the **Description** section for enhanced clarity:

```
1. AWSTemplateFormatVersion: "2010-09-09"
2. Description: |
3.   This CloudFormation template creates an AWS infrastructure for a
     web application.It provisions an Amazon VPC and EC2 instances.
4.   Version: 1.2.3 (Date: 2023-12-01)
```

In this specific example, the **Description** section serves as a concise yet informative summary, articulating the primary objective of the CloudFormation template. It not only communicates the template's purpose but also delineates the specific AWS Resources that will be created during its execution. Furthermore, the **Description** includes a versioning note, offering additional context about the template's evolution. This showcases the pivotal role of a well-crafted **Description** in facilitating collaboration among team members and fostering a deeper understanding of the template's intent. Such clarity contributes significantly to the overall effectiveness of managing and maintaining the infrastructure defined by the CloudFormation template.

> **Tip: Consider including the author's name in the template Description as a best practice, especially in collaborative team settings. This practice enhances documentation and fosters effective collaboration, particularly when multiple users are involved in working on or reviewing the template. I personally adhere to this style when creating templates.**

Introduction to Resources

As explored in *Chapter 2, CloudFormation Template Fundamentals*, the Resources section plays a pivotal role in driving infrastructure provisioning and management within a CloudFormation template. This is a mandatory section of the CloudFormation template. A resource is a fundamental building block defined within a CloudFormation template, representing an AWS entity or service that you want to create or configure. Resources encapsulate various AWS components, such as compute instances, storage buckets, databases, and more.

Let us briefly explore some key attributes of Resources:

- **Type**: Each resource is associated with a specific AWS resource type, defining its nature and purpose. For example, an Amazon EC2 instance, an S3 bucket, or a **Relational Database Services (RDS)** database. We will explore this in detail.

- **Properties**: Properties of a Resource specify its configurable settings, such as the size of an EC2 instance, the access control rules for an S3 bucket, or the engine type for an RDS database.

- **Logical ID**: Resources are uniquely identified within a template by a logical ID. This ID is crucial for referencing and interacting with the resource within the template.

Let us swiftly look into a sample excerpt from the Resources section, where we can identify and understand these attributes. Here, we are trying to create an EC2 instance:

```
1.  Resources:
2.    MyEC2Instance:
3.      Type: AWS::EC2::Instance
4.      Properties:
5.        InstanceType: t2.micro
6.        ImageId: ami-12345678
```

In this illustration, a resource named **MyEC2Instance** is established, serving as a logical ID of type **AWS::EC2::Instance**. This resource comes with defined properties, including the instance type and AMI.

For a more comprehensive understanding of these attributes, we will delve into further details in the upcoming section. The concept of logical ID has been covered in the previous chapter so we will not discuss it again.

> **Tip:** AWS CloudFormation templates offer configuration options for over 700 distinct types of resources within the AWS ecosystem. Resources can refer to one another for integration and configuration, a topic that will be explored in greater detail later in this chapter.

Amazon Web Services Resource types

In the Resources section, AWS Resource types are a crucial aspect that defines the type of AWS resource to be created or managed within a template. Each resource type corresponds to a specific AWS service or entity, such as an EC2 instance, S3 bucket, RDS database, and more. These resource types serve as the blueprint for the creation and configuration of the associated AWS service.

When specifying a resource within the template, the type attribute is used to indicate the AWS Resource type. This attribute has a special format which is as follows:

```
1. AWS::Service::data-type-name
```

In the preceding syntax, the term **Service** denotes the AWS service to which the resource is associated, and **data-type-name** specifies the resource within that service. Referring to the example snippet we explored previously, the service is represented by EC2, while the **data-type-name** is specifically denoted as an instance.

The AWS Resource types possess several key characteristics that contribute to their functionality and versatility. Let us have a look at a few of them:

- **Service association**: As we discussed earlier, each resource type is associated with a specific AWS service. For example, an EC2 instance is associated with the EC2 service, an S3 bucket with the S3 service, and so on.

- **Resource specification**: The resource type specifies the specific category or classification of a resource within its associated service. In the previous example, we highlighted the resource type as **Instance**, a classification falling under the EC2 service. However, EC2 encompasses various other resource types, such as security groups, volumes, **Elastic Network Interfaces (ENIs)**, and more. Each of these resource types represents a distinct aspect or component that can be configured and managed within the broader EC2 service.

- **Configuration properties**: Each AWS resource type has a set of specific properties or attributes that can be configured. These properties define the characteristics of the resource, such as its size, configuration settings, and dependencies. For instance, in the preceding example of instance resource types under EC2 service, the set of properties include **InstanceType** and **ImageID**. We will explore this topic extensively later in the chapter.

- **Dependency resolution**: Resources can have dependencies on each other. AWS resource types and CloudFormation handle dependency resolution, ensuring that resources are created or updated in the correct order to maintain consistency.

- **Extensibility**: AWS allows for the creation of custom resource types, offering extensibility to cater to specific use cases not covered by standard AWS resources. Custom resources can be defined using AWS Lambda-backed custom resources. We will delve into this topic extensively later in our book.

- **Resource lifecycle management**: CloudFormation leverages AWS resource types to manage the entire lifecycle of resources, including resource creation, updating, and deletion, providing a unified approach to infrastructure management. We will explore this topic later in this chapter.

Let us briefly explore some of the services and their respective AWS Resource types through the following table:

AWS service	Resource type	Description
Amazon EC2	`AWS::EC2::Instance`	Represents a virtual server in the cloud.
Amazon S3	`AWS::S3::Bucket`	Creates a storage bucket for storing and retrieving any amount of data.
Amazon RDS	`AWS::RDS::DBInstance`	Represents a relational database instance in Amazon RDS.
Amazon VPC	`AWS::EC2::VPC`	Defines a **virtual private cloud (VPC)** for launching AWS resources.
Amazon DynamoDB	`AWS::DynamoDB::Table`	Defines a DynamoDB table for storing and retrieving data.
AWS Lambda	`AWS::Lambda::Function`	Defines a Lambda function, allowing you to run code without managing servers.
AWS Elastic Beanstalk	`AWS::ElasticBeanstalk::Application`	Defines an Elastic Beanstalk application for deploying and managing applications in the AWS Cloud.
AWS **SNS (Simple Notification Service)**	`AWS::SNS::Topic`	Defines an SNS topic for sending messages to subscribers.
AWS CloudFront	`AWS::CloudFront::Distribution`	Creates a CloudFront distribution for content delivery.
AWS Kinesis	`AWS::Kinesis::Stream`	Defines a kinesis stream for collecting and processing real-time data.

Table 3.1: AWS services and Resource types

For other service Resource types, you can visit the official documentation of AWS. The link is as follows:

(https://docs.aws.amazon.com/AWSCloudFormation/latest/UserGuide/aws-template-resource-type-ref.html)

Resource properties

We have seen that the Resources section plays a pivotal role in defining the AWS infrastructure components you want to create or manage. Within this section, each resource type is equipped with a distinctive set of properties, providing users with the flexibility to tailor their configuration based on specific requirements. In the preceding section, we explored Resource types. Now, let us dive deeper into the subsequent aspect, Resource properties.

Resource properties in CloudFormation define the characteristics and configurations of specific AWS resources. These properties allow users to customize the behavior of resources during creation. For instance, when creating an EC2 instance, properties may include specifying the instance type, security groups, or key pair. Similarly, when defining RDS instance (database), properties may include configurations such as the database engine, allocated storage, and master username/password. In essence, understanding and effectively utilizing resource properties is fundamental to crafting templates that align seamlessly with specific use cases and requirements.

Note: When defining a resource, it is essential to consult the AWS documentation for the CloudFormation service. Pre-defined modules are available for comprehensive resource declarations. By referencing these Resource modules, we can easily customize our own modules by specifying the required set of properties. The link for the is as follows:

(https://docs.aws.amazon.com/AWSCloudFormation/latest/UserGuide/aws-template-resource-type-ref.html)

Upon clicking on the provided link, a list of various AWS service resources, each with a hyperlink, will be displayed. Simply choose the specific AWS service resource you intend to instantiate using your template. Upon selecting the relevant hyperlink, you will be directed to the page containing all pertinent Resource types associated with the chosen AWS service.

Subsequently, pick the desired Resource type and obtain the default resource configuration, which can be directly incorporated into your template. To complete the definition, you only need to specify the actual values along with the necessary properties.

Let us dive into this concept through an example. Suppose we aim to launch an EC2 instance using a CloudFormation template. The following steps outline the process of obtaining the AWS-defined syntax for the EC2 service from the AWS documentation:

1. Navigate to the provided URL, and the following page will be displayed:

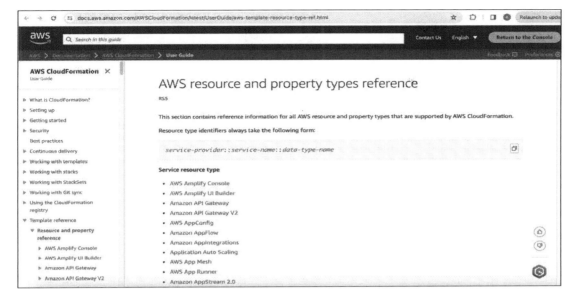

Figure 3.1: *AWS documentation for AWS Resource and property types*

2. Following the previous example of EC2, we will locate the EC2 service on the page and click on the corresponding hyperlink. The following page will appear. Choose the **AWS::EC2::Instance** Resource type:

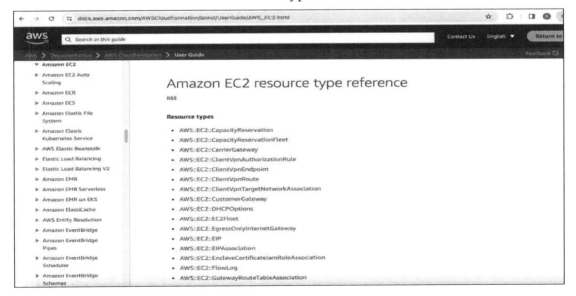

Figure 3.2: *AWS EC2 Resource type reference*

3. Upon selecting the hyperlink for the **AWS::EC2::Instance** Resource type, the subsequent page will present the AWS-defined default syntax for this resource:

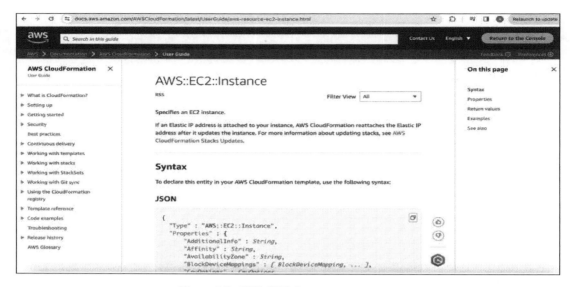

Figure 3.3: AWS::EC2::Instance syntax page

Here, you will encounter the syntax presented in both JSON and YAML formats. For clarity, we will concentrate on the YAML syntax. The YAML syntax is conveniently accessible on the same page with the following information:

1. Type: AWS::EC2::Instance
2. Properties:
3. AdditionalInfo: String
4. Affinity: String
5. AvailabilityZone: String
6. BlockDeviceMappings:
7.   - BlockDeviceMapping
8. CpuOptions:
9.   CpuOptions
10. CreditSpecification:
11.   CreditSpecification
12. DisableApiTermination: Boolean
13. EbsOptimized: Boolean
14. ElasticGpuSpecifications:
15.   - ElasticGpuSpecification
16. ElasticInferenceAccelerators:
17.   - ElasticInferenceAccelerator
18. EnclaveOptions:
19.   EnclaveOptions
20. HibernationOptions:

```
21.    HibernationOptions
22.  HostId: String
23.  HostResourceGroupArn: String
24.  IamInstanceProfile: String
25.  ImageId: String
26.  InstanceInitiatedShutdownBehavior: String
27.  InstanceType: String
28.  Ipv6AddressCount: Integer
29.  Ipv6Addresses:
30.    - InstanceIpv6Address
31.  KernelId: String
32.  KeyName: String
33.  LaunchTemplate:
34.    LaunchTemplateSpecification
35.  LicenseSpecifications:
36.    - LicenseSpecification
37.  Monitoring: Boolean
38.  NetworkInterfaces:
39.    - NetworkInterface
40.  PlacementGroupName: String
41.  PrivateDnsNameOptions:
42.    PrivateDnsNameOptions
43.  PrivateIpAddress: String
44.  PropagateTagsToVolumeOnCreation: Boolean
45.  RamdiskId: String
46.  SecurityGroupIds:
47.    - String
48.  SecurityGroups:
49.    - String
50.  SourceDestCheck: Boolean
51.  SsmAssociations:
52.    - SsmAssociation
53.  SubnetId: String
54.  Tags:
55.    - Tag
56.  Tenancy: String
57.  UserData: String
58.  Volumes:
59.    - Volume
```

At this point, we observe that there are numerous properties available for the **Instance** Resource type.

> **Note: It is not mandatory to use all the properties of an AWS CloudFormation Resource type. The properties you include in your template depend on your specific requirements. You can choose to specify only the properties that are relevant to your use case. For example, if you are launching a simple EC2 instance and are satisfied with the default values for certain properties, you might only need to specify InstanceType and ImageId. On the other hand, if you have specific networking or security requirements, you may include additional properties like SubnetId, SecurityGroupIds, etc.**

Based on our needs, we can choose specific properties while either retaining default values or omitting those that are not required. Further details on this topic will be explored in the subsequent section on Resource creation and management later in the chapter.

4. Next, we will copy the syntax, including the relevant attributes for **Properties**, and proceed to tailor our template to align with the project requirements. Following this step, our resource syntax will be prepared for use in the project. This is the final step.

   Similarly, we can choose the default syntax and subsequently modify it to suit the requirements of the other AWS service we intend to configure in our template.

Sample excerpts

Let us explore some examples of Resources excerpts for a better understanding of properties. Each of them has a unique set of properties that defines the resource type setup, like:

- **EC2 instance properties**: The sample for EC2 instance resource type is as follows:
  ```
  Resources:
    MyEC2Instance:
      Type: "AWS::EC2::Instance"
      Properties:
        InstanceType: t2.micro
        ImageId: ami-12345678
        KeyName: myKeyPair
  ```

  In this context, the defined properties include **InstanceType**, **ImageId**, and **KeyName**.

- **S3 bucket instance properties**: The sample for S3 bucket resource type is as follows:

```
o  Resources:
o    MyS3Bucket:
o      Type: "AWS::S3::Bucket"
o      Properties:
o        BucketName: my-unique-bucket
o        AccessControl: PublicRead
```

In this context, the defined properties include **BucketName** and **AccessControl**.

- **VPC properties**: The sample for VPC resource type is as follows:

```
o  Resources:
o    MyVPC:
o      Type: "AWS::EC2::VPC"
o      Properties:
o        CidrBlock: 10.0.0.0/16
o        EnableDnsSupport: true
```

In this context, the defined properties include **CidrBlock** and **EnableDnsSupport**.

- **Lambda function properties**: The sample for Lambda resource type is as follows:

```
o  Resources:
o    MyLambdaFunction:
o      Type: "AWS::Lambda::Function"
o      Properties:
o        FunctionName: my-lambda-function
o        Runtime: nodejs14.x
o        Handler: index. Handler
```

In this context, the defined properties include **FunctionName**, **Runtime** and **Handler**.

- **SQS queue properties**: The sample for SQS resource type is as follows:

```
o  Resources:
o    MySQSQueue:
o      Type: "AWS::SQS::Queue"
o      Properties:
o        QueueName: my-queue
o        DelaySeconds: 0
o        MaximumMessageSize: 262144
```

In this context, the defined properties include **QueueName**, **DelaySeconds** and **MaximumMessageSize**.

Resource creation and management

In AWS CloudFormation, resource creation and management form a fundamental aspect of the IaC paradigm. This process involves defining, provisioning, and configuring AWS resources through CloudFormation templates. To understand more about this, let us explore a few example scenarios that can help us understand the concepts of resource creation and management in AWS CloudFormation.

Scenario one

We need to perform a simple EC2 instance deployment using the default VPC properties:

- **Objective**: The objective is to deploy an Apache based web server on an EC2 instance. It will use the default VPC configuration we already have in our account in us-east-1 region.

- **Template**: The sample template for the same is as follows:

```
1.  AWSTemplateFormatVersion: '2010-09-09'
2.  Description: "Deploy a basic apache
    web server using EC2 instance"
3.  Resources:
4.    MyEC2Instance:
5.      Type: AWS::EC2::Instance
6.      Properties:
7.        ImageId: ami-xxxxxxxxxxxxxxxxx
8.  # Replace with an available AMI ID
9.        InstanceType: t2.micro
10.       KeyName: YourKeyPairName
11. # Replace with your key pair name for SSH access
12.       UserData:
13.         Fn::Base64: |
14.           #!/bin/bash
15.           yum update -y
16.           yum install -y httpd
17.           service httpd start
18.           chkconfig httpd on
19.       SecurityGroups:
20.         - YourSecurityGroupName
       # Replace with your security group name for EC2 instance
```

In this example:

- Replace **ami-xxxxxxxxxxxxxxxxx** with the actual AMI ID of an Amazon Machine Image that is available in your AWS Region.

- Replace **YourKeyPairName** with the name of your existing EC2 key pair that you want to use for SSH access.

- Replace **YourSecurityGroupName** with the name of your existing security group that allows HTTP traffic (port 80).

This template creates an EC2 instance with the specified AMI, installs Apache during the instance launch using the UserData script, and starts the Apache service. It makes use of the default VPC configuration like VPC ID, subnets etc. as we have not declared them specifically. Ensure that your security group allows inbound traffic on port 80 to access the web server.

Let us attempt to execute this template using the real values for **ImageId**, **KeyName**, and **SecurityGroups** present in our AWS account (us-east-1 region) for testing purposes. The template, post-configuration with the authentic values, is as follows:

```
1.  AWSTemplateFormatVersion: 2010-09-09
2.  Description: Deploy a Apache web server using EC2|Default VPC
3.  Resources:
4.    MyEC2Instance:
5.      Type: 'AWS::EC2::Instance'
6.      Properties:
7.        ImageId: ami-0e9107ed11be76fde
8.        InstanceType: t2.micro
9.        KeyName: mynewkey
10.       UserData:
11.         'Fn::Base64': |
12.           #!/bin/bash
13.           yum update -y
14.           yum install -y httpd
15.           service httpd start
16.           chkconfig httpd on
17.       SecurityGroups:
18.         - launch-wizard-1
```

We will try to spin up this template using AWS CloudFormation console as we attempted in earlier chapters. Please refer to the following snippet for the final status of our stack:

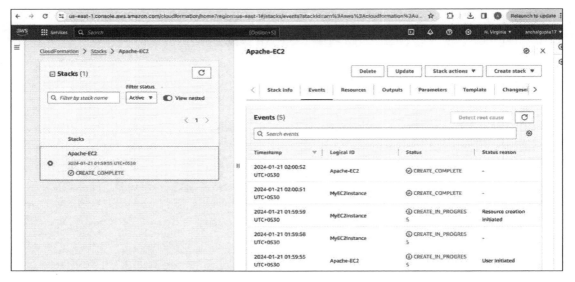

Figure 3.4: *Apache-EC2 stack status*

From the **Resources** section on the console page, we will get the EC2 instance detail. Please refer to following figure:

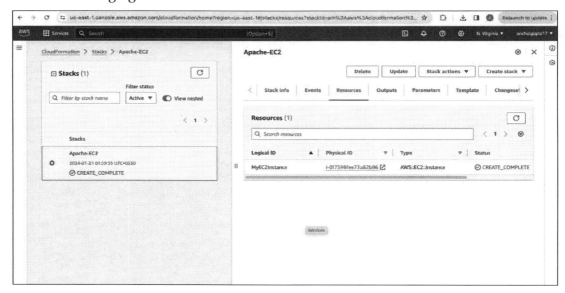

Figure 3.5: *EC2 instance detail*

Here we will click on the EC2 **Physical ID** hyperlink which will redirect us to the EC2 console page. From there, we will get the public IP information. Please refer to *Figure 3.6:*

Figure 3.6: *EC2 console page*

To further validate it, let us try to directly hit the web page for our installed Apache web server. We will try to hit the public IP of our newly commissioned EC2 instance which should land us to the default page of our web server and will confirm if our setup was done right or not. Please refer to the following figure:

Figure 3.7: *Apache Web server validation*

Thus, the confirmation of the default message indicates the successful creation of the necessary EC2 instance, along with the installation and configuration of the required web server through the CloudFormation template. This marks the validation of our setup.

A crucial point to observe is that we have utilized fundamental properties for the instance Resource type, while retaining other values as their default settings. This reiterates that it is not mandatory to configure every attribute listed under the properties section.

Summary

In the provided configuration, we have instantiated a single resource, an EC2 instance, utilizing our CloudFormation template. This represents a straightforward scenario where we create and configure a solitary resource using our template, incorporating only a few Parameters. In this case, we are not addressing additional elements such as VPC ID, subnets, etc., as we are relying on default values, simplifying the resource's management. Likewise, we can create individual resource templates for other AWS services tailored to our specific requirements.

Scenario two

Now, let us attempt to deploy the same EC2 setup with the S3 bucket in a single template:

- **Objective**: The objective is to deploy an Apache-based web server on an EC2 instance along with other resources like S3 bucket in us-east-1 region of AWS.

- **Template**: The sample template for the same is as follows:

```
1.  AWSTemplateFormatVersion: '2010-09-09'
2.  Description: "Deploy a S3 and Apache web server"
3.  Resources:
4.    MyEC2Instance:
5.      Type: AWS::EC2::Instance
6.      Properties:
7.        ImageId: ami-0e9107ed11be76fde
8.        InstanceType: t2.micro
9.        KeyName: mynewkey
10.       UserData:
11.         Fn::Base64: |
12.           #!/bin/bash
13.           yum update -y
14.           yum install -y httpd
15.           service httpd start
16.           chkconfig httpd on
17.       SecurityGroups:
18.         -  launch-wizard-1
19.
20.   MyS3Bucket:
21.     Type: AWS::S3::Bucket
22.     Properties:
23.       BucketName: mytestbucket2424
24.       AccessControl: PublicRead
25.
```

Now, we will try to spin up this template using AWS CloudFormation console similar to the earlier attempted. Please refer to following snippet for the final status of our stack:

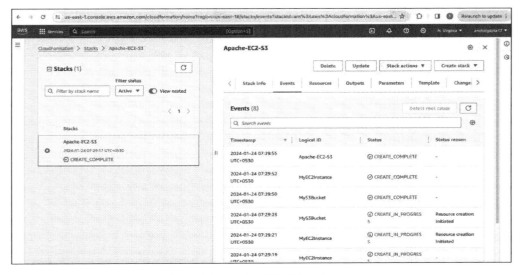

Figure 3.8: *Apache-EC2-S3 stack status*

Next, let us move to the **Resources** section, where we will discover the **Resources** we have just created along with their associated details. Please consult the following figure for reference:

Figure 3.9: *Template Resource section*

In this section, we observe that two resources have been successfully generated using the provided template, each accompanied by corresponding hyperlinks for additional verification. Selecting the EC2 hyperlink redirects us to the recently established EC2 instance, offering access to pertinent details, including the public IP address like *Scenario one*. We can validate the successful installation and configuration of our Apache web server by accessing this IP.

Likewise, by clicking on the S3 bucket hyperlink, we are directed to the dedicated S3 bucket console page. Here, we can inspect our newly created S3 bucket, complete with essential details for validation.

For additional details, kindly refer to the subsequent set of figures:

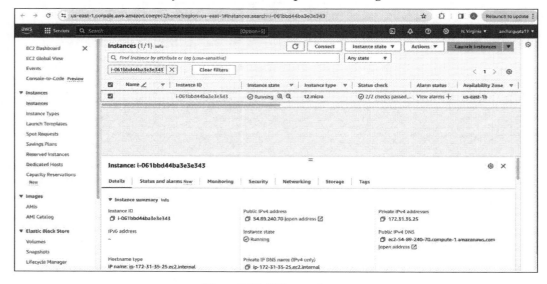

Figure 3.10: EC2 console page

Now, refer to *Figure 3.11*:

Figure 3.11: Apache Web server validation

Refer to the following figure for more details:

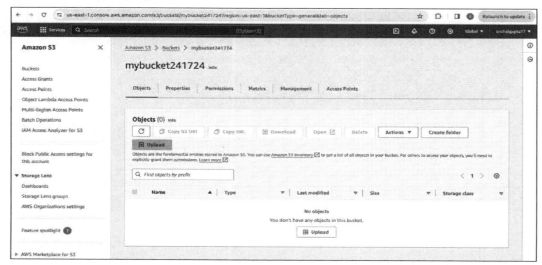

Figure 3.12: S3 bucket console page

Summary

In this example, we have effectively created two separate resources using a single template, highlighting their ability to exist independently without affecting each other's settings. Both resources were neatly described in the **Resources** section. This emphasizes our flexibility in choosing to define individual resources or combine multiple ones in a single CloudFormation template. The choice depends on the unique requirements of our project and the environment we are working in.

Optimizing multi-resource templates

When dealing with templates that define multiple resources, take note of the following guidelines:

- **Organize Resources clearly**: Ensure that your template is well-organized, with each Resource clearly defined. Use indentation and formatting to enhance readability.

- **Use meaningful Resource names**: Choose descriptive and meaningful names for your Resources. This makes it easier for you and others to understand their purpose.

- **Documentation is key**: Include comments or documentation within the template to explain the purpose and configuration of each resource. This is especially helpful for anyone reviewing or modifying the template in the future.

- **Consider dependencies**: If there are dependencies between resources, make sure to define them appropriately. CloudFormation allows you to specify dependencies to ensure resources are created in the correct order. We will explore this in detail in the next section.

- **Test incrementally**: When developing templates with multiple resources, test and validate incrementally. Create and test individual resources before combining them into a larger template. This helps identify and resolve issues more effectively.

- **Split templates**: When dealing with many resources, it is recommended to break down your templates to enhance resource management.

- **Continuous improvement**: Regularly review and update your templates as your infrastructure evolves. Incorporate lessons learned from previous deployments to enhance the efficiency and reliability of your CloudFormation templates.

> Note: The provided guidelines offer valuable insights into effective management of CloudFormation templates with multiple resources. While these pointers serve as a foundation, it is crucial to acknowledge that the optimal approach may vary based on the specific requirements of your project. Flexibility and adaptability should be exercised to tailor the implementation to the unique needs and intricacies of each individual project.

Resource dependencies

Resource dependencies form a pivotal aspect of orchestrating the seamless creation and configuration of diverse cloud resources. The term dependency in this context refers to the relationship between resources where the successful creation or configuration of one resource relies on the existence or state of another. The orchestration of these dependencies guarantees that resources are created and configured in a carefully orchestrated order, preventing issues related to unfulfilled prerequisites or misaligned configurations.

This dependency can be divided into two categories:

- Implicit dependency
- Explicit dependency

Let us explore more about each of them in detail.

Implicit dependency

Implicit dependencies are relationships between resources that CloudFormation recognizes automatically based on the template's configuration. This means we are not going to define them specially. Our template will automatically detect the dependency and orchestrate the creation of resources in the necessary order to avoid any issues.

Let us look at the detailed example to enhance our comprehension:

- **Use case**: Our objective is to establish a VPC along with a specified subnet nested within this VPC in us-east-1 region.

- **Template**: The sample template for the same is as follows:

```
1.  AWSTemplateFormatVersion: "2010-09-09"
2.
3.  Resources:
4.    MyVPC:
5.      Type: "AWS::EC2::VPC"
6.      Properties:
7.        CidrBlock: "10.0.0.0/16"
8.        EnableDnsSupport: "true"
9.        EnableDnsHostnames: "true"
10.
11.   MySubnet:
12.     Type: "AWS::EC2::Subnet"
13.     Properties:
14.       VpcId: !Ref MyVPC
15.       CidrBlock: "10.0.0.0/24"
```

In this template, our goal is to generate a custom VPC based on our specified CIDR, incorporating only a subset of properties. Additionally, we aim to craft a subnet within this VPC. To gain insights into the sequence of execution that AWS CloudFormation will follow in creating the necessary resources, let us execute this template on the AWS CloudFormation console. The following figure outlines this process:

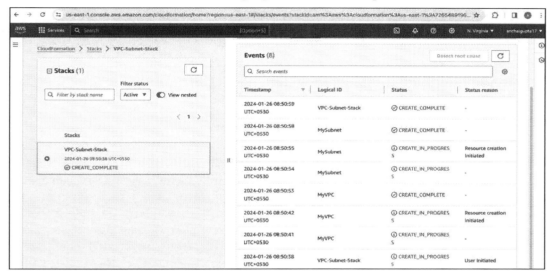

Figure 3.13: Intrinsic dependency illustration

In this sequence, CloudFormation prioritized the creation of the VPC resource (**MyVPC**), waiting for its status to transition to **CREATE_COMPLETE** before proceeding with the Subnet (**MySubnet**). It is noteworthy to revisit *Figure 3.8*, where we attempted to create an EC2 instance alongside an S3 bucket. In that scenario, both resources entered the **CREATE_IN_ PROGRESS** state concurrently, disregarding the state of other resources. However, in the current example, CloudFormation autonomously determined the order in which resources should be created, considering dependencies for their setup and configuration.

Now, let us dive into how CloudFormation discerns the optimal resource creation order. In the **MySubnet** module of the template, we have specified properties, including VPC ID, which designates the VPC under which the subnet will be created. Since we are simultaneously creating the VPC, we cannot hardcode the VPC ID, as it is not available to us yet. Therefore, we employ the intrinsic function **!Ref**, signaling to CloudFormation that, during subnet creation, it should reference the VPC ID from the newly created VPC resource. The snippet of the module from the defined template is as follows:

```
MySubnet:
  Type: "AWS::EC2::Subnet"
  Properties:
    VpcId: !Ref MyVPC
    CidrBlock: "10.0.0.0/24"
```

To achieve this substitution of the actual VPC ID, CloudFormation must create the VPC resource first before proceeding with the subnet. This decision is automatically identified by CloudFormation upon parsing the template.

> **Note: !Ref stands as one of the intrinsic functions, signifying Refer to. A detailed exploration of this function will be presented later in this chapter. Further intrinsic functions, instrumental in establishing intrinsic dependencies, will be uncovered in a dedicated chapter, where we will delve into their distinct use cases and functionalities.**

This dynamic sequencing proves invaluable, especially when managing multiple interdependent resources within a template.

Explicit dependency

Explicit dependency in AWS CloudFormation refers to the precise definition of relationships between resources within a template. Unlike implicit dependencies, where CloudFormation automatically determines the order of resource creation based on property references, explicit dependencies provide explicit instructions on the order in which resources should be created or updated. By explicitly declaring dependencies, you gain greater control over the orchestration of your infrastructure, ensuring that resources are provisioned or modified in a specified sequence. This level of precision becomes invaluable when dealing with complex architectures and interdependencies, allowing you to define the exact flow of resource creation or updates to meet specific project requirements. In this section, we will explore how to understand explicit dependencies in CloudFormation templates to achieve a more controlled and predictable infrastructure deployment.

Explicit dependencies are explicitly defined in the CloudFormation template using the **DependsOn** attribute. Let us explore an example to understand this in detail:

- **Use case**: Our objective is to establish a coordinated deployment of resources, specifically an S3 bucket, an EC2 instance, and an RDS instance in us-east-1 region, utilizing extrinsic dependencies in AWS CloudFormation. Extrinsic dependencies will be leveraged to define the precise order in which these resources are provisioned or updated.

- **Template**: The sample template for the same is as follows:

```
1.  AWSTemplateFormatVersion: '2010-09-09'
2.  Description: "Setup S3 and EC2"
3.
4.  Resources:
5.    MyS3Bucket:
6.      Type: AWS::S3::Bucket
7.      Properties:
8.        BucketName: mybucket262425
9.    MyEC2Instance:
```

```
10.      Type: AWS::EC2::Instance
11.      DependsOn: MyS3Bucket
12.# Explicit dependency on the S3 bucket
13.
14.      Properties:
15.        ImageId: ami-0a3c3a20c09d6f377
16.        InstanceType: t2.micro
17.        KeyName: mynewkey
18.        UserData:
19.          Fn::Base64: |
20.            #!/bin/bash
21.            echo "My EC2 instance depends on the S3 bucket."
```

In this AWS CloudFormation template, we are defining the setup for an S3 bucket (**MyS3Bucket**) and an EC2 instance (**MyEC2Instance**). The explicit dependency is established by using the **DependsOn** attribute in the definition of the EC2 instance, specifically pointing to the S3 bucket. Unlike intrinsic dependencies typically declared in the properties section of a Resource, this explicit dependency is defined outside the properties section. This design ensures that CloudFormation will ensure the S3 bucket is created before proceeding with the EC2 instance. Now, let us execute this template on the AWS CloudFormation console and explore the generated events. The following figures provide a detailed overview of the process:

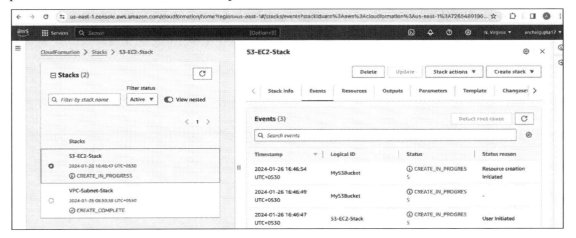

Figure 3.14: Creation of S3 bucket

Now, upon reviewing the **Events** section, it becomes apparent that the AWS CloudFormation service is currently in the process of setting up the S3 bucket exclusively (with status **CREATE_IN_PROGRESS**), without initiating the creation of the EC2 instance. This is facilitated by the **DependsOn** attribute, allowing the service to identify the resource that needs to be created first (in this scenario, the S3 bucket). Once the S3 bucket creation is completed, the service will then only proceed to configure the EC2 instance. For a visual representation of this process, please refer to *Figure 3.16*:

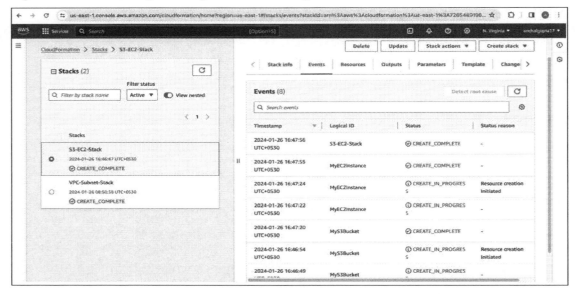

Figure 3.15: Creation of EC2 instance

In *Figure 3.16*, we can see that the AWS CloudFormation service starts creating the EC2 instance only after successfully setting up the S3 bucket (when the status changes to **CREATE_COMPLETE**).

Resource deletion and update

Updating and deleting resources in AWS CloudFormation are integral aspects of managing your IaC. The CloudFormation service provides mechanisms to modify existing resources and gracefully handle their removal. Let us understand these processes and explore how AWS CloudFormation empowers users to adapt to evolving requirements and maintain robust infrastructure.

Resource deletion

AWS CloudFormation offers deletion policies that define how resources should be handled during stack removal. These policies play a pivotal role in orchestrating the deletion sequence and managing dependencies. The **DeletionPolicy** attribute can be declared under the Resource section. The primary deletion policies options include the following:

- **Delete**: This represents the default policy. In cases where no specific deletion policy is specified, AWS CloudFormation, during stack deletion, will remove all the resources outlined in the stack. However, there are certain exceptional scenarios where the default deletion policy may not yield the desired behavior. A few instances are:

- o **S3 bucket**: The default behavior of AWS CloudFormation is to delete an S3 bucket during stack deletion. Yet, if the bucket holds objects or versioned objects, the default deletion policy may fall short. To successfully delete an S3 bucket containing objects, it is necessary to first remove the objects within the bucket. Only after this step, the deletion policy will effectively proceed to delete the bucket; otherwise, the deletion operation may encounter failures.

- o **RDS::DBCluster**: The default policy for this resource is Snapshot (we will discuss it next).

- o **RDS::DBInstance**: If the **DBClusterIdentifier** property is not mentioned in the properties section of this resource, the default policy is snapshot.

- **Retain**: As the name suggests, CloudFormation has the ability to retain resources during stack deletion by using the Retain deletion policy. This policy ensures that the specified resource, along with its contents, remains intact even after the stack deletion is completed. You can apply the Retain deletion policy to various resource types. While the stack transitions to the **Delete_Complete** state, the retained resources persist and continue to accrue associated charges until you explicitly delete them.

- **Snapshot**: With this option, CloudFormation generates snapshots for resources that support this feature before initiating their deletion. Even after the stack deletion is finalized, and the stack enters the **Delete_Complete** state, any snapshots created using this policy persist. It is important to note that these Retained snapshots continue to exist and accumulate associated charges until you explicitly delete them.

  Here is a compilation of resources that offer support for snapshots:

  - o **AWS::DocDB::DBCluster**
  - o **AWS::EC2::Volume**
  - o **AWS::ElastiCache::CacheCluster**
  - o **AWS::ElastiCache::ReplicationGroup**
  - o **AWS::Neptune::DBCluster**
  - o **AWS::RDS::DBCluster**
  - o **AWS::RDS::DBInstance**
  - o **AWS::Redshift::Cluster**

Syntax

We will explore an example involving an S3 bucket to comprehend the syntax and application of the deletion policy in the resource section. Please refer to the following snippet of the template:

```
1. AWSTemplateFormatVersion: '2010-09-09'
2. Resources:
3.    myS3Bucket:
4.       Type: AWS::S3::Bucket
5.       DeletionPolicy: Retain
```

In this scenario, we want to preserve the S3 bucket even after the stack is deleted. To achieve this, we set the **DeletionPolicy** option to **Retain** for our bucket (**myS3Bucket**). By specifying this value, we ensure that deleting the stack, which includes this S3 bucket, will not result in the removal of the bucket. The **Retain** option prevents the deletion of this specific resource during the stack deletion process.

If no specific syntax is provided, the default option is assumed to be delete, ensuring that the resource can be directly deleted.

Likewise, for resources such as RDS instances, which support snapshots, the Snapshot syntax would appear as follows:

```
1. Resources:
2.    MyRDSInstance:
3.       Type: AWS::RDS::DBInstance
4.       DeletionPolicy: Snapshot
5.       Properties:
6.          DBInstanceIdentifier: my-rds-instance
7.          AllocatedStorage: 10
8.          DBInstanceClass: db.t2.micro
9.          Engine: mysql
10.         MasterUsername: admin
11.         MasterUserPassword: password
```

In this example, the **DeletionPolicy** attribute for the RDS instance (**MyRDSInstance**) is set to **Snapshot**. This means that when the stack is deleted, AWS CloudFormation will Retain the RDS instance and create a final DB Snapshot before deleting it.

Tip: While AWS CloudFormation offers different options for resource deletion during stack removal, it is crucial to refer to the resource-specific documentation for detailed insights. Each AWS Resource type may have unique behaviors, and the documentation serves as a comprehensive guide to understanding deletion policies, syntax, and special considerations. Staying informed about each AWS resource's specifics ensures precise configuration in CloudFormation templates, aligning with AWS best practices and adapting to any changes or updates in AWS services.

Stack deletion

Let us explore the process of deleting a stack using the AWS management console for the CloudFormation service. Through the following steps, we will remove the **VPC-Subnet-Stack** created earlier during our discussion on intrinsic dependencies:

1. **Navigate to AWS CloudFormation console**: Access the AWS management console, locate the **CloudFormation** service, and open the console.

2. **Identify the current stack state**: Observe the current state of the stack in the AWS **CloudFormation** console. Ensure the stack you wish to **delete**, such as **VPC-Subnet-Stack**, is visible. Please refer to the following figure:

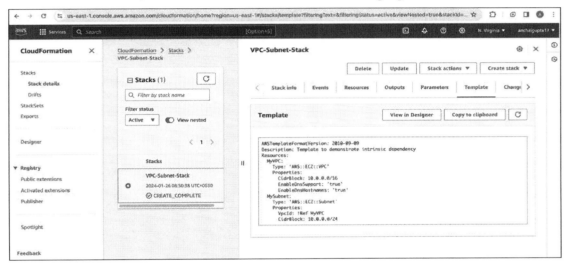

Figure 3.16: Current state of stack

3. **Examine the template section**: Review the **Template** section for the chosen stack. If no specific deletion policy option is defined in the template, the default behavior is assumed. This default behavior involves deleting resources as part of the stack deletion process. Please refer to the preceding figure.

4. **Initiate stack deletion**: Proceed to initiate the stack deletion process by selecting the desired stack (for example, **VPC-Subnet-Stack**) and choosing the **Delete** option. This is a crucial step, as we need to be cautious in scenarios where we have multiple stacks. Always double check the stack selection and then click on **Delete** option.

5. **Follow deletion confirmation steps**: Follow the on-screen prompts to confirm the deletion. AWS CloudFormation will perform the deletion based on defined deletion policies or the default behavior if none are specified. Kindly refer to *Figure 3.18* for the same:

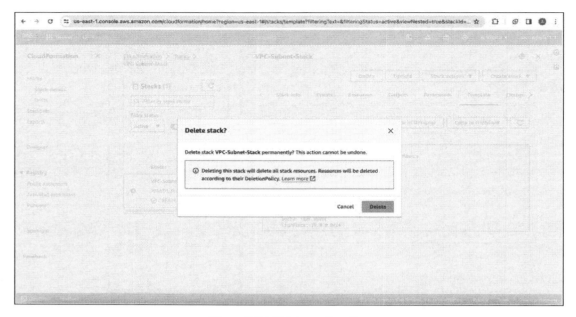

Figure 3.17: Delete confirmation

6. **Monitor deletion progress**: Monitor the deletion progress in the **CloudFormation** console. The status will transition through various stages until the stack deletion is complete. Kindly refer to the following figures:

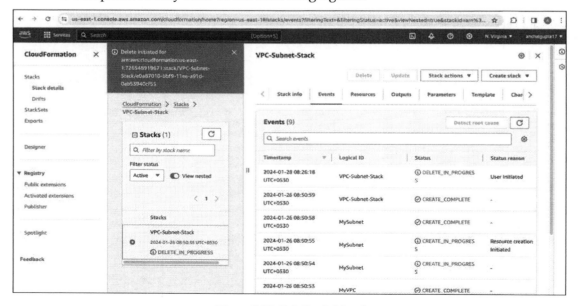

Figure 3.18: Deletion initiated

As we proceed with deleting our stack, it is essential to monitor the removal of associated resources. Once the deletion process is initiated, the status of the events related to resource deletion will transition to **DELETE_IN_PROGRESS**. This status signifies that the CloudFormation service is actively working on removing the specified resources:

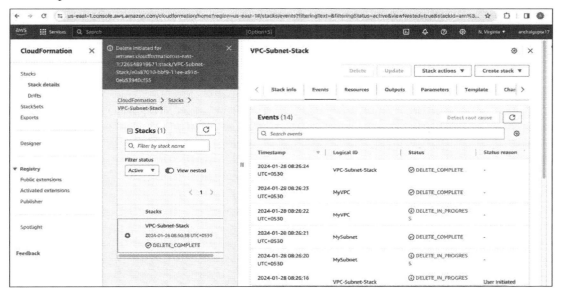

Figure 3.19: *Deletion completed*

As soon as it deletes the resource, the event's status will change to **DELETE_ COMPLETE** state. Kindly refer to preceding figure.

One thing to notice is that the deletion order and whether resources are deleted concurrently or sequentially depends on the dependencies and relationships defined in the CloudFormation template. Resources with no dependencies or with dependencies that can be resolved concurrently may be deleted simultaneously.

However, it is important to note that certain resources may have dependencies on others, and CloudFormation will handle deletions based on these dependencies. Resources with dependencies on each other may be deleted sequentially to maintain proper order. For instance, in the current scenario, the subnet was deleted first due to its dependency on the VPC created earlier. Only after the subnet was successfully deleted did the deletion process proceed to the VPC.

Resource update

AWS CloudFormation empowers you to modify your infrastructure seamlessly by updating existing Resources, providing a fundamental capability for adapting to changes, implementing enhancements, and optimizing your AWS environment. A comprehensive understanding of how Resource updates function within CloudFormation is essential for the effective maintenance of a reliable and up to date infrastructure.

When triggering an update to a CloudFormation stack, the service intelligently recognizes alterations made in your template and applies those modifications to the relevant resources. CloudFormation evaluates the current state of resources vis-a-vis the desired state outlined in the updated template.

Update replace policy

In conjunction with deletion policies that proficiently handle resource removal, CloudFormation employs update replace policies to govern the approach for executing resource updates. The resource update policies define how the service should handle changes to resources during stack updates. These policies give you granular control over the update process, allowing you to specify the desired behavior for each resource in your template. The **UpdateReplacePolicy** attribute can be declared under the Resource section for any resource. The primary update policy options include the following:

- **Delete**: This is the default option. CloudFormation deletes the old resource and creates a new one with a new physical ID.

- **Retain**: It Retains the existing resource, even if it is being replaced. This can be useful to preserve data or configurations during updates. The key observation here is that while it Retains the resource, it removes it from the CloudFormation scope.

- **Snapshot**: Applies to resources that support snapshots (e.g., Amazon RDS instances). It creates a Snapshot of the existing resource before deleting it. The following list of resources support snapshots option:
    - **AWS::EC2::Volume**
    - **AWS::ElastiCache::CacheCluster**
    - **AWS::ElastiCache::ReplicationGroup**
    - **AWS::Neptune::DBCluster**
    - **AWS::RDS::DBCluster**
    - **AWS::RDS::DBInstance**
    - **AWS::Redshift::Cluster**

> **Note: If you specify the Snapshot option in the UpdateReplacePolicy for a resource that does not support snapshots, CloudFormation will fall back to default behavior, which is Delete.**

Let us delve into an example template where we aim to create and update a RDS instance. In this exploration, we will observe how this attribute interacts with our resource:

Template: The sample template for the same is as follows:

```
 1.  AWSTemplateFormatVersion: 2010-09-09
 2.  Description: Demo of Retain Update Policy for RDS Instance
 3.  Resources:
 4.    MyRDSInstance:
 5.      Type: 'AWS::RDS::DBInstance'
 6.      DeletionPolicy: Retain
 7.      UpdateReplacePolicy: Retain
 8.      Properties:
 9.        DBInstanceIdentifier: my-rds-instance
10.        AllocatedStorage: 10
11.        DBInstanceClass: db.t2.micro
12.        Engine: mysql
13.        MasterUsername: admin
14.        MasterUserPassword: password
```

Let us execute this template. After completion, the stack deployment details will be available. Please refer to the following figure for specific information:

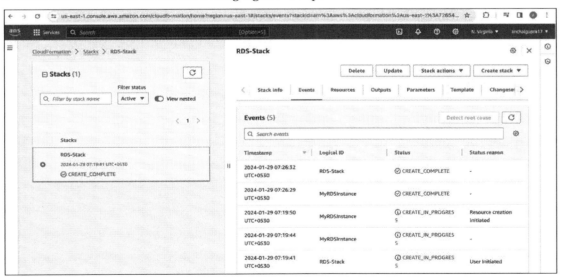

Figure 3.20: *RDS stack creation completed*

Now, let us proceed to the **Resources** section on the console page, where we can find details about the newly established RDS instance. Please consult the following figure for specifics on the RDS instance:

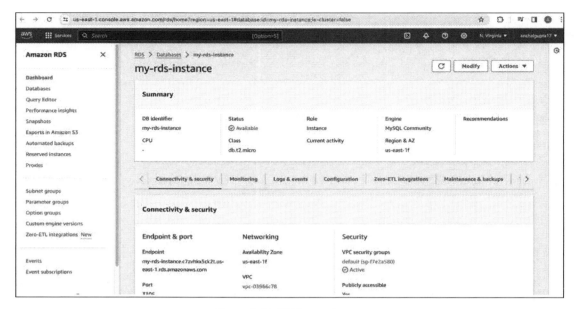

Figure 3.21: *RDS console page*

Upon successful deployment, our RDS instance is now up and running, identified by **my-rds-instance** in the **DB identifier** field.

Now, we will attempt to update the RDS instance by modifying this **DB identifier** field in our template and observe how the update process unfolds.

Following is the updated template:

```
1. AWSTemplateFormatVersion: 2010-09-09
2. Description: Demo of Retain Update Policy for RDS Instance
3. Resources:
4.   MyRDSInstance:
5.     Type: 'AWS::RDS::DBInstance'
6.     DeletionPolicy: Retain
7.     UpdateReplacePolicy: Retain
8.     Properties:
9.       DBInstanceIdentifier: updated-rds-instance
10.      AllocatedStorage: 10
11.      DBInstanceClass: db.t2.micro
12.      Engine: mysql
```

```
13.        MasterUsername: admin
14.        MasterUserPassword: password
```

With the **DBInstanceIdentifier** property now set to **updated-rds-instance**, we aim to update our existing stack using this modified template. Given that our **UpdateReplacePolicy** attribute is configured as **Retain**, the expectation is that it would not delete the original RDS instance but create a new one with the updated DB identifier. Let us return to the AWS CloudFormation console and initiate the template update.

The current state of our stack before we begin the update process is as follows:

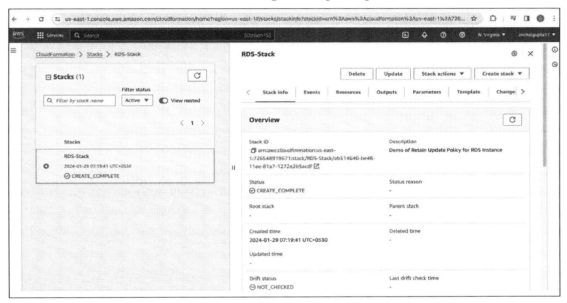

Figure 3.22: Current state of stack

Now, with the current stack selected, the **Update** button is enabled. A simple click on **Update** will redirect us to the next page, prompting us to proceed with the template update. Please refer to the following figure for a visual guide:

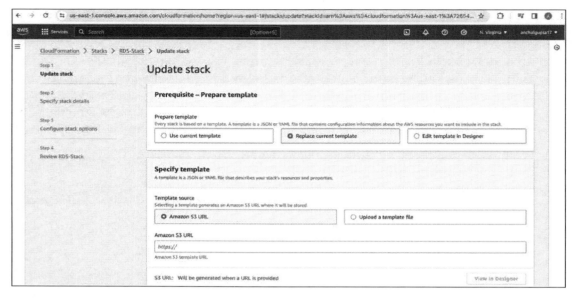

Figure 3.23: Replace current template

We will now choose, **Replace current template** to update the new template from our local system directly. Other options will be explored later in the book. After uploading the new template, we will proceed with the next steps, similar to the initial stack creation process. On the final page, where we click the **Submit** button at the bottom of the page, we will find a section for **Changeset preview**. Please refer to the following figure for details:

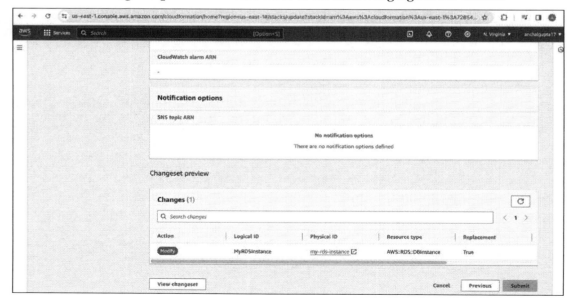

Figure 3.24: Preview changes

Additional details on Change sets will be covered in a later in the book. However, for our current understanding, let us focus on the information generated here. In this section, we can observe that the CloudFormation service has identified the **Action** as **Modify**, indicating that the existing setup needs to be modified according to the new template. Now, let us click on the **Submit** button and observe the actions performed by the CloudFormation service:

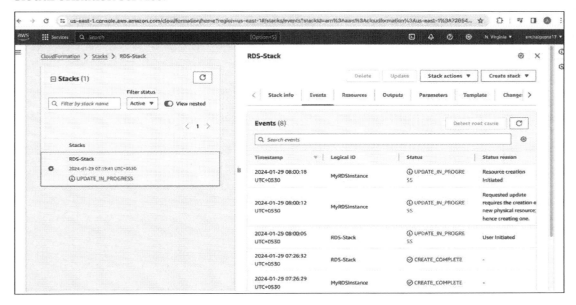

Figure 3.25: Update in progress

Next, we observe a new event, **UPDATE_IN_PROGRESS**, indicating that the stack is currently being updated with the new changes. Notably, the status reason states, **Requested update required the creation of a new physical resource; hence creating one.** This implies the creation of a new instance without deleting the existing one. This behavior is a result of the **UpdateReplacePolicy** attribute set to **Retain** in our original template. After the completion of the stack update, navigating to the RDS console page reveals the existence of both our original and updated RDS instances. Please refer to the following figure:

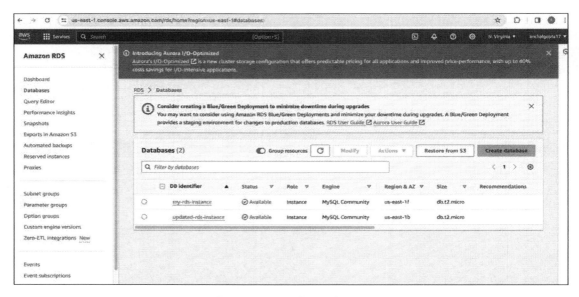

Figure 3.26: RDS console page

Conclusion

In conclusion, this chapter has provided a comprehensive overview of essential concepts in AWS CloudFormation, guiding you through the fundamental elements of template creation and management. Starting with the declaration of the **AWSTemplateFormatVersion** and Description sections, we looked into the core components of defining resources using various AWS resource types.

We explored the diverse properties and attributes associated with resources, gaining insights into their configuration and customization. The chapter also elucidated the intricacies of resource dependencies, emphasizing the importance of understanding and managing the order in which resources are created. Furthermore, the discussion extended to resource updates and deletions, where we explored policies governing modifications and removals. Understanding the nuances of these processes is integral to effectively managing and evolving your infrastructure as code. As you move forward, the knowledge gained in this chapter will form a solid foundation for harnessing the power of AWS CloudFormation, enabling you to design, deploy, and manage AWS resources seamlessly.

In the forthcoming chapters, we will explore advanced subjects such as Parameters, Metadata, Mappings, and Conditions, offering a more nuanced comprehension of CloudFormation's extensive capabilities and industry best practices.

Multiple choice questions

1. **What does the AWSTemplateFormatVersion section in an AWS CloudFormation template define?**

   a. The AWS account ID

   b. The version of the CloudFormation template format

   c. The name of the template

   d. The AWS Region

2. **What section of a CloudFormation template is used to provide additional information about the template, such as its purpose and contents?**

   a. AWSTemplateFormatVersion

   b. Metadata

   c. Resources

   d. Description

3. **What is the primary function of the DependsOn attribute in AWS CloudFormation?**

   a. To specify the version of the CloudFormation template

   b. To define the order of resource creation

   c. To manage deletion policies

   d. To control resource updates

4. **In CloudFormation, what is the purpose of the AWS::EC2::Instance resource type?**

   a. Create an S3 bucket

   b. Define an IAM role

   c. Create an EC2 instance

   d. Establish a VPC

5. **If the UpdateReplacePolicy attribute is not specified in a CloudFormation template, what is the default behavior during stack updates?**

   a. Retain

   b. Delete

   c. Snapshot

   d. Modify

Answers

1. a
2. d
3. b
4. c
5. b

Join our book's Discord space

Join the book's Discord Workspace for Latest updates, Offers, Tech happenings around the world, New Release and Sessions with the Authors:

https://discord.bpbonline.com

CHAPTER 4

Parameters, Metadata, Mappings and Conditions

Introduction

This chapter explores the intricate components of Parameters, Metadata, Mappings, and Conditions within the AWS CloudFormation template, pivotal elements that underpin the framework for orchestrating cloud resources on AWS platforms. Through an in-depth examination, readers will gain insight into how these foundational elements empower users to customize deployments, enhance template readability, optimize resource configuration, and precisely tailor deployments to meet specific criteria. By understanding the functionalities and practical applications of Parameters, Metadata, Mappings, and Conditions, readers will be equipped with the knowledge to navigate the complexities of cloud resource management with confidence and efficiency.

Structure

The chapter covers the following topics:

- Parameters
- Additional DataType
- Metadata
- Learning to use Metadata
- Mappings

- Learning to use Mappings
- Conditions
- Practical use of different Conditions

Objectives

This chapter serves as an exploration into the intricacies of Parameters, Metadata, Mappings, and Conditions within AWS CloudFormation. These foundational elements are integral to template-driven infrastructure deployment, providing a structured framework for defining and orchestrating cloud resources on AWS platforms.

Parameters serve as the cornerstone of this customization, enabling users to input values at deployment time and seamlessly adapt templates to varying environments.

We will also explore the significant role of Metadata in enhancing the readability and maintainability of CloudFormation templates. Whether it is providing contextual information within resource sections or effectively structuring template documentation,

Additionally, Mappings emerge as a potent tool for abstracting and streamlining template logic, facilitating dynamic resource configuration based on input Parameters. By exploring Mappings, readers will gain insights into optimizing template design and fortifying reusability across a spectrum of deployment scenarios.

Conditions emerge as a pivotal concept in governing resource creation during stack deployment. As we navigate through this chapter, readers will gain a deeper understanding of how Conditions can be leveraged to tailor deployments with precision.

Overall, by the end of this chapter, readers will gain a comprehensive understanding of how these elements contribute to the efficiency and versatility of managing cloud resources.

Parameters

Parameters in AWS CloudFormation templates allow you to customize and make your templates more flexible. They allow users to input values during the stack creation or update process, making the template adaptable to various scenarios. They also serve as placeholders for values that can be specified at runtime, allowing for greater reusability and dynamic configurations.

Usage of Parameters

Let us take a brief look at how using Parameters benefits the design of a CloudFormation template. Here are the key features:

- **Adaptability**: Parameters allow users to tailor the template to different scenarios. For example, an EC2 instance type or the number of desired instances can be parameterized to accommodate diverse use cases.

- **Flexibility**: Parameters enable user input during the stack creation or update process. This dynamic interaction ensures that users can provide specific values for their deployment needs.

- **Reusability**: By parameterizing values that may change between deployments, templates become more reusable. This modularity facilitates the reuse of a single template across various environments or projects.

- **Sensible defaults**: Including default values in Parameters enhances user experience. Users can proceed with the stack creation without providing specific values and relying on sensible defaults for most situations.

- **Dynamic configurations**: Parameters empower users to make on-the-fly adjustments to the template configurations without modifying the underlying code. This agility is particularly useful in dynamic and evolving cloud environments.

Syntax

In AWS CloudFormation templates, Parameters are declared in the Parameters section, specifying their characteristics such as type, description, default value, and more. The basic syntax for defining Parameters along with their purpose is as follows:

```
1.  Parameters:
2.    ParameterName:
3.      Type: DataType
4.  # Specify the data type (String, Number, List, etc.)
5.      Description: Description of the parameter
6.      Default: DefaultValue
7.  # Optional: Provide a default value
8.      AllowedValues:
9.  # Optional: Specify a list of allowed values
10.       - AllowedValue1
11.       - AllowedValue2
12.     AllowedPattern: "[a-zA-Z0-9]*"
13. # Optional: Specify a regular expression pattern
14.     NoEcho: BooleanValue
15. # Optional: A Boolean value to hide/expose the parameter value
    during stac creation/update.
16.     MinLength: MinimumLength
17. # Optional: Specify minimum length for String type
18.     MaxLength: MaximumLength
19. # Optional: Specify maximum length for String type
20.     MinValue: MinimumValue
```

```
21. # Optional: Specify minimum value for Number type
22.    MaxValue: MaximumValue
23. # Optional: Specify maximum value for Number type
24.    ConstraintDescription: A constraint description
25. # Optional: Displayed when constraint is violated
```

Now, let us dive into some example syntax where we will combine previously mentioned attributes according to our requirements. This exploration will deepen our comprehension of each attribute and illustrate how they synergize in various scenarios. The examples are as follows:

Basic parameter

Let us look at a sample parameter module to understand how it works:

```
1. Parameters:
2.    MyParameter:
3.      Type: String
4.      Description: "This is a basic string parameter."
```

In this example, the parameter named **MyParameter** is configured with a data type of **String**, indicating that it expects string values during stack creation or update. Users initiating the stack deployment, whether through the CloudFormation console or command line interface, will be prompted to provide a string value for the **MyParameter** parameter. The provided string value will then be assigned to the parameter as part of the stack creation or update process. This setup ensures user interaction when customizing string Parameters based on specific requirements during deployment.

Parameter with a default value

Let us explore an example module with a default parameter configuration:

```
1. Parameters:
2.    MyParameter:
3.      Type: Number
4.      Default: 10
5.      Description: "This parameter has a default value of 10."
```

In this example, the parameter named **MyParameter** is configured with a data type of **Number**, indicating that it should accept numerical values. The **Default** attribute is set to **10**, establishing a default value for the parameter. If a user deploying the stack does not explicitly provide a value for **MyParameter**, it will automatically default to the number **10**. The accompanying **Description** attribute offers additional context, stating that the parameter has a default value of 10. This setup provides flexibility for users to customize the parameter during stack deployment while ensuring a predefined default value when no explicit input is provided.

Parameter with allowed values

Let us explore an example to understand how Parameters with allowed values work:

```
1.  Parameters:
2.    MyParameter:
3.      Type: String
4.      AllowedValues: ["V1", "V2"]
5.      Description: "This parameter can only take values V1 or V2
```

In this example, the parameter named **MyParameter** is configured with a data type of **String**. Additionally, the **AllowedValues** attribute restricts the valid input to either **V1** or **V2**. This setup ensures that during the stack creation or update process, users are prompted to provide a value for **MyParameter**, but only values **V1** or **V2** are permissible. The **Description** provides a clear understanding of the constraint on the parameter, indicating that it is designed to accept only the specified values **V1** or **V2**. This allows for a more controlled and predefined set of options, ensuring consistency and adherence to specific requirements.

Parameter with NoEcho

Let us explore an example with **NoEcho** attribute:

```
1.  Parameters:
2.    MySensitiveParameter:
3.      Type: String
4.      NoEcho: true
5.      Description: "Sensitive Value"
```

In this example, the **MySensitiveParameter** is configured as a string type parameter with the attribute **NoEcho** set to **true**. The **NoEcho** attribute ensures that the parameter's value will not be displayed or echoed during stack creation or update. This is particularly useful for handling sensitive information, such as passwords or secret keys, where you want to keep the value confidential.

Minimum and maximum length string Parameters

Let us explore an example to understand the minimum and maximum length string attributes:

```
1.  Parameters:
2.    MyStringLengthParameter:
3.      Type: String
4.      MinLength: 5
5.      MaxLength: 10
6.      Description: Enter a string between 5 and 10 characters.
```

In this example, we introduce a parameter **MyStringLengthParameter** within an AWS CloudFormation template. The parameter is defined with the data type **String**, indicating that it expects string input. Two additional attributes, **MinLength** and **MaxLength**, impose constraints on the allowable length of the string. The **MinLength** attribute is set to **5**, specifying that the entered string must be at least five characters long. Conversely, the **MaxLength** attribute is set to **10**, indicating that the string should not exceed ten characters in length. This combination of attributes ensures that the **MyStringLengthParameter** parameter offers flexibility within defined length boundaries while providing clear guidance to users during stack creation or update.

Pattern constrained parameter

Let us explore an example for the understanding of AllowedPattern attribute:

```
1. Parameters:
2.   MyPatternParameter:
3.     Type: String
4.     AllowedPattern: "[a-zA-Z]+"
5.     Description: Enter an alphabetical string.
```

In this example, the **MyPatternParameter** is configured with a data type of **String**. It expects users to input a string during stack creation or update. The parameter is constrained to ensure that the value provided for **MyPatternParameter** adheres to a specific regular expression pattern, defined here as **[a-zA-Z]+**. This pattern restricts the input to only alphabetical characters, both uppercase and lowercase. Consequently, any input that fails to match this pattern will be rejected during stack creation or update.

Parameter with constraint description

Let us explore an example module to understand the usage of constraint description attributes:

```
1. Parameters:
2.   MyConstrainedParameter:
3.     Type: Number
4.     MinValue: 1
5.     MaxValue: 100
6.     ConstraintDescription: Value must be between 1 and 100 only.
7.     Description: Enter a numeric value between 1 and 100.
```

In this example, **MyConstrainedParameter** is specified as a **Numeric** type with constraints applied. The parameter must adhere to the constraints defined by **MinValue** and **MaxValue**, which are set to **1** and **100**, respectively. Additionally, a **ConstraintDescription** is provided to guide users in inputting values within the specified range. In this case, if a user attempts to provide a value outside the specified range of 1 to 100 for the

MyConstrainedParameter, CloudFormation will reject the input and display the constraint description. For example, if a user tries to input a value of 150, CloudFormation will reject it and display the constraint description: **Value must be between 1 and 100 only**. This helps users understand why their input was not accepted and prompts them to provide a valid value within the defined range.

Referencing Parameters in templates

Now that we have a solid understanding of how to define Parameters within the template let us learn how to reference them effectively. Parameters are referenced using the **Ref** intrinsic function, followed by the logical name of the parameter. This approach allows us to dynamically incorporate user provided values into our resource configurations, enhancing the flexibility and adaptability of our CloudFormation templates. Following is the example syntax for the same:

- **Syntax**: An example module with the required syntax:

```
1.  Resources:
2.    MyEC2Instance:
3.      Type: AWS::EC2::Instance
4.      Properties:
5.        InstanceType: !Ref InstanceTypeParameter
6.        KeyName: !Ref KeyNameParameter
7.        ImageId: !Ref AMIid
8.
```

- **Explanation**: This example illustrates the **Resources** section of the template, designed to deploy an EC2 instance based on user provided input specified through Parameters within the properties attribute. Here, the **Ref** intrinsic function is utilized to reference Parameters, with **InstanceTypeParameter**, **KeyNameParameter**, and **AMIid** representing the logical names of the referenced Parameters.

- **Usage**: Now, let us examine the template that includes the syntax provided previously. Following is the template where we define the instance type and key name for an EC2 instance:

```
1.  AWSTemplateFormatVersion: '2010-09-09'
2.  Description: "Example template
      demonstrating parameter referencing"
3.  Parameters:
4.    InstanceTypeParameter:
5.      Type: String
6.      Default: t2.micro
7.      Description: Enter the EC2 instance type.
```

```
8.    KeyNameParameter:
9.      Type: String
10.      Default: my-key-pair
11.      Description: Enter the EC2 key pair name.
12.    AMIid:
13.      Type: AWS::EC2::Image::Id
14.      Default: ami-1234567890abcdef0
15.      Description: Enter the AMI ID for the EC2 instance.
16. Resources:
17.    MyEC2Instance:
18.      Type: AWS::EC2::Instance
19.      Properties:
20.        InstanceType: !Ref InstanceTypeParameter
21.        KeyName: !Ref KeyNameParameter
22.        ImageId: !Ref AMIid
```

In this template, the visible terms mean the following:

- **InstanceType**: The property of the EC2 instance is set to the value provided by the **InstanceTypeParameter** parameter.

- **KeyName**: The property is set to the value provided by the **KeyNameParameter** parameter.

- **ImageId**: The property is set to the value provided by the **AMIid** parameter.

Note: In this template, default values for Parameters are set to arbitrary values while still allowing users to input required values during stack execution. This setup demonstrates how the actual values provided during execution can override the default ones.

Next, let us deploy this template using the AWS CloudFormation console. The following steps are required for execution:

1. Upon logging into the CloudFormation console, proceed to upload the template directly from your local system:

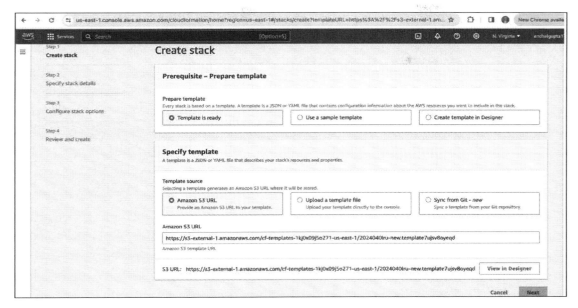

Figure 4.1: CloudFormation console

2. Clicking on the **Next** button will navigate us to the subsequent page:

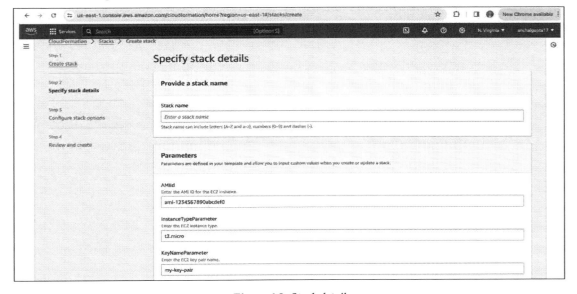

Figure 4.2: Stack detail

Now, in contrast to previous examples discussed in earlier chapters, we encounter a new section titled **Parameters** alongside the provision for specifying a **Stack name**. This section includes pre-populated default values for various Parameters defined in our template. However, users have the flexibility to modify these values as needed. If no values are provided, the stack deployment will default to the values specified in the template.

3. Next, we will input a stack name and provide new values for each parameter, overriding the default settings. Refer to the following screenshot for visual guidance:

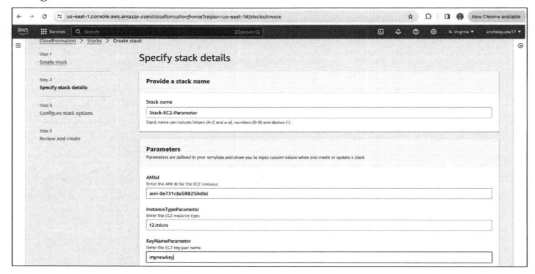

Figure 4.3: Parameters input

4. Once we have entered the desired values in the **Parameters** section, we will proceed and click on the **Next** button. See the following figure for reference:

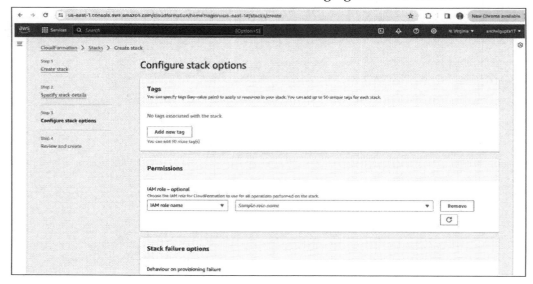

Figure 4.4: Configure stack options

Currently, we will proceed by leaving all options with their default values and clicking on the **Next** button.

5. Upon completing the previous steps, we will arrive at the final page, where we will review the template attributes and options. Here, the **Parameters** section will display the values we provided in the earlier steps. Please refer to the following figure:

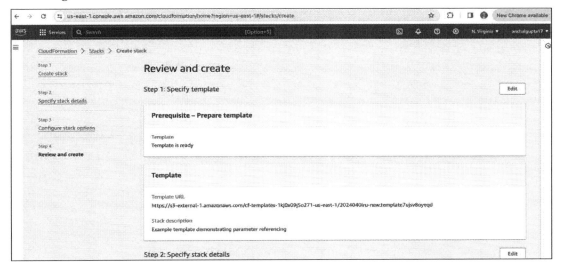

Figure 4.5: *Review stack options*

6. Next, we will click on the **Submit** button to initiate creation of our EC2 instance stack:

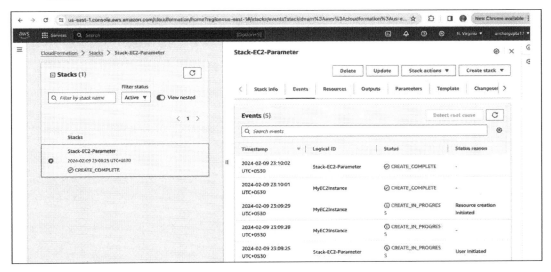

Figure 4.6: *Stack completion*

7. We can verify the parameter values in the **Parameters** section of this stack. Here, we will see the values provided during runtime, confirming that the resource was created using the user provided parameter values rather than the default ones specified in the template. This concludes our discussion on referencing Parameters in templates.

Additional DataType

Earlier in our discussion of the parameter section, we observed an attribute called type in the parameter syntax. This attribute, known as DataType, determines the data type that the parameter will accept during stack execution. A few of them, like string and number, were already discussed while we were discussing the syntax. Let us now dive into other types of data types available to us and understand their usage. They are as follows:

- **CommaDelimitedList**: **CommaDelimitedList** is a data type in AWS CloudFormation used to represent a list of comma separated string values. It allows users to specify multiple string values within a single parameter, separated by commas. This data type is commonly used when there is a need to provide multiple values for a parameter, such as a list of security group IDs, subnet IDs, env etc.

  Let us have a look at the following example to understand in detail:

  ```
  AWSTemplateFormatVersion: '2010-09-09'
  Description: "Example template with a CommaDelimitedList"
  Parameters:
    SecurityGroups:
      Type: CommaDelimitedList
      Description: The list of SecurityGroupIds in your VPC
      Default: sg-a123456, sg-b456789
  Resources:
    MyEC2Instance:
      Type: 'AWS::EC2::Instance'
      Properties:
        ImageId: ami-0e731c8a588258d0d
        KeyName: mynewkey
        SecurityGroupIds: !Ref SecurityGroups
  ```

  Here we have defined the parameter named as **SecurityGroups**, which is of type **CommaDelimitedList**. This parameter is used to specify a list of **SecurityGroupIds** in the VPC. The **Default** attribute provides default values for the parameter. Within the **Resources** section, an EC2 instance named **MyEC2Instance** is defined. It references the **SecurityGroups** parameter to specify the **SecurityGroupIds** associated with the instance. Through this template, users can flexibly specify **SecurityGroupIds** as a comma-separated list during the stack creation process.

- **List<Number>**: It is a data type that represents an array of integers or floats that are separated by commas. AWS CloudFormation validates the parameter value as numeric input; however, when referenced elsewhere in the template (such as through the **Ref** intrinsic function), the parameter value is interpreted as a list of strings.

Let us explore an example to understand the same in detail:

```
AWSTemplateFormatVersion: 2010-09-09
Description: Example template with a
List<Number> type parameter
Parameters:
  Numbers:
    Type: List<Number>
    Description: List of numbers
    Default: 1,2,3,4,5
  BucketName:
    Type: String
    Description: Name for the S3 bucket
    Default: my-example-bucket
Resources:
  MyBucket:
    Type: 'AWS::S3::Bucket'
    Properties:
      BucketName: !Ref BucketName
      Tags:
        - Key: Number
          Value: !Select [2, !Ref Numbers]
```

In this example of CloudFormation template, we define a parameter **Numbers** of type **List<Number>**, allowing users to input a list of numbers. Additionally, we introduce a parameter **BucketName**, enabling users to specify the name for an S3 bucket. The template creates an S3 bucket named according to the provided **BucketName** parameter. Furthermore, it assigns a tag to the bucket using the intrinsic function Select, with the value being the third number from the list provided by the numbers parameter. We will discuss this intrinsic function in detail in the later chapters.

- **AWS-specific parameter types**: The AWS-specific parameter types in AWS CloudFormation templates are custom parameter types provided by AWS to streamline the provisioning and administration of AWS resources. These parameter types are designed to interact with AWS services and resources, enabling users to define Parameters customized to specific AWS resources with pre-established validation rules and default values. For instance, consider the `AWS::EC2::VPC::Id` parameter type, which necessitates users to input an existing VPC ID within the respective account and region when creating the stack. Here are several other examples of AWS-specific parameter types, each tailored to serve a distinct purpose, simplifying resource provisioning and management:

- o **AWS::EC2::AvailabilityZone::Name**
- o **AWS::EC2::Instance::Id**
- o **AWS::EC2::KeyPair::KeyName**
- o **AWS::EC2::SecurityGroup::GroupName**
- o **AWS::EC2::SecurityGroup::Id**
- o **AWS::EC2::Subnet::Id**
- o **AWS::EC2::Volume::Id**
- o **AWS::EC2::VPC::Id**
- o **AWS::Route53::HostedZone::Id**
- o **List<AWS::EC2::AvailabilityZone::Name>**
- o **List<AWS::EC2::Image::Id>**
- o **List<AWS::EC2::Instance::Id>**
- o **List<AWS::EC2::SecurityGroup::GroupName>**
- o **List<AWS::EC2::SecurityGroup::Id>**
- o **List<AWS::EC2::Subnet::Id>**
- o **List<AWS::EC2::Volume::Id>**
- o **List<AWS::EC2::VPC::Id>**
- o **List<AWS::Route53::HostedZone::Id>**

For more detailed information on each of these data types, please refer to the official AWS documentation page. You can find the documentation at the following link:

(https://docs.aws.amazon.com/AWSCloudFormation/latest/UserGuide/ parameters-section-structure.html)

- **SSM parameter types**: The **Systems Manager (SSM)** parameter type in AWS CloudFormation templates enables integration with the AWS Systems Manager Parameter Store. This parameter type facilitates secure storage and management of sensitive configuration data, such as passwords, database strings, or API tokens.

  When using the SSM parameter type, CloudFormation retrieves the parameter value from the Parameter Store during stack creation or update. If a designated parameter is not found within the Parameter Store under the requester's AWS account, AWS CloudFormation will issue a validation error.

Let us examine an example where we aim to launch an EC2 instance. We have stored the relevant AMI ID parameter in the AWS Systems Manager Parameter Store. We will incorporate this parameter into our template. The template is as follows:

- `AWSTemplateFormatVersion: '2010-09-09'`
- `Description: "Example template demonstrating the usage of AWS SSM Parameter Types"`
- `Parameters:`
- `  ImageId:`
- `    Type: 'AWS::SSM::Parameter::Value<AWS::EC2::Image::Id>'`
- `    Default: /EC2/AMI_ID`
- `Resources:`
- `  MyInstance:`
- `    Type: AWS::EC2::Instance`
- `    Properties:`
- `      ImageId: !Ref ImageId`
- `      InstanceType: t3.micro`

In this template, we have stored the value for the parameter **ImageId** within AWS SSM Parameters. The **Default** attribute specifies the path **/EC2/AMI_ID** from which this value can be retrieved. Within the **Resources** section, we reference the **ImageId** parameter. Upon execution of this template, it will retrieve the necessary information from the SSM parameter and utilize it to launch the EC2 instance. Following are the screenshots for the SSM parameter where we have stored the parameter before executing the template:

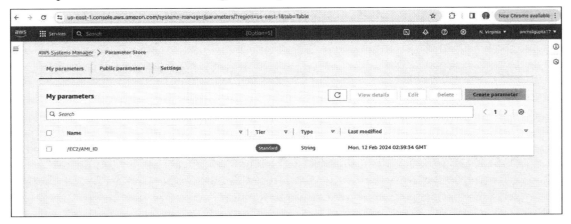

Figure 4.7: SSM parameter

In the following figure, the parameter value corresponds to an AMI ID, which will subsequently be utilized to initiate the EC2 instance:

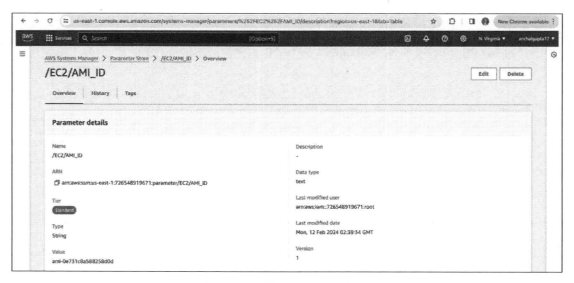

Figure 4.8: SSM parameter detail

In the depicted figure, the parameter value corresponds to an AMI ID, which will subsequently be utilized to initiate the EC2 instance.

Note: When creating or updating stacks and generating Change sets, AWS CloudFormation utilizes the values present in the Parameter Store at the moment of operation execution. If a specified parameter is not found in the Parameter Store within the caller's AWS account, AWS CloudFormation issues a validation error.

Supported SSM parameter types

A few supported SSM parameter types that can be used as part of template designing are as follows:

- **AWS::SSM::Parameter::Name**: This type represents the name of a SSM parameter key. It is useful for passing the parameter key and validating its existence.

- **AWS::SSM::Parameter::Value<String>**: This type corresponds to a SSM parameter with a string value, akin to the string parameter type in parameter store.

- **AWS::SSM::Parameter::Value<List<String>>**: This type denotes Systems Manager Parameters with values structured as lists of strings. This corresponds to the StringList parameter type in parameter store.

- **AWS::SSM::Parameter::Value<CommaDelimitedList>**: Similar to the previous type, this denotes Systems Manager Parameters with values formatted as comma-delimited lists of strings. This also corresponds to the **StringList** parameter type in parameter store.

- **`AWS::SSM::Parameter::Value<AWS-specific parameter type>`**: Such Parameters have values corresponding to AWS specific parameter types, such as **`AWS::EC2::KeyPair::KeyName`**.

- **`AWS::SSM::Parameter::Value<List<AWS-specific parameter type>>`**: These Parameters store lists of AWS specific parameter types. For instance, a list of **`AWS::EC2::KeyPair::KeyName`** types.

Unsupported SSM parameter type

AWS CloudFormation does not support certain SSM parameter types, including lists of SSM parameter types such as **`List<AWS::SSM::Parameter::Value<String>>`**. Additionally, CloudFormation does not allow defining template Parameters as SecureString Systems Manager parameter types. However, you can still specify SecureStrings as parameter values for specific resources using dynamic parameter patterns.

> **Note: While we have discussed the usage of SSM parameter types in AWS CloudFormation templates, it is important to highlight that this book will not dive into the detailed functionalities of the SSM service itself. The focus here is specifically on how SSM parameter types are integrated and utilized within AWS CloudFormation templates for resource provisioning and management. For a comprehensive understanding of SSM service features and capabilities, please refer to the official AWS documentation and resources dedicated to the SSM.**

Metadata

Metadata in AWS CloudFormation provides a mechanism to include additional information or instructions within your templates. It offers flexibility in defining various attributes and settings that can enhance the functionality and management of your resources.

Purpose of Metadata

Let us explore a few key points to understand how Metadata can be useful within a CloudFormation template:

- **Enhanced resource configuration**: Metadata allows you to define additional configurations and properties for your resources beyond what is specified in the resource properties section.

- **Automation and customization**: It enables automation and customization of resource deployments by providing instructions or scripts to be executed during stack creation or update.

- **Dynamic resource handling**: Metadata can be used to handle dynamic resource configurations or perform actions based on specific Conditions or events.

Components of Metadata

Metadata in an AWS CloudFormation template consists of key-value pairs and can be defined at different levels within the template hierarchy which are as follows:

- **Template level Metadata**: Metadata defined at the top level of the template applies globally to the entire stack.

- **Resource level Metadata**: Metadata associated with specific resources provides additional instructions or configurations tailored to those resources.

Use cases

Let us explore some common scenarios where utilizing Metadata can be advantageous. These scenarios are as follows:

- **Bootstrapping instances**: Metadata can include user data scripts or initialization commands to be executed during instance launch, enabling automated setup and configuration.

- **Custom configuration**: It allows for custom configuration settings or environment variables to be passed to resources.

- **Dependency handling**: Metadata can specify dependencies or ordering instructions for resources, ensuring proper sequencing during stack creation or update.

- **Resource tagging**: Metadata can include default tags or tagging strategies to apply consistent tags to resources within the stack.

Learning to use Metadata

Let us understand how to use Metadata in our CloudFormation templates. As discussed above, Metadata provides additional information about the template or its resources, which can include implementation details, dependencies, runtime configurations, or any other relevant information necessary for managing the infrastructure defined in the template. This Metadata can be in the form of JSON or YAML objects, allowing users to structure and organize the information in a readable and meaningful way, as shown in the following example syntax:

- **JSON**: The JSON structure for the **Metadata** module is as follows:

```
o   "Metadata" : {
o     "S3" : {"Description" : "Detail about the S3 bucket"},
o     "VPC" : {"Description" : "Detail about the VPC"}
o   }
```

- **YAML**: The YAML structure for the **Metadata** module is as follows:

```
o   Metadata:
o     S3:
o       Description: "Detail about the S3 bucket"
o     VPC:
o       Description: "Detail about the VPC"
```

Let us explore an example template where we will try to use Metadata both in the template section and in the resources section. We will try to spin this template in the us-east-1 region of our AWS account. Corresponding AMI ID is available in the us-east-1 region only. The template is as follows:

```
1.  AWSTemplateFormatVersion: '2010-09-09'
2.  Description: 'Simple CloudFormation template with metadata'
3.
4.  Metadata:
5.    TemplateMetadata:
6.      Description: 'This template defines a simple EC2 instance.'
7.
8.  Resources:
9.    MyEC2Instance:
10.     Type: 'AWS::EC2::Instance'
11.     Metadata:
12.       ResourceMetadata:
13.         Description: 'This EC2 instance is used for testing only'
14.     Properties:
15.       ImageId: ami-0e731c8a588258d0d
16.       InstanceType: t2.micro
```

Now, in this example:

- The **Metadata** section at the template level provides information about the entire CloudFormation template. Here, **TemplateMetadata** describes the template's purpose.

- The **Metadata** section within the **MyEC2Instance** resource provides Metadata specific to that EC2 instance. Here, **ResourceMetadata** describes additional details about the purpose of the EC2 instance.

If we spin up this template on the AWS CloudFormation management console, the stack will proceed as usual and will create an EC2 instance, similar to before the introduction of Metadata in our template. However, the addition of Metadata enhances the template description, providing users with a deeper understanding of its contents and inclusions. The final snippet of the console output, after our stack executions is successfully completed, is as follows:

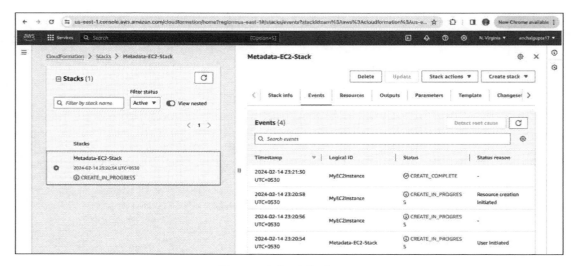

***Figure 4.9**: Stack final status*

This example demonstrates how Metadata can be used both at the template and the resource level to provide additional information and context about the resources defined in the CloudFormation template without affecting the resource.

Metadata keys

AWS CloudFormation provides a set of Metadata keys that are specific to AWS services and resources, offering additional functionalities and configurations tailored to the AWS environment. These keys enable users to fine-tune the behavior of resources and optimize their deployment within AWS infrastructure. Here are some AWS specific Metadata keys commonly used in CloudFormation templates:

- **AWS::CloudFormation::Init**: This Metadata key is crucial for configuring EC2 instances using AWS CloudFormation. It allows users to specify initialization actions during instance startup, such as running scripts or installing packages. Under the hood, **cfn-init**, a component of the AWS CloudFormation helper scripts, reads and executes instructions from this key. It performs tasks like fetching and parsing Metadata from the CloudFormation template, installing packages, writing files to disk, and managing services. This capability streamlines instance setup and customization, enhancing the automation and management of infrastructure as code on AWS.

  Let us explore the following example template to understand this concept in a better way:

  ```
  1. AWSTemplateFormatVersion: 2010-09-09
  2. Description: Example template with
     CloudInit metadata for an EC2.
  ```

```
3.  Resources:
4.    MyEC2Instance:
5.      Type: 'AWS::EC2::Instance'
6.      Metadata:
7.        'AWS::CloudFormation::Init':
8.          config:
9.
10.          packages:
11.            yum:
12.              httpd: []
13.          files:
14.            /var/www/html/index.html:
15.              content: |
16.                echo "Hello, I am alive";
17.              mode: '000755'
18.              owner: root
19.              group: root
20.
21.          services:
22.            sysvinit:
23.              httpd:
24.                enabled: 'true'
25.                ensureRunning: 'true'
26.      Properties:
27.        InstanceType: t2.micro
28.        ImageId: ami-0e731c8a588258d0d
```

In the given template, we can observe the following pointers:

o **Metadata** under **AWS::CloudFormation::Init** specifies a series of configurations for the EC2 instance.

o It installs the Apache HTTP server using the **packages** section.

o It creates an **index.html** file with a simple message **Hello, I am alive**.

This Metadata configures the EC2 instance during launch based on the specified directives, allowing you to customize the instance with packages, files, and services as needed.

• **AWS::CloudFormation::Interface**: The **AWS::CloudFormation::Interface** Metadata key is a powerful tool in AWS CloudFormation that allows users to customize how Parameters are presented and organized in the CloudFormation console. By leveraging this Metadata key, you can enhance the user experience by grouping Parameters logically, providing descriptive labels, and specifying the order in which they appear. When creating or updating stacks using the CloudFormation console, Parameters are typically listed alphabetically by their logical IDs. However, this default ordering may not always provide the most intuitive experience for users, especially when dealing with complex templates that include numerous Parameters.

The **AWS::CloudFormation::Interface** Metadata key allows you to define custom grouping, labelling, and ordering for Parameters, making it easier for users to understand and input the required values during stack creation or update.

Let us explore the following example template to understand this concept better:

```
1.  AWSTemplateFormatVersion: '2010-09-09'
2.  Description: "Template with AWS::CloudFormation::Interface"
3.  Parameters:
4.    InstanceType:
5.      Type: String
6.      Description: "Enter the instance type."
7.    KeyName:
8.      Type: String
9.      Description: "Enter the EC2 Key Pair name."
10.   ImageId:
11.     Type: String
12.     Description: "Enter the AMI id"
13.   BucketName:
14.     Type: String
15.     Description: "Enter the S3 Bucket name."
16.
17. Resources:
18.   MyEC2Instance:
19.     Type: 'AWS::EC2::Instance'
20.     Properties:
21.       InstanceType: !Ref InstanceType
22.       KeyName: !Ref KeyName
23.       ImageId: !Ref ImageId
24.   MyS3Bucket:
25.     Type: 'AWS::S3::Bucket'
26.     Properties:
27.       BucketName: !Ref BucketName
```

```
28.
29. Metadata:
30.    AWS::CloudFormation::Interface:
31.      ParameterGroups:
32.        - Label:
33.            default: "Amazon EC2 Configuration"
34.          Parameters:
35.            - InstanceType
36.            - KeyName
37.            - ImageId
38.        - Label:
39.            default: "S3 Bucket Configuration"
40.          Parameters:
41.            - BucketName
42.
43.      ParameterLabels:
44.        BucketName:
45.          default: "Enter the unique bucket name"
```

This CloudFormation template utilizes the **AWS::CloudFormation::Interface** Metadata key to enhance the parameter organization and presentation in the AWS CloudFormation console. Let us explore the **Metadata** section defined in our template:

The **Metadata** section includes **AWS::CloudFormation::Interface** Metadata, which is further divided into two sub-sections. These are as follows:

o   **ParameterGroups**: Organizes Parameters into logical groups, each with a corresponding label. For example, EC2 related Parameters (**InstanceType**, **KeyName**, and **ImageId**) are grouped together under the label **Amazon EC2 Configuration**, while the **BucketName** parameter is grouped separately under the label **S3 Bucket Configuration**.

o   **ParameterLabels**: Provides user friendly labels for each parameter, enhancing clarity and usability in the CloudFormation console. For instance, the **BucketName** parameter is labelled **Enter the unique bucket name**.

Following is the console screenshot showcasing the Parameters section while we try to deploy the template. The Parameters are neatly grouped according to the associated resources, facilitating user comprehension. Additionally, the label for the bucket name under **S3 Bucket Configuration** provides clear guidance for users, ensuring ease of use and clarity throughout the process:

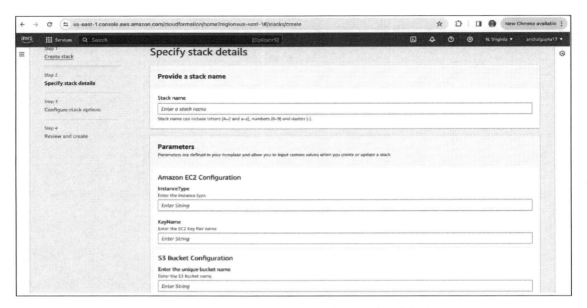

Figure 4.10: Parameter section as per the Metadata definition

- **AWS::CloudFormation::Designer**: The **AWS::CloudFormation::Designer** Metadata is a special section within a CloudFormation template that allows users to provide additional information specifically for visualization purposes within the CloudFormation Designer tool. This **Metadata** section enhances the visual representation of the template in the CloudFormation Designer interface, helping users better understand the architecture and relationships between resources. We will dive further into this topic in subsequent chapters dedicated to CloudFormation Designer.

Mappings

Mappings in AWS CloudFormation are a powerful feature used to define a set of static values that can be referenced within a template. They enable you to map keys to a corresponding set of named values, providing a convenient way to manage configurations, such as AMI IDs, region-specific values, or instance types, in a single location within your CloudFormation template. Let us have a look at a few key points related to Mappings:

- **Static key-value pairs**: Mappings consist of a collection of key-value pairs, where each key is associated with a set of values. These values can be strings or complex data structures, including lists or nested Mappings.

- **Centralized configuration**: Mappings allow you to centralize configuration data within your CloudFormation template, making it easier to manage and update values that are reused across multiple resources.

- **Conditional logic**: You can use Mappings to implement conditional logic within your template. By referencing a specific key based on Condition or Parameters, you can dynamically select the appropriate value from the Mapping.

- **Use cases**: Mappings are commonly used to define AMI IDs based on regions, specify instance types or sizes, configure environment specific settings, or manage resource-specific Parameters.

Syntax

The syntax of Mappings in AWS CloudFormation follows a specific structure within a template. Following is a breakdown of the syntax:

```
1. Mappings:
2.   MappingLogicalName1:
3.     Key1:
4.       Value1: Value1
5.       Value2: Value2
6.     Key2:
7.       Value3: Value3
8.       Value4: Value4
9.   MappingLogicalName2:
10.    Key1:
11.      Value1: Value1
12.      Value2: Value2
13.    Key2:
14.      Value3: Value3
15.      Value4: Value4
```

Let us try to understand the different components present in our syntax. They are as follows:

- **Mappings**: Begins with the keyword **Mappings**, which indicates the start of the **Mappings** section within the template.

- **MappingLogicalName**: Each Mapping is identified by a unique name, followed by a colon (:) and indentation.

- **Key**: Within each Mapping, keys are defined, followed by a colon (:) and indentation. These keys represent identifiers or categories.

- **Value**: Under each key, one or more values are specified, followed by a colon (:) and indentation. Values can be strings, numbers, lists, or nested Mappings.

Syntax rules

Here are some key rules to consider when designing the syntax:

- Mappings are defined at the top level of the CloudFormation template.
- Each Mapping is structured as a series of key-value pairs, where each key is associated with one or more values.
- Indentation is used to organize Mappings, keys, and values within the template.
- Each Mapping's logical name must be unique within the **Mappings** section of the template.
- Key names within a Mapping must also be unique.

Example

Consider the following example for your understanding:

```
1. Mappings:
2.   RegionMap:
3.     us-east-1:
4.       AMI: "ami-12345678"
5.     us-west-2:
6.       AMI: "ami-87654321"
```

In this example:

- **RegionMap** is a logical name for Mapping.
- Under **RegionMap**, keys such as **us-east-1** and **us-west-2** are associated with corresponding AMI IDs. This ensures AWS Region to AMI ID Mapping.

Learning to use Mappings

Now that we have explored the concept and purpose of Mappings within a CloudFormation template, let us delve into a practical example to understand how Mappings are employed in a real scenario.

Consider a scenario where you need to deploy an EC2 instance using CloudFormation across multiple regions, each requiring a specific AMI based on its availability. In this scenario, Mappings come to the rescue by allowing you to define region-specific AMIs centrally within your CloudFormation template.

Let us explore the following template in detail:

```
1. AWSTemplateFormatVersion: '2010-09-09'
2. Description: Deploy an EC2 instance with region-specific AMIs
3.
4. Parameters:
5.   InstanceType:
6.     Type: String
7.     Default: t2.micro
8.     AllowedValues:
9.       - t2.micro
10.       - t2.small
11.     Description: Choose the instance type for the EC2 instance.
12.
13. Mappings:
14.   RegionAMIMap:
15.     us-east-1:
16.       AMI: "ami-0e731c8a588258d0d"
17.     us-west-2:
18.       AMI: "ami-0c20d88b0021158c6"
19.
20. Resources:
21.   MyEC2Instance:
22.     Type: 'AWS::EC2::Instance'
23.     Properties:
24.       InstanceType: !Ref InstanceType
25.       ImageId: !FindInMap [RegionAMIMap, us-east-1, AMI]
```

In this CloudFormation template, **Mappings** are prominently utilized to streamline the deployment of EC2 instances with region-specific AMIs. The **Mappings** section defines a Mapping named **RegionAMIMap**, where we have defined two AWS Regions, namely **us-east-1** and **us-west-2**, associating each with a specific AMI ID. This Mapping allows for centralized management of **AMI** configurations, facilitating updates and ensuring consistency across regions.

Inside the **Resources** section, the **FindInMap** function dynamically retrieves the appropriate AMI ID based on the AWS Region where the stack is being deployed, ensuring that the correct **AMI** is used for each region. **FindInMap** is an intrinsic function in AWS CloudFormation that retrieves the value of a specified key from a specific Mapping declared in the template. It allows you to reference values from Mappings within your CloudFormation templates dynamically.

The syntax for Fn::**FindInMap** is as follows:

```
1. !FindInMap [ MapName, TopLevelKey, SecondLevelKey ]
```

In the provided syntax:

- **MapName**: Denotes the logical name of the Mapping in the CloudFormation template.
- **TopLevelKey**: Refers to the key at the top level of the Mapping.
- **SecondLevelKey**: Signifies the key nested within the specified top-level key.

Now, revisiting the template, let us examine how these concepts are applied. Within the resources section, particularly in the properties subsection, we have specified the **ImageId** property. This property dictates the AMI ID to be used for the EC2 instance. In this context, we are making use of a Mapping previously defined elsewhere in our template.

The specific syntax used to reference this Mapping is as follows:

ImageId: !FindInMap [RegionAMIMap, us-east-1, AMI]

In this expression, the following terms mean:

- **MapName** is represented by **RegionAMIMap**.
- **TopLevelKey** corresponds to **us-east-1**.
- **SecondLevelKey** is identified as **AMI**.

By employing this syntax, we dynamically retrieve the **AMI** ID associated with the **us-east-1** region from the **RegionAMIMap** Mapping. This ensures that the EC2 instance is launched with the correct AMI according to the targeted region. This utilization of Mappings enhances the template's adaptability, facilitating seamless deployment across diverse AWS Regions.

Deployment

Now, let us proceed to deploy this template on the AWS CloudFormation Management Console. We will initiate the deployment in the **us-east-1** region, as specified within our Mapping. This ensures that the EC2 instance will be provisioned with the AMI mapped specifically for the **us-east-1** region.

We will not discuss all initial steps for template uploading and execution as they remain the same to the previous examples. We will directly jump to the final output page where our stack is created. Kindly refer to the following figure:

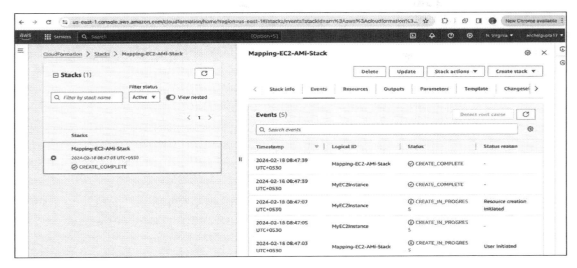

Figure 4.11: Stacks status

Now, we can see at the top of the page that the region is North Virginia, which corresponds to us-east-1. Therefore, our target EC2 instance should ideally spin up with the AMI ID ami-0e731c8a588258d0d, which belongs to the us-east-1 region of AWS. To confirm this, we will navigate to the Resources section to retrieve the instance details.

Please refer to the following screenshot:

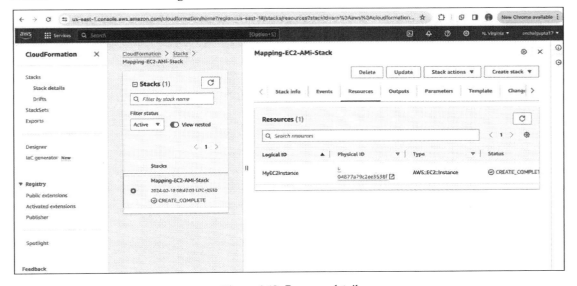

Figure 4.12: Resource detail

On this page, we will click on the highlighted instance ID, which will redirect us to the EC2 management console page. From there, we will navigate to the Details section of our newly set up EC2 instance, where we can locate the AMI ID. Upon inspection, we will find that our template utilized the relevant AMI ID associated with the AWS Region for spinning up the EC2 instance. This confirmation validates that the Mappings functioned as expected.

> **Note: In the preceding example, we have hardcoded the value for the `TopLevelKey`, but we can also parameterize it as demonstrated. We can include an additional parameter corresponding to the `TopLevelKey`, which we can pass during the stack execution step.**

```
ImageId: !FindInMap [RegionAMIMap, !Ref 'Region', AMI]
```

> **Here, `Region` is an additional parameter where we can provide the actual value. Based on the input value provided, it will consider the specified region for selecting the appropriate AMI ID. This parameterization adds flexibility to our template, allowing us to dynamically choose the region and the associated AMI ID during deployment.**

Conditions

Conditions in AWS CloudFormation allow you to define conditional statements based on input Parameters, Mappings, and other factors. These Conditions determine whether certain entities must be created or configured during the stack deployment. For instance, you can link the condition with the creation of a resource like EC2 only if the certain condition is set to be true. If not you can skip the creation.

Conditions are defined using conditional intrinsic functions such as **Fn::Equals**, **Fn::Not**, **Fn::And**, **Fn::Or**, etc. They evaluate expressions and return **true** or **false**, depending on the outcome. Conditions can be applied to resources, resource properties, outputs, and other sections within the CloudFormation template. Conditions add flexibility to CloudFormation templates, enabling you to create dynamic deployments that adapt based on specific Conditions or requirements.

Syntax

Let us have a look at the following syntax definition for including **Conditions** in a CloudFormation template:

```
1. Conditions:
2.    ConditionName:
3.       Intrinsic function
```

In this syntax:

- **Conditions**: This is the section header indicating the start of the **Conditions** section in the CloudFormation template. All condition definitions will be listed under this section.

- **ConditionName**: This line defines a unique logical name for the condition being defined. The **ConditionName** is used to reference the condition elsewhere in the template.

- **Intrinsic function:** This line specifies an intrinsic function, such as **Fn::Equals**, **Fn::Not**, **Fn::And**, **Fn::Or**, etc., used to evaluate the condition. The intrinsic function determines the logic that will be applied to the Parameters provided within the function.

Condition intrinsic functions

Let us now explore the capabilities of condition intrinsic functions. Through the following detailed syntax explanations and illustrative examples, we will dive into their power and versatility within AWS CloudFormation templates:

- **Fn::Equals**: Compares two values and returns **true** if they are equal. The syntax for the same is as follows:

  o   ConditionName:
  o   Fn::Equals:
  o   - ValueToCompare1
  o   - ValueToCompare2

  Example: Let us go through the following example for better understanding:

  o   IsProdEnvironment:
  o   Fn::Equals:
  o   - !Ref EnvironmentType
  o   - prod

  Correlating the provided syntax with the example:

  o   **ConditionName**: Assigns the logical name **IsProdEnvironment** to the condition.

  o   **Fn::Equals**: Specifies the intrinsic function used to evaluate if the two values are equal.

  o   **ValueToCompare1**: References the **EnvironmentType** parameter.

  o   **ValueToCompare2**: Compares the **EnvironmentType** parameter value with the string **prod**. If they are equal, the condition is evaluated as **true**.

- **Fn::Not**: Negates the result of a condition. The syntax for the same is as follows:

  o   ConditionName:
  o   Fn::Not:
  o   - Condition: ConditionToNegate

  Example: Let us go through the following example for better understanding:

```
o    IsNotProdEnvironment:
o      Fn::Not:
o        - Condition: IsProdEnvironment
```

Correlating the provided syntax with example:

- o **ConditionName**: Assigns the logical name **IsNotProdEnvironment** to the negated condition.

- o **Fn::Not**: Indicates the intrinsic function used to negate the result of the specified condition.

- o **ConditionToNegate**: Specifies the condition. If **IsProdEnvironment** evaluates to **true**, **IsNotProdEnvironment** evaluates to **false**, and vice versa.

- **Fn::And**: Evaluates multiple conditions and returns **true** only if all are true. The syntax for the same is as follows:

```
o    ConditionName:
o      Fn::And:
o        - Condition1
o        - Condition2
o        - ...
```

Example: Let us go through the following example for better understanding:

```
o    IsProdAndHighTraffic:
o      Fn::And:
o        - Condition: IsProdEnvironment
o        - Condition: IsHighTraffic
```

Correlating the provided syntax with the example:

- o **ConditionName**: Assigns the logical name **IsProdAndHighTraffic** to the combined condition.

- o **Fn::And**: Specifies the intrinsic function used to evaluate if all provided Conditions are true.

- o **Condition1, Condition2**: Specifies the Conditions **IsProdEnvironment** and **IsHighTraffic**. The **IsProdAndHighTraffic** condition evaluates to **true** only if both **IsProdEnvironment** and **IsHighTraffic** Conditions are true.

- **Fn::Or**: Evaluates multiple Conditions and returns **true** if at least one is true. The syntax for the same is as follows:

```
o    ConditionName:
o      Fn::Or:
o        - Condition1
```

```
o        - Condition2
o        - ...
```

Example: Let us go through the following example for better understanding:

```
o    IsProdOrTestEnvironment:
o      Fn::Or:
o        - Condition: IsProdEnvironment
o        - Condition: IsTestEnvironment
```

Correlating the provided syntax with example:

o **ConditionName**: Assigns the logical name **IsProdOrTestEnvironment** to the combined condition.

o **Fn::Or**: Specifies the intrinsic function used to evaluate if any of the provided conditions are true.

o **Condition1, and condition2**: Specifies the Conditions **IsProdEnvironment** and **IsTestEnvironment**. The **IsProdOrTestEnvironment** evaluates to **true** if either **IsProdEnvironment** or **IsTestEnvironment** condition is true.

- **Fn::If**: Returns one value if a condition is true and another if it is false. The syntax for the same is as follows.

```
o    ConditionName:
o      Fn::If:
o        - Condition
o        - ValueIfTrue
o        - ValueIfFalse
```

Example: Let us go through the following example for better understanding:

```
o    InstanceType:
o      Fn::If:
o        - IsProdEnvironment
o        - t2.large
o        - t2.micro
```

Correlating the provided syntax with example:

o **ConditionName**: Assigns the logical name **InstanceType** to the condition.

o **Fn::If**: Specifies the intrinsic function used to return one value if a condition is true and another value if it is false.

o **Condition**: Specifies the condition **IsProdEnvironment**. If **IsProdEnvironment** evaluates to **true**, **InstanceType** is set to **t2.large**; otherwise, it is set to **t2.micro**.

> **Note: For additional details on condition intrinsic functions, you can explore further documentation available at:**

(https://docs.aws.amazon.com/AWSCloudFormation/latest/UserGuide/intrinsic-function-reference-conditions.html#intrinsic-function-reference-conditions-and)

Usage overview

Now that we understand the significant role Conditions can play in managing various entities within a template, it is essential to include statements in specific template sections to implement them effectively. The following sections include specific scenarios that will aid in comprehending the diverse use cases:

- **Parameters**: In the **Parameters** section, define the input Parameters that your Conditions will evaluate. These Parameters form the basis for evaluating Conditions, as Conditions assess whether certain criteria are met based on the values of these Parameters. Consider the following example of a Parameters section in a template:

```
o  Parameters:
o    EnvironmentType:
o      Type: String
o      Default: dev
o      AllowedValues:
o        - dev
o        - test
o        - prod
o      Description: Specify the environment
   type for resource provisioning.
```

In this template, the **Parameters** section allows users to input the environment type (**dev**, **test**, or **prod**) during stack execution, which can then be used in Conditions to control resource provisioning based on the specified environment.

> **Note: We can also use pseudo parameters to define the Conditions. Subsequent chapters will provide detailed explanations and practical examples demonstrating their usage in Conditions.**

- **Resources**: In the **Resources** section, associate the defined Conditions with the resources that you want to create conditionally. Use the condition key along with the logical ID of the condition to link it with a resource. AWS CloudFormation will create resources associated with Conditions evaluated as **true** and ignore those associated with Conditions evaluated as **false**. Consider the following example of a resources section along with the previous parameter section:

```
o  Parameters:
```

```
o    EnvironmentType:
o      Type: String
o      Default: dev
o      AllowedValues:
o        - dev
o        - test
o        - prod
o      Description: Specify the environment type for resource
o    Resources:
o      MyEC2Instance:
o        Type: 'AWS::EC2::Instance'
o        Properties:
o          InstanceType: t2.micro
o          ImageId: !If
o            - IsProdEnvironment
o            - ami-0440d3b780d96b29d
o            - ami-0cf10cdf9fcd62d37
o    Conditions:
o      IsProdEnvironment:
o        'Fn::Equals':
o          - !Ref EnvironmentType
o          - prod
```

In this example:

- o The **EnvironmentType** parameter allows the user to specify the environment type for resource provisioning.

- o The **MyEC2Instance** resource is conditionally created based on the value of the **EnvironmentType** parameter.

- o The **IsProdEnvironment** condition checks if the **EnvironmentType** parameter is set to **prod**.

- o If the **EnvironmentType** is **prod**, the **ImageId** property of the EC2 instance is set to **ami-0440d3b780d96b29d**. Otherwise, it is set to **ami-0cf10cdf9fcd62d37**.

- **Outputs**: In the **Outputs** section, associate the defined Conditions with the outputs that you want to create conditionally. Use the condition key along with the logical ID of the condition to link it with an output. AWS CloudFormation will include outputs associated with Conditions evaluated as **true** and exclude those associated with Conditions evaluated as **false**. Consider the following example of outputs section in continuation to the previous template structure:

```
o  Outputs:
o     EnvironmentInfo:
o        Description: Information about the environment
o        Value: !If
o           - IsProdEnvironment
o           - 'Production environment'
o           - 'Non-production environment'
```

In this example:

- o The **Outputs** section includes an output named **EnvironmentInfo**, which provides information about the environment.

- o The value of the **EnvironmentInfo** output is conditionally set based on the evaluation of the **IsProdEnvironment** condition. If the condition is **true**, the output value is **Production environment**; otherwise, it is **Non-production environment**.

> Note: The **Outputs** section will be explored comprehensively in the upcoming chapters. For now, our primary focus is on understanding how to incorporate Conditions within this section.

Practical use of different Conditions

So far, we understood that Conditions in AWS CloudFormation provide a powerful mechanism for controlling the creation and configuration of AWS resources based on specified criteria. By leveraging Conditions, you can create flexible and dynamic templates that adapt to various scenarios. Here, we explore a few practical use cases demonstrating the versatility of Conditions in CloudFormation:

- **Multi-environment deployments**:
  - o **Scenario**: You have a CloudFormation template that deploys resources to different environments such as development, staging, and production. Each environment may require a different configuration or set of resources.

  - o **Solution**: Use Conditions to define environment specific Parameters and resources. For instance, you can define a condition that checks the environment type (e.g., dev, staging, prod) and configure resources accordingly. This allows you to maintain a single template while adapting it to multiple environments.

- **Instance type selection:**

  o **Scenario**: You need to deploy an Amazon EC2 instance, but the instance type varies depending on the workload or application requirements.

  o **Solution**: Utilize Conditions to specify different instance types based on Conditions such as workload type, performance needs, or cost considerations. By defining Conditions for instance type selection, you can ensure optimal resource allocation for different use cases without maintaining separate templates.

- **Region specific configuration**:

  o **Scenario**: You deploy resources across multiple AWS Regions, and certain configurations differ based on the region's capabilities or compliance requirements.

  o **Solution**: Employ Conditions to handle region-specific configurations efficiently. For example, you can set Conditions to enable or disable features that are only available in specific regions. This ensures consistent deployment across regions while accommodating variations in resource availability or compliance regulations.

- **Feature toggle**:

  o **Scenario**: You want to enable or disable specific features or functionalities during deployment based on user preferences or application requirements.

  o **Solution**: Leverage Conditions to implement feature toggles within your CloudFormation templates. By defining Conditions that control the creation or configuration of resources related to specific features, you can easily enable or disable those features without modifying the underlying template structure.

- **Security configuration**:

  o **Scenario**: Your application requires different security configurations based on compliance standards or risk assessments.

  o **Solution**: Utilize Conditions to enable or disable security configurations based on compliance requirements or risk assessments. For example, you can define Conditions to enable encryption options, restrict access based on IP ranges, or enforce specific authentication methods only when necessary, ensuring that security measures are tailored to each deployment scenario.

Conclusion

In conclusion, this chapter has provided a comprehensive overview of essential elements in AWS CloudFormation templates, empowering users to create dynamic and customizable infrastructure deployments. We explored the significance of Parameters, allowing for user input and customization while delving into additional data types to handle complex data structures efficiently. The discussion on Metadata sheds light on its role in providing supplementary information and facilitating template management.

Next, we explored the practical application of Metadata, showcasing its effectiveness in improving template organization and enhancing clarity. Mappings were also introduced as a potent mechanism for handling key-value pairs, facilitating simplified resource configuration across diverse scenarios.

Finally, we understood concepts of Conditions that emerged as a pivotal aspect in controlling resource creation and configuration based on specified criteria. Through practical examples, we showcased the versatility of Conditions in adapting deployments to diverse environments.

In the upcoming chapter, we will dive into advanced topics such as macros, transform, and outputs. These elements play crucial roles in enhancing the flexibility, scalability, and extensibility of CloudFormation templates. By exploring macros, which enable template transformations and automation, and transforms, which allow for the inclusion of external template snippets, we will unlock additional capabilities for managing and deploying infrastructure. Additionally, we will examine outputs, which provide valuable information about the deployed stack, facilitating post-deployment actions and integrations. You will find an in-depth exploration of these essential features in the next chapter.

Multiple choice questions

1. **Which AWS CloudFormation feature allows users to define input values that can be customized during stack creation?**

    a. Metadata

    b. Mappings

    c. Conditions

    d. Parameters

2. **How does Metadata contribute to AWS CloudFormation templates?**

    a. By enabling streamlined resource allocation across various scenarios.

    b. By defining input values that can be customized during stack creation.

    c. By enhancing template organization and clarity.

    d. By specifying Conditions for resource creation.

3. **In what scenario would you use Conditions in AWS CloudFormation?**

   a. To handle user input and customization during stack creation.

   b. To manage key-value pairs for resource configuration.

   c. To specify Conditions for resource creation based on certain criteria.

   d. To define Metadata for resources.

4. **Which intrinsic functions can be used in AWS CloudFormation to conditionally create resources or define resource properties based on certain Conditions?**

   a. Fn::If

   b. Fn::And

   c. Fn::Or

   d. All of the above

5. **What capabilities does AWS CloudFormation Init provide to users?**

   a. It allows users to visually design CloudFormation templates using a drag-and-drop interface.

   b. It automatically configures EC2 instances launched as part of a CloudFormation stack according to specified configuration data.

   c. It facilitates the management of AWS Lambda functions within CloudFormation stacks.

   d. It enables users to monitor and visualize the execution of CloudFormation stacks in real-time.

Answers

1. a

2. c

3. c

4. d

5. b

References

A list of essential URLs that we have referenced in this chapter are:

- **https://docs.aws.amazon.com/AWSCloudFormation/latest/UserGuide/parameters-section-structure.html**

Join our book's Discord space

Join the book's Discord Workspace for Latest updates, Offers, Tech happenings around the world, New Release and Sessions with the Authors:

https://discord.bpbonline.com

Chapter 5

Macros, Transform and Outputs

Introduction

As we advance further into CloudFormation, we will encounter pivotal concepts like macros, transforms, and Outputs. Having thoroughly explored foundational elements such as resources, Parameters, Mappings, and Metadata in the previous chapter, we now stand equipped with a robust comprehension of these fundamentals. This knowledge forms a solid foundation for our forthcoming exploration of macros, transforms, and Outputs that epitomize advanced functionalities, empowering users to wield CloudFormation with unparalleled flexibility and efficiency.

Within this chapter, we dive into the intricacies of macros, dynamic transformations, and output mechanisms within CloudFormation templates. Macros extend CloudFormation's native syntax and functionality, enabling users to craft custom transformations and automate complex processes seamlessly. Transforms empower developers to leverage pre-built templates and macros, streamlining the provisioning of intricate architectures while enhancing reusability and scalability. Additionally, Outputs help share important info from your CloudFormation setup with other systems outside. This makes it easy to integrate everything smoothly and handle tasks after deploying your resources. Through comprehensive elucidation and practical examples, we navigate these advanced concepts, enriching our understanding and proficiency in CloudFormation orchestration.

Structure

The chapter covers the following topics:

- Unleashing the macros
- Transform and pre-processing
- AWS::Serverless
- AWS::Include
- Mastering Outputs definitions

Objectives

This chapter will familiarize you with advanced features in CloudFormation: macros, transforms, and Outputs. It builds upon foundational knowledge and provides practical insights into leveraging macros for custom transformations, transforms for streamlining architecture provisioning, and Outputs for seamless integration and post-deployment tasks. Through concise explanations and examples, readers will gain proficiency in employing these features effectively within their CloudFormation setups.

Unleashing the macros

Macros offer a versatile mechanism for customizing CloudFormation templates to suit specific requirements. They empower users to execute a wide range of operations, ranging from basic find-and-replace actions to comprehensive transformations that overhaul entire templates. At its core, a macro allows you to define a set of instructions or logic that CloudFormation applies to your template during the provisioning process. This means you can automate repetitive tasks, implement complex business logic, or integrate with external systems seamlessly.

Workings of macro

In CloudFormation, macros are implemented using AWS Lambda functions. To use macros, you first need to define a Lambda function that contains the logic for the custom processing you want to perform on your templates.

Here is a breakdown of the process:

1. **Define a Lambda function**: You create a Lambda function containing the logic for your macro. This function will receive the CloudFormation template as input,

perform the desired processing or transformation, and return the modified template.

2. **Create a macro resource**: In your CloudFormation template, you define a resource of type **AWS::CloudFormation::Macro**. This resource references the Lambda function created in the previous step and specifies other properties, such as the name and description of the macro. The syntax for the same is as follows:

```
1. Resources:
2.   MyCustomMacro:
3.     Type: 'AWS::CloudFormation::Macro'
4.     Properties:
5.       Name: 'MyCustomMacroName'
6.       Description: 'Description of my custom Macro'
7.       FunctionName: 'arn:aws:lambda:region:account-id:function:function-name'
```

3. **Invoke the macro**: Once the macro is defined, you can use it in your CloudFormation templates by referencing its name. When CloudFormation processes the template, it automatically invokes the associated macro Lambda function to perform the custom processing on the template before proceeding with stack creation or update. Further details on the invocation will be explored in the upcoming section, transform and pre-processing.

Foundational template for macro declaration

Let us examine the simple foundational template, where we will define a macro with the associated Lambda resource. In this setup, we will assume that our Lambda code resides in an S3 bucket, which will be directly referenced for retrieval. We will not explore the code or logic of Lambda functions for macros since this is outside the scope of this book.

Note: There may be variations in how macros are implemented based on specific requirements and preferences. For example, the Lambda function's code and permissions, as well as the macro's configuration, can be customized further in the template depending on the use case. In this context, we are focusing on a basic implementation for our comprehension.

The foundational template is as follows:

```
1. AWSTemplateFormatVersion: '2010-09-09'
2.
3. Resources:
4.   MyMacroFunctionRole:
5.     Type: AWS::IAM::Role
6.     Properties:
```

```
7.          AssumeRolePolicyDocument:
8.            Version: '2012-10-17'
9.            Statement:
10.             - Effect: Allow
11.               Principal:
12.                 Service: lambda.amazonaws.com
13.               Action: sts:AssumeRole
14.         Policies:
15.           - PolicyName: LambdaExecutionPolicy
16.             PolicyDocument:
17.               Version: '2012-10-17'
18.               Statement:
19.                 - Effect: Allow
20.                   Action:
21.                     - logs:CreateLogGroup
22.                     - logs:CreateLogStream
23.                     - logs:PutLogEvents
24.                     - s3:GetObject
25.                   Resource: '*'
26.
27.   MyMacroFunction:
28.     Type: AWS::Lambda::Function
29.     Properties:
30.       Handler: index.handler
31.       Role: !GetAtt MyMacroFunctionRole.Arn
32.       Code:
33.         S3Bucket: my-bucket
34.         S3Key: lambda.zip
35.       Runtime: nodejs14.x
36.
37.   MyMacro:
38.     Type: AWS::CloudFormation::Macro
39.     Properties:
40.       Name: MyMacro
41.       Description: A custom macro for transformation
42.       FunctionName: !GetAtt MyMacroFunction.Arn
```

In this template:

- **MyMacroFunctionRole** defines the IAM role required for the Lambda function. It grants permissions for the Lambda function to write logs and access objects from S3.

- **MyMacroFunction** creates the Lambda function. It specifies the function's runtime (assuming Node.js based code), handler, IAM role, and the location of the code file stored in an S3 bucket.

- **MyMacro** creates the CloudFormation macro, linking it to the Lambda function created earlier. This allows the macro to execute the logic defined in the Lambda function during stack creation or update.

Transform and pre-processing

In the preceding section, we explored the creation of macros; now, we will understand how to invoke them. We have two options to achieve the same depending on our requirements:

- If you want to process just a subsection of a template, use **Fn::Transform**.

- If you want to process the entire template, reference the macro in the Transform section of the template. This section is optional. It is declared at the same level as other primary template sections, like Parameters and resources.

Let us discuss each of them in detail:

Fn::Transform

The **Fn::Transform** is an intrinsic function in AWS CloudFormation that allows you to process template snippets at specific locations in your CloudFormation template using a macro. The following is the YAML syntax for the same:

```
1. Fn::Transform:
2.   Name: MacroName
3.   Parameters:
4.     Param1Name: Param1Value
5.     Param2Name: Param2Value
6.     ...
```

The preceding syntax can also be written as:

```
1. !Transform:
2.   Name: MacroName
3.   Parameters:
4.     Param1Name: Param1Value
5.     Param2Name: Param2Value
6.     ...
```

In the preceding syntax, the following mean:

- **Name (required)**: It specifies the name of the macro that you want to invoke.

- **Parameters (optional)**: It specifies Parameters (key-value format) to pass to the macro. These Parameters are accessible within the macro code for processing.

- **Fn::Transform** is equivalent to **!Transform** (in YAML). It is the short format used to reference the function.

Let us investigate an example template to grasp this concept more effectively. We will assume that we already have a macro in place:

```
1.  AWSTemplateFormatVersion: '2010-09-09'
2.
3.  Parameters:
4.    InputString:
5.      Type: String
6.      Default: "Hello, world!"
7.
8.  Resources:
9.    S3Bucket:
10.     Type: "AWS::S3::Bucket"
11.     Properties:
12.       Tags:
13.         - Key: "UpperCaseTag"
14.           Value:
15.             'Fn::Transform':
16.               - Name: 'StringMacro'
17.                 Parameters:
18.                   InputString: !Ref InputString
19.                   Operation: Upper
```

The preceding example template includes the following:

- It introduces a **Parameters** section, allowing users to customize input values during stack creation or updates. This example includes a single parameter named **InputString**, which is a type **String** and has a default value of **Hello, world!**.

- In the **Resources** section, the template creates an S3 bucket named **S3Bucket**. Within the bucket's configuration, a tag named **UpperCaseTag** is defined. What is noteworthy is the value transformation applied to this tag, achieved through a custom macro named **StringMacro**. The transformation, specified using **Fn::Transform**, utilizes the input string parameter provided by the user and converts it to uppercase. This dynamic transformation ensures that the tag's value reflects the uppercase version of the InputString parameter, providing consistency and standardization across resources.

Note: In essence, this template showcases the creation of an S3 bucket with a tag whose value is dynamically transformed based on user input, demonstrating the flexibility and extensibility of CloudFormation templates through custom macros.

Transform section

The Transform section is a top-level attribute within the CloudFormation template. It allows users to apply a single transformation to the entire template, which is useful when we need to process our template at multiple locations. It is an optional section. It is declared at the same level as other primary template sections, like Parameters and resources. the following is the YAML syntax for the same:

```
1. Transform: MacroName
```

In the preceding syntax:

- **Transform** is the keyword indicating the start of the Transform section.

- **MacroName** is the name of the transformation or macro that you want to apply to the CloudFormation template.

Let us explore the syntax for declaring multiple macros. This is crucial, particularly in production setups, where various scenarios demand the utilization of multiple macros to meet specific requirements. The syntax is as follows:

```
1. Transform:
2.   - MyMacro1
3.   - MyMacro2
4.   - MyMacro3
```

In the preceding syntax:

- **MyMacro1**, **MyMacro2** and **MyMacro3** are the names of the macros or transformations you want to apply.

- Each macro or transformation is listed as a separate item in the list.

> **Note:** It is crucial to understand that in this scenario, the three macros will not execute simultaneously. Instead, they follow a sequential execution order. Initially, **Macro1** is executed, and its output serves as the input for **Macro2**, which is then executed. Subsequently, the output of **Macro2** becomes the input for **Macro3**, concluding the sequence. This sequential process ensures that each macro operates on the template after the transformations applied by the preceding macro, enabling a controlled and predictable flow of transformations. This facilitates complex template customization and automation with clarity and precision.

Now, let us explore an example template to enhance our understanding of this concept. We will assume that a macro is already in place. This template will provision multiple EC2 instances using the transform section with the relevant macro:

```
1. AWSTemplateFormatVersion: '2010-09-09'
2. Transform: CountMacro
3.
```

```
 4. Resources:
 5.    EC2Instance:
 6.       Type: AWS::EC2::Instance
 7.       Properties:
 8.          InstanceType: t2.micro
 9.          ImageId: ami-12345678
10.          Count: 3
```

In the preceding example template:

- In the Transform section, the line specifies that the CloudFormation template will utilize a custom macro named **CountMacro**. Here, **CountMacro** is likely a custom macro designed to handle the creation of multiple resources based on a specified count.

- In the **Resources** section, we define the creation of the EC2 instance. However, what is noteworthy is the **Count** property. Instead of specifying a fixed number of instances, the **Count** property indicates that the number of instances to be created will be determined dynamically by the **CountMacro** transformation. This transformation enables the creation of multiple instances based on a single resource definition.

> **Note: In essence, the transform: CountMacro directive instructs CloudFormation to apply the logic defined within the CountMacro macro during template processing. This macro likely evaluates the Count property specified for resources and generates multiple instances accordingly. This approach streamlines the template by abstracting away the complexity of managing multiple resource definitions and enhances its flexibility and scalability.**

Predefined macros

AWS CloudFormation supports transforms, which are predefined macros provided by the AWS CloudFormation service. It is important to distinguish between transforms and the Transform section in a CloudFormation template. The former refers to the ready-to-use macros available for direct referencing within the template, while the latter refers to the section of the template where both custom and pre-built macros are specified for processing. For our understanding, we will use the word transforms in lowercase to refer to the predefined macros available for ready use.

One important thing to note is that transforms in AWS CloudFormation do not necessitate special permissions for usage as they are hosted by CloudFormation itself. They are accessible across various accounts within the CloudFormation environment without incurring associated costs. Moreover, transforms are handled similarly to other macros by CloudFormation with respect to their evaluation order and scope.

A list of inbuilt macros or transforms available within AWS CloudFormation for use are:

- `AWS::CodeDeployBlueGreen transform`
- `AWS::Include transform`
- `AWS::LanguageExtensions transform`
- `AWS::SecretsManager transform`
- `AWS::Serverless transform`
- `AWS::ServiceCatalog transform`

Out of these, **`AWS::Include`** transform, and **`AWS::Serverless`** transform are the most common and frequently used for template designing. We will discuss them in detail in a separate section. The other transforms offer specialized functionalities catering to specific use cases. We will briefly discuss each of these to provide an overview of their capabilities.

AWS::CodeDeployBlueGreen transform

The **`AWS::CodeDeployBlueGreen`** transform is specifically tailored to enable blue-green deployments for Amazon **Elastic Container Service (ECS)** applications using AWS CodeDeploy within AWS CloudFormation templates. Blue-green deployments are a deployment strategy used to mitigate risk and minimize downtime during application updates. With the **`AWS::CodeDeployBlueGreen`** transform, you can seamlessly implement blue-green deployments for ECS services, ensuring smooth transitions between different application versions. It automates creating two ECS service sets (blue and green) and configuring CodeDeploy to manage traffic routing between them during deployments.

To enable CloudFormation for blue/green deployments within a stack, ensure the following information is included in its stack template:

- Incorporate a **Transform** section within your template, invoking the **`AWS::CodeDeployBlueGreen`** **transform**.

- Add a Hook section to invoke the **`AWS::CodeDeploy::BlueGreen`** hook.

The syntax for declaring it in the template is as follows:

```
1.  Transform:
2.    - 'AWS::CodeDeployBlueGreen'
```

For additional insights into executing ECS blue/green deployments using this transform, please refer to the following documentation:

https://docs.aws.amazon.com/AWSCloudFormation/latest/UserGuide/blue-green.html

AWS::LanguageExtensions transform

The **`AWS::LanguageExtensions`** transform, hosted within AWS CloudFormation, serves as a powerful tool for incorporating additional functionalities and intrinsic functions not inherently available in CloudFormation. By integrating this transform into your templates, you can unlock a range of capabilities beyond the default CloudFormation features.

When **AWS::LanguageExtensions** is referenced within a template, and stacks are created or updated via Change sets, CloudFormation seamlessly updates any intrinsic functions defined by the transform to their resolved values within the template. This dynamic functionality streamlines the template creation and update processes, ensuring intrinsic functions are appropriately evaluated and integrated. Integrating the **AWS::LanguageExtensions** transform into your AWS CloudFormation templates enables the utilization of intrinsic functions as Parameters for **Ref** and **Fn::GetAtt**. This flexibility empowers users to leverage advanced functions and streamline resource definitions, enhancing the overall efficiency and effectiveness of CloudFormation deployments.

The syntax for declaring it in the template is as follows:

```
1. Transform: AWS::LanguageExtensions
```

Ensure that the **AWS::LanguageExtensions** transform is applied at the top level of your template. It cannot be utilized as an embedded transform within another template section.

For additional insights into its usage, please refer to the following documentation:

https://docs.aws.amazon.com/AWSCloudFormation/latest/UserGuide/transform-aws-languageextensions.html

AWS::SecretsManager transform

The **AWS::SecretsManager** transform is a powerful macro hosted by AWS CloudFormation aimed at simplifying the management of secrets and their rotation tasks within your infrastructure. It streamlines the process of defining and managing secrets, such as database credentials, API keys, and other sensitive information, while simultaneously facilitating automated rotation tasks for enhanced security.

The syntax for the same is as follows:

```
1. Transform: AWS::SecretsManager-2020-07-23
```

Leverage the **AWS::SecretsManager** transform to define an AWS Lambda function responsible for secret rotation tasks. When initiating a Change set or updating stacks via Change sets, AWS CloudFormation automatically generates the necessary AWS Lambda function for executing secrets rotation if the template references **AWS::SecretsManager**.

To specify the attributes of the desired AWS Lambda function, utilize the **HostedRotationLambda** property type within the **AWS::SecretsManager::RotationSchedule** resource. The AWS Lambda function is embedded within a Nested stack, represented by an **AWS::CloudFormation::Stack** resource, within the processed template. This resource establishes a connection to the appropriate function template available in the AWS Secrets Manager rotation Lambda functions repository, depending on the specified **RotationType** within the **AWS::SecretsManager::RotationSchedule** resource.

An example snippet of the **AWS::SecretsManager::RotationSchedule** resource is as follows:

```
1.  MyCustomSecretRotation:
2.    Type: AWS::SecretsManager::RotationSchedule
3.    Properties:
4.      SecretId: !Ref MyCustomSecret
5.      HostedRotationLambda:
6.        RotationType: CustomRotationFunction
7.        RotationLambdaName: MyCustomRotationFunction
8.        VpcSecurityGroupIds: !GetAtt MyVPC.SecurityGroups
9.        VpcSubnetIds:
10.         - !Ref MySubnet1
11.         - !Ref MySubnet2
12.     RotationRules:
13.       AutomaticallyAfterDays: 7
```

In the preceding snippet the following perform functions, like:

- **MyCustomSecretRotation**: It defines the resource and the relevant type that is responsible for managing the rotation schedule of a secret.

- **SecretId**: References the logical ID of the secret to be rotated, specified by **!Ref MyCustomSecret**.

- **HostedRotationLambda**: Configures the hosted rotation Lambda function that is responsible for executing the rotation logic.

- **RotationType**: Specifies the type of rotation to be performed. In this example, it is set to **CustomRotationFunction**.

- **RotationLambdaName**: Defines the name of the custom rotation Lambda function, named **MyCustomRotationFunction**.

- **VpcSecurityGroupIds**: Specifies the security group IDs associated with the VPC where the rotation Lambda function will execute, retrieved using **!GetAtt MyVPC. SecurityGroups**.

- **VpcSubnetIds**: Defines the subnet IDs within the VPC where the rotation Lambda function will execute. Here, it refers to the logical IDs of **MySubnet1** and **MySubnet2**.

- **RotationRules**: Configures the rotation rules, specifying that the secret should be automatically rotated after seven days.

For additional insights into its usage, please refer to the following documentation:

https://docs.aws.amazon.com/AWSCloudFormation/latest/UserGuide/transform-aws-secretsmanager.html

AWS::ServiceCatalog transform

The **AWS::ServiceCatalog** transform facilitates the referencing of Outputs from provisioned products within CloudFormation templates. By including this transform at the top of the template, users can specify the names of provisioned products and their corresponding output keys. During stack provisioning, the transform retrieves these output values and substitutes them into the template, streamlining resource configuration and enhancing automation. This capability allows for simplified infrastructure deployments, promoting efficiency and reliability in AWS Service Catalog environments.

The syntax for the same is as follows:

```
1. Transform: AWS::ServiceCatalog
```

To reference Outputs from existing provisioned products, users must include the **AWS::ServiceCatalog** transform at the top of their CloudFormation templates. Within the template, specify the provisioned product names and output key names where output values are required. Multiple provisioned products and key names can be referenced within a single template, with a maximum limit of 20 references per template.

For additional insights into its usage, please refer to the following documentation:

https://docs.aws.amazon.com/AWSCloudFormation/latest/UserGuide/transform-aws-servicecatalog.html

AWS::Serverless

The **AWS::Serverless** transform, an essential macro within CloudFormation, serves as a gateway to the **AWS Serverless Application Model (AWS SAM)** syntax. By invoking this transform, users can encapsulate an entire AWS SAM template within CloudFormation and seamlessly expand it into a fully compliant CloudFormation template. This transformation process bridges the gap between AWS SAM's simplified syntax and CloudFormation's extensive capabilities, empowering developers to harness the agility and productivity benefits of serverless architecture while leveraging the robustness and scalability of CloudFormation for deployment.

The syntax for the same is as follows:

```
1. Transform: "AWS::Serverless-2016-10-31"
```

Before we discuss this transform in more detail, let us try to understand the SAM.

Serverless Application Model

SAM is indeed a framework provided by AWS for building serverless applications. It extends AWS CloudFormation with simplified shorthand syntax and additional features tailored for serverless development. It provides developers with an intuitive and concise way to define serverless resources such as AWS Lambda functions, Amazon API Gateway

APIs, Amazon DynamoDB tables, and others. It abstracts the complexity of resource configuration and management, enabling developers to focus on writing application logic rather than infrastructure provisioning. In essence, SAM is a toolkit that enhances the developer experience of creating and operating serverless applications on AWS. By declaring the previous defined syntax, we are informing the CloudFormation that our template defines a serverless app.

In general, AWS SAM consists of the following two parts:

- **AWS SAM templates**: It offers a concise syntax for defining IaC tailored for serverless applications.

- **AWS SAM command line interface**: It is a developer tool designed to swiftly create, develop, and deploy serverless applications.

Serverless resource types

Let us now explore some commonly used Serverless resources and their practical application, which are as follows:

- **AWS Lambda (`AWS::Serverless::Function`)**: AWS Lambda is a serverless compute service that lets you run code without provisioning or managing servers. With AWS SAM, you can easily define Lambda functions using the `AWS::Serverless::Function` resource type. This resource type allows you to declare Lambda functions along with their configurations and event sources.

  When using **`AWS::Serverless::Function`**, you specify essential properties such as the function's handler, runtime, and the location of the deployment package in an Amazon S3 bucket.

  Kindly refer to the following example for more understanding:

```
1.  AWSTemplateFormatVersion: '2010-09-09'
2.  Transform: AWS::Serverless-2016-10-31
3.
4.  Resources:
5.    MyServerlessFunc:
6.      Type: AWS::Serverless::Function
7.      Properties:
8.        Handler: index.lambda_handler
9.        Runtime: python3.9
10.       CodeUri: s3://<my-bucket>/my-function-code.zip
```

  In the preceding example, the **`AWS::Serverless-2016-10-31`** transform allows you to define serverless applications using simplified syntax, while in the **Resources** section; **`AWS::Serverless::Function`** indicates the creation of a Lambda function. Overall, this CloudFormation template defines a Lambda function named **MyServerlessFunc**, sets its handler to **index.lambda_handler**, specifies Python 3.9 as the runtime environment and specifies the location of the deployment package in an S3 bucket.

For further details on additional options available, please refer to the following link:

https://docs.aws.amazon.com/serverless-application-model/latest/ developerguide/sam-resource-function.html

> **Note: It is noteworthy that we have utilized a high-level abstraction to define the Lambda function, simplified the syntax and minimized the boilerplate code required for its creation. This streamlined approach reduces the verbosity of the template.**

- **Amazon API Gateway API (AWS::Serverless::Api):** The Amazon API Gateway API resource type, designated as **AWS::Serverless::Api**, serves as a fundamental component for declaring and managing collections of API Gateway resources and methods within AWS SAM. This resource enables developers to define HTTP endpoints and corresponding routes, offering a streamlined approach to building RESTful APIs as part of serverless applications.

  Kindly refer to the following example for more understanding:

  ```
  1. AWSTemplateFormatVersion: '2010-09-09'
  2. Transform: AWS::Serverless-2016-10-31
  3. Resources:
  4.   MyAPI:
  5.     Type: AWS::Serverless::Api
  6.     Properties:
  7.       StageName: dev
  8.       DefinitionUri: swagger.yml
  ```

  In the given example, the **AWS::Serverless-2016-10-31** transform allows you to define serverless applications using simplified syntax. At the same time, in the **Resources** section, **AWS::Serverless::Api** indicates the creation of an API Gateway resource and method that can be invoked through HTTPS endpoints.

  An important thing to note here is the **DefinitionUri** attribute under the **Properties** section. Here, we directly provide the path of the Swagger file, which can be present in the S3 bucket, like in the previous example for Lambda. The content of this file defines the routes, methods, and integration details for the API Gateway API. By referencing an external Swagger or OpenAPI definition file, developers can separate the API configuration from the AWS SAM template, allowing for greater flexibility and manageability.

For further details on additional options available, please refer to the following link:

https://docs.aws.amazon.com/serverless-application-model/latest/ developerguide/sam-resource-api.html

> **Note: We will not explore Swagger in detail as it falls outside the scope of this book.**

- **Amazon DynamoDB table (`AWS::Serverless::SimpleTable`):** Amazon DynamoDB is a fully managed NoSQL database service provided by AWS, offering a low-latency performance at any scale. The **`AWS::Serverless::SimpleTable`** resource allows you to define a DynamoDB table within your serverless application using the AWS CloudFormation template.

  Kindly refer to the following example for more understanding:

  ```
  1. AWSTemplateFormatVersion: '2010-09-09'
  2. Transform: AWS::Serverless-2016-10-31
  3. Resources:
  4.   MyDynamoDBTable:
  5.     Type: AWS::Serverless::SimpleTable
  6.     Properties:
  7.       TableName: MyTable
  8.       PrimaryKey:
  9.         Name: MyPartitionKey
  10.         Type: String
  ```

  In the given example, the **`AWS::Serverless-2016-10-31`** transform allows you to define serverless applications using simplified syntax, while in the Resources section, **`AWS::Serverless::SimpleTable`** indicates the creation of a DynamoDB table using AWS SAM. Here we are creating a DynamoDB table named **MyTable** with a primary key composed of a single attribute named **MyPartitionKey** of type **String**. This table will be provisioned with the default read and write capacity settings.

  For further details on additional options available, please refer to the following link:

  https://docs.aws.amazon.com/serverless-application-model/latest/ developerguide/sam-resource-simpletable.html

AWS::Include

The **`AWS::Include`** transform is a powerful feature provided by AWS CloudFormation, allowing you to include reusable, shared templates or macros directly within your CloudFormation templates. This enables you to modularize your IaC by breaking it into smaller, manageable components that can be reused across multiple stacks or projects. When creating or updating stacks, AWS CloudFormation inserts the contents of the file present in the S3 bucket.

The syntax for the same is as follows:

```
1. 'Fn::Transform':
2.    Name: 'AWS::Include'
```

Here are some guidelines and considerations for using the **AWS::Include** transform in your CloudFormation templates:

- **Amazon S3 URL requirement**: Currently, only Amazon S3 URIs are supported for including snippets. Other formats, such as Amazon S3 ARNs, are not supported. The included resource must reside in an Amazon S3 bucket and cannot be sourced from locations like GitHub repositories.

- **Inclusivity**: Once a snippet is made available at an Amazon S3 URL, anyone with access to that URL can include the snippet in their CloudFormation template, fostering collaboration and reuse among team members.

- **JSON validity**: Template snippets included using **AWS::Include** must adhere to the JSON format, ensuring compatibility and consistency across deployments.

- **Key-value format**: Snippets must be structured in a valid key-value format within the JSON objects. Each key-value pair must adhere to the required syntax for CloudFormation templates.

- **Limitations on nested inclusions**: You cannot reference a template snippet that itself uses **AWS::Include**, preventing potential circular dependencies and ensuring predictable behaviour during stack creation.

- **Manual updates**: If the contents of your included snippets change, your CloudFormation stack does not automatically reflect those changes. You must explicitly update the stack with the updated snippets. It is crucial to verify any changes before updating the stack, ideally by reviewing the generated Change set.

- **Template language compatibility**: While creating templates and snippets, you can use a combination of YAML and JSON template languages, allowing you to leverage the strengths of each as needed.

- **YAML shorthand notation**: The use of shorthand notations for YAML snippets is not supported now. Ensure that YAML snippets adhere to the full YAML syntax requirements.

- **Cross-region replication**: You can include snippets with cross-region replication Amazon S3 URIs using AWS::Include. However, ensure careful consideration of Amazon S3 bucket names and access permissions, particularly when accessing cross-region replication objects.

Workings of AWS::Include

The **AWS::Include** transform capability simplifies the management and reuse of common configurations across your infrastructure as code. Let us now try to understand how it works.

With **AWS::Include**, we create a reference for a specific template snippet residing in an S3 bucket. This snippet encapsulates a portion of configuration or resource definitions that you wish to include in your main CloudFormation template. Now, during operations such as creating a Change set or updating stacks using Change sets, AWS CloudFormation automatically handles the inclusion of referenced **AWS::Include** templates. When your main template references an **AWS::Include**, CloudFormation seamlessly inserts the contents of the specified file at the location of the transform within the template.

The main advantage of the **AWS::Include** function is that it streamlines your CloudFormation templates, abstracting repetitive configurations and promoting consistency across your infrastructure deployments. This feature empowers you to efficiently manage complex infrastructure configurations while adhering to best practices in infrastructure as code development.

In the next section, we will explore a use case to understand the effective use of this transform.

Example

Let us understand this concept through an example. We aim to launch an EC2 instance while storing some of its configurations as a snippet in an S3 bucket. We will employ the **AWS::Include** transform in our main CloudFormation template. This straightforward example will provide clarity on how this mechanism operates.

Here is the snippet that we will store in our S3 bucket for later retrieval:

```
1.  Resources:
2.    EC2Instance:
3.      Type: AWS::EC2::Instance
4.      Properties:
5.        InstanceType: t2.micro
6.        ImageId: ami-0f403e3180720dd7e
7.        KeyName: mynewkey
8.        SecurityGroupIds:
9.          - sg 075b58dd04ac73731
10.       SubnetId: subnet-4590de7a
```

In the snippet provided, we have outlined a complete **Resource** section for an EC2 instance, allowing direct referencing in our main template. All essential attribute information for spinning up the EC2 instance is provided, obviating the necessity of duplicating the **Resource** section in our main template. This snippet file is named **ec2-snippet.yaml**.

Note: We will deploy in the AWS us-east-1 region, so that we have hardcoded values for various attributes according to the environment. We can change them accordingly as per the region choice.

Now let us have a look at our the template we will be spinning up on the CloudFormation console:

```
1. AWSTemplateFormatVersion: 2010-09-09
2. Transform:
3.   Name: 'AWS::Include'
4.   Parameters:
5.   Location: 's3://myexamplecf/ec2-snippet.yaml'
```

In the preceding template, the `AWS::Include` transform is utilized, enabling the inclusion of reusable code from an external location, specifically an S3 bucket. Additionally, the parameter attribute specifies the location of the code file along with the necessary S3 bucket information where it resides. This is where CloudFormation will fetch additional template content during stack creation or update.

Now, we will proceed to deploy this template using the CloudFormation console. We will directly upload the template from our local system to create the stack. Please follow the outlined steps for a clearer understanding:

1. After logging into the AWS Console, navigate to the S3 bucket for uploading the snippet file:

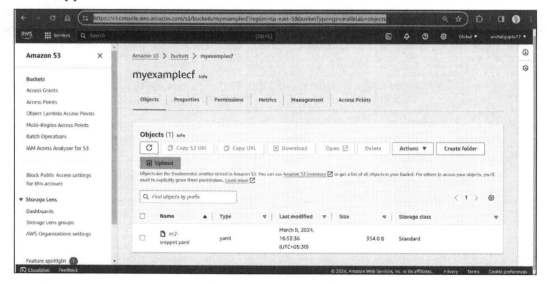

Figure 5.1: S3 bucket snippet uploading

In the provided screenshot, you can observe the successful upload of the snippet file to the S3 bucket. We will employ this file later in the transform process.

2. Following that, we will now proceed to the **CloudFormation** console to deploy the stack using the template we have just reviewed:

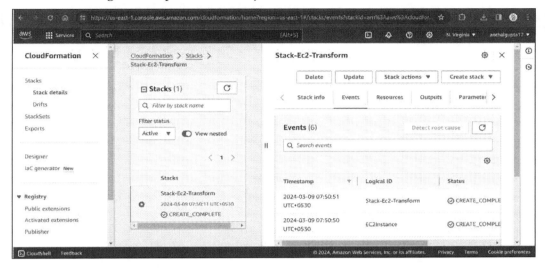

Figure 5.2: CloudFormation Console

We have uploaded the template from our local system to create the stack named **Stack-Ec2-Transform**, indicating the utilization of the Transform section to instantiate the EC2 instance. The stack was created successfully without any issues, indicating its ability to retrieve the snippet from the S3 bucket for EC2 configuration. Let us promptly verify the **Resource** and **Template** sections on the console page for quick validation:

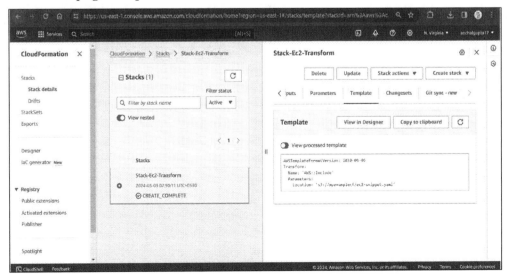

Figure 5.3: Template overview

The **Resources** section is as follows:

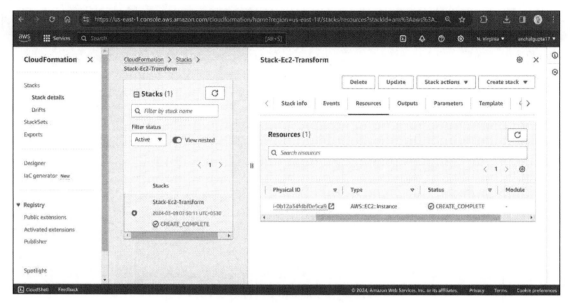

Figure 5.4: Resource section

3. In *Figure 5.3*, we can swiftly review our uploaded template, while in the subsequent one, that is, *Figure 5.4*, we can observe the physical ID of the freshly configured EC2 instance. Clicking on the EC2 instance ID will direct us to the EC2 console page. For further clarification, please consult the following figure:

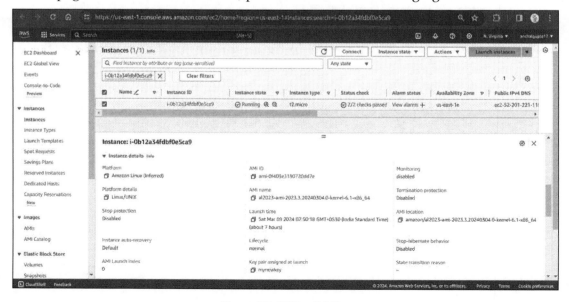

Figure 5.5: EC2 validation

4. In *Figure 5.5*, it is evident that the newly launched EC2 instance is configured with Parameters such as **AMI ID** and key pair, as specified in the snippet stored in the S3 bucket. This indicates the successful completion of the entire setup process.

Note: Please note that while snippets of CloudFormation templates can be stored in S3 for enhanced efficiency and accessibility, it is important to be aware of a crucial limitation: the parameter section cannot be included as part of these stored snippets. This exclusion is due to the dynamic nature of Parameters, which require direct input during stack creation to customize configurations according to specific needs and environments.

Mastering Outputs definitions

In CloudFormation, Outputs provide a means to retrieve information about the resources created during stack deployment. They are crucial for communicating important details or resource attributes to other parts of the infrastructure or external systems. Mastering Outputs definitions in CloudFormation templates is essential for gaining full control over stack deployments and effectively managing the resources within.

Understanding Outputs

The Outputs section, while optional, serves a pivotal role in CloudFormation templates by declaring values that can be imported into other stacks for cross-stack references, returned in responses to describe stack calls, or conveniently viewed on the AWS CloudFormation console. As an illustration, you might choose to output the EC2 instance ID for a stack, facilitating its retrieval and use in subsequent operations.

The syntax is as follows:

```
1.  Outputs:
2.    OutputLogicalID:
3.      Description: Description of the output
4.      Value: Value to be outputted
5.      Export:
6.        Name: ExportedOutputName
```

In the preceding syntax, the following means:

- **OutputLogicalID**: A unique identifier for the output.
- **Description**: (Optional) A brief description of what the output represents.
- **Value**: (Optional) The value to be outputted, which can be a resource attribute, a literal value, or a function.
- **Export**: (Optional) Allows exporting the output value to be used in other stacks.

Examples

Let us see a few example snippets to gain a deeper understanding of how this section can be effectively utilized:

- **Cross stack output reference**: The following example snippet represents an **Outputs** section in a CloudFormation template, specifically defining an output named **MyS3BucketName**:

```
1. Outputs:
2.   MyS3BucketName:
3.     Description: The name of the S3 bucket
4.     Value: !Ref MyS3Bucket
5.     Export:
6.       Name: !Sub "${AWS::StackName}-S3BucketName"
```

Let us break down each part:

- o **Outputs**: This denotes the start of the **Outputs** section in the CloudFormation template.

- o **MyS3BucketName**: This is the logical name given to the output. It represents the name of the S3 bucket in this example.

- o **Description**: This provides a brief description of the output. In this case, it describes that this output represents **The name of the S3 bucket**.

- o **Value**: This specifies the value to be outputted. In CloudFormation templates, **!Ref** is an intrinsic function used to reference other resources in the template. **MyS3Bucket** is assumed to be the logical ID of the S3 bucket resource.

- o **Export**: This section is optional and allows exporting the output value for use in other CloudFormation stacks. It enables cross-stack references. The **Name** attribute specifies the name of the exported value. Here, **!Sub** is another intrinsic function used for string substitution. **${AWS::StackName}** retrieves the name of the current CloudFormation stack, and **-S3BucketName** is appended to create a unique name for the exported value.

> **Note: The intrinsic function !Sub will be thoroughly explored in Chapter 6, Intrinsic Functions and Pseudo Parameters. Additionally, the method for importing exported values for cross-stack references will be discussed later. For now, we will concentrate on understanding how to export values within the current context.**

- **Simple stack output**: This example demonstrates an **Outputs** section in a CloudFormation template, specifically defining an output named **MyVPCID** which represents a newly set VPC ID:

```
7.  Outputs:
8.    MyVPCID:
9.      Description: The ID of the VPC
10.     Value: !Ref MyVPC
```

Let us break down each part:

- o **Outputs**: This denotes the start of the **Outputs** section in the CloudFormation template.

- o **MyVPCID**: This is the logical name given to the output. It represents the identifier for the VPC in this example.

- o **Description**: This provides a brief description of the output. In this case, it describes that this output represents **The ID of the VPC**.

- o **Value**: This specifies the value to be outputted. In CloudFormation templates, **!Ref** is an intrinsic function used to reference other resources in the template. **MyVPC** is assumed to be the logical ID of the VPC resource.

Limitations of the Output section

While the Outputs section in CloudFormation templates provides a convenient way to extract information about resources created during stack deployment, it also has the following limitations:

- **Limited export**: Although Outputs can be exported for cross-stack references, this export is limited to other stacks within the same AWS account and region. Cross-region or cross-account exports are not supported.

- **No built-in versioning**: CloudFormation does not provide built-in versioning or history tracking for Outputs. Once an output value is overwritten or deleted, its previous state is not preserved within CloudFormation.

- **Limited to stack completion**: Outputs are only available once the stack has completed creation or update. There is no real-time access to Outputs during stack creation or update processes.

- **Dependency constraints on deletion**: You cannot delete a stack if another stack references one of its Outputs. This can introduce complexities in managing stack dependencies and deletions, especially in complex multi-stack architectures.

- **Unique export names within a region**: For each AWS account, Export names must be unique within a region. This constraint ensures the uniqueness and proper referencing of exported values across different CloudFormation stacks within the same region.

Conclusion

Throughout this chapter, we understood several fundamental aspects of CloudFormation templating. We began by delving into the powerful capabilities of macros, understanding how they allow for dynamic transformations within our templates. With a focus on transformation and preprocessing, we explored the nuances of AWS's serverless and include transforms, leveraging them to streamline our infrastructure deployment processes.

A significant portion of our discussion was dedicated to mastering Outputs definitions, where we learned how to effectively extract critical information from our stacks for use in cross-stack references and other applications. By grasping the intricacies of Outputs, we gained greater control over our CloudFormation stacks, enhancing their modularity and interoperability.

As we conclude this chapter, we stand equipped with a deeper understanding of these essential concepts, poised to leverage them in our CloudFormation journey. With a solid foundation laid, we now turn our attention to the exploration of intrinsic functions and pseudo-Parameters. In the next chapter, we will understand the power and versatility of these tools, further expanding our toolkit for crafting robust and scalable infrastructure as code solutions.

Multiple choice questions

1. **Which of the following options represents a type of transform in AWS CloudFormation for serverless applications?**

    a. AWS::Lambda

    b. AWS::EC2

    c. AWS::Serverless

    d. AWS::RDS

2. **What is the primary function of Outputs definitions in AWS CloudFormation?**

    a. To define input Parameters for CloudFormation stacks.

    b. To specify the Outputs produced after the successful creation of CloudFormation stacks.

    c. To manage resource dependencies within CloudFormation templates.

    d. To define Conditions for resource creation in CloudFormation stacks

3. **What is the primary purpose of AWS::Include in AWS CloudFormation?**

    a. To include external AWS services within CloudFormation templates.

    b. To incorporate reusable code snippets or entire templates into CloudFormation stacks.

    c. To transform YAML templates into JSON format for easier deployment.

    d. To define Parameters and Outputs for CloudFormation stacks.

4. **What is the main purpose of AWS SAM?**

    a. To provide a framework for managing traditional server-based applications on AWS.

    b. To simplify the deployment and management of serverless applications on AWS.

    c. To optimize networking configurations for AWS services.

    d. To enhance security features for CloudFormation stacks.

5. **What role do macros play in AWS CloudFormation?**

    a. Macros are used to define custom resource types in CloudFormation templates.

    b. Macros are used to preprocess data before deploying CloudFormation stacks.

    c. Macros enable the use of custom transformations and manipulations of templates.

    d. Macros facilitate the definition of input Parameters for CloudFormation stacks.

Answers

1. c
2. b
3. b
4. b
5. c

Join our book's Discord space

Join the book's Discord Workspace for Latest updates, Offers, Tech happenings around the world, New Release and Sessions with the Authors:

https://discord.bpbonline.com

CHAPTER 6

Pseudo Parameters and Intrinsic Functions

Introduction

In this chapter, we embark on a comprehensive exploration of CloudFormation's pseudo parameters and intrinsic functions. As foundational components of the IaC paradigm, these features play a pivotal role in the orchestration and management of cloud resources within the AWS ecosystem. Pseudo parameters furnish essential contextual information about the deployment environment, facilitating template adaptability across various regions and accounts. Meanwhile, intrinsic functions imbue templates with dynamic capabilities, enabling the injection of logic and dynamic values to streamline configuration processes. We will learn how to harness these pre-defined variables to customize our templates and make them context-aware. Together, these elements form the backbone of CloudFormation's declarative approach, empowering users to construct scalable, resilient architectures with unparalleled efficiency and precision.

Structure

The chapter covers the following topics:

- Unveiling intrinsic functions
- Types of intrinsic functions and their usage
- Pseudo parameters
- Customizing templates with pseudo parameters

Objectives

The objective of this chapter is to provide a comprehensive understanding of CloudFormation's intrinsic functions and pseudo parameters, integral components in the realm of IaC deployment within AWS environments. Through this exploration, readers will uncover the intricacies of intrinsic functions, learning about their various types and usage scenarios to empower dynamic template creation and configuration. Additionally, this chapter aims to elucidate the significance of pseudo parameters, elucidating their role in furnishing contextual information about deployment environments and demonstrating techniques for customizing templates with these invaluable placeholders. By delving into these topics, readers will gain the necessary insights and expertise to leverage intrinsic functions and pseudo parameters effectively, enabling the construction of resilient, scalable cloud architectures with unparalleled precision and efficiency.

Unveiling intrinsic functions

In CloudFormation, intrinsic functions serve as indispensable tools for passing runtime values to Parameters within templates, enabling dynamic and flexible configurations tailored to specific deployment requirements. These functions serve as the backbone of template customization.

To illustrate this concept further, let us delve into one of the most commonly utilized intrinsic functions: **Ref**. As previously discussed in earlier chapters, **Ref** retrieves the value of a designated parameter or resource attribute. This function proves invaluable for referencing other resources within the template, thereby streamlining inter-resource communication and dependency management. Through leveraging **Ref**, developers can seamlessly integrate resource identifiers—such as instance IDs or security group names—into their templates without the need for hardcoded values, enhancing template flexibility and maintainability.

This example of **Ref** demonstrates how intrinsic functions serve as powerful mechanisms for injecting dynamic behavior into CloudFormation templates. However, it is crucial to understand where and when these intrinsic functions can be utilized within the CloudFormation template structure, like:

- **Conditions section**: Intrinsic functions find their application within the Conditions section, an optional segment of the CloudFormation template dedicated to specifying criteria under which stack resources are created. Here, developers can leverage intrinsic functions to define Conditions that dynamically determine the inclusion or exclusion of resources based on runtime evaluations.

- **Resources section**: Intrinsic functions play a vital role within the Resources section, the mandatory segment of the CloudFormation template responsible for defining all AWS resources intended for deployment within the stack. In this section, intrinsic functions can be used to dynamically configure resource properties, facilitating the creation of adaptive and scalable infrastructure configurations.

- **Outputs section**: Intrinsic functions extend their utility to the Outputs section, another optional segment utilized for passing values to other stack templates or for displaying resource and stack-related information within the AWS Management Console. Here, developers can employ intrinsic functions to generate dynamic Outputs based on runtime Conditions or resource attributes, enhancing the interoperability and visibility of CloudFormation stacks.

- **Metadata section**: Intrinsic functions can also be used in the Metadata section. In this section of a CloudFormation template, intrinsic functions can be employed to provide dynamic Metadata for the template or its resources. This Metadata can include information such as version numbers, author details, or any other relevant data associated with the template or its resources. By using intrinsic functions within the Metadata section, developers can ensure that this information remains up-to-date and reflective of the current state of the template or its resources.

Types of intrinsic functions and their usage

Now, let us take an in-depth look at the various types of intrinsic functions available in AWS CloudFormation and explore how each one is utilized within our templates. They are as follows:

- **Ref function**: As discussed earlier, the intrinsic function **Ref** serves a crucial role in AWS CloudFormation by retrieving the value of a specified parameter or resource. When referring to a parameter's logical name, **Ref** returns the corresponding parameter value. Similarly, when specifying a resource's logical name, **Ref** provides a value typically used to reference that resource, such as its physical ID. Likewise **Ref** can be employed to retrieve the output of other intrinsic functions. This capability adds a layer of versatility, enabling dynamic template configurations.

  The syntax for the same is as follows:

```
1. MyResource:
2.   Type: AWS::Some::ResourceType
3.   Properties:
4.     SomeProperty: !Ref LogicalNameOfParameterOrResource
```

  In this syntax:

  o **MyResource** is the logical name assigned to the resource being declared in the CloudFormation template.

  o **AWS::Some::ResourceType** represents the AWS resource type being declared. This can vary depending on the resource being created.

  o **SomeProperty** is a placeholder for one of the properties of the resource being configured. This could be any valid property for the specified resource type.

o **!Ref LogicalNameOfParameterOrResource** is where the **Ref** intrinsic function is used. Here, **LogicalNameOfParameterOrResource** should be replaced with the logical name of the parameter or resource whose value you want to reference.

Let us explore the following example snippet to get more clarity:

```
1.  MyInstance:
2.    Type: AWS::EC2::Instance
3.    Properties:
4.      InstanceType: !Ref InstanceType
```

The preceding example is for an EC2 resource where **Ref** function is used to set the value of the **InstanceType** parameter when creating the **MyInstance** resource.

- **Fn::Sub function**: **Fn::Sub** is a versatile intrinsic function within AWS CloudFormation. Its purpose is to seamlessly substitute variables in a given input string with specified values. This functionality becomes invaluable when you need to dynamically construct commands or Outputs within your templates, incorporating values that may only become available during stack creation or updates.

The syntax for the same is as follows:

```
1.  Fn::Sub:
2.    - String
3.    - Var1Name: Var1Value
4.      Var2Name: Var2Value
```

Another version for defining this function in short format applicable for all intrinsic functions is as follows:

```
1.  !Sub
2.    - String
3.    - Var1Name: Var1Value
4.      Var2Name: Var2Value
```

In the preceding syntax:

o **String** represents the input string where variables are to be substituted. This is the first parameter of **Fn::Sub**. Variables in this string are represented by **${VarName}** or **$VarName**. These placeholders will be replaced with their corresponding values.

o **{ Var1Name: Var1Value, Var2Name: Var2Value, ... }**: This is the second parameter of **Fn::Sub** and provides a Mapping of variable names to their values. This map specifies the values that will replace the variables in the input string. Variable names (For example, **Var1Name**, **Var2Name**) are referenced within the input string, and their corresponding values (For example, **Var1Value**, **Var2Value**) will be substituted accordingly.

Let us explore the following example snippet to get more clarity on this:

```
1. Fn::Sub:
2.    - "This is a ${Environment} environment with ${InstanceType}"
3.    - { Environment: "production", InstanceType: "t2.micro" }
```

In this example:

- o **This is a ${Environment} environment with ${InstanceType}** is the input string with placeholders for variables.

- o **{ Environment: "production", InstanceType: "t2.micro" }** is a map specifying the values for **Environment** and **InstanceType**. These values will be substituted into the input string.

After substitution, the resulting string will be as follows:

```
1. "This is a production environment with t2.micro."
```

An alternative approach involves parameterizing the Mapping rather than hard-coding the values, as demonstrated in the following example:

```
1. Fn::Sub:
2.    - "This is a ${Environment} environment with ${InstanceType}"
3.    - { Environment: !Ref envtype, InstanceType: "t2.micro" }
```

Here, **envtype** is a parameter declared in our CloudFormation template which is later referenced in the preceding Mapping.

- **Fn::GetAtt function**: The **Fn::GetAtt** function is an intrinsic function in AWS CloudFormation used to retrieve the value of an attribute from a resource in the template. This function allows you to access specific attributes of AWS resources and use them elsewhere in the template.

The syntax for the same is as follows:

```
1. Fn::GetAtt: [ logicalNameOfResource, attributeName ]
```

In the preceding syntax:

- o **logicalNameOfResource** specifies the logical name of the resource from which you want to retrieve the attribute value.

- o **attributeName** specifies the name of the attribute whose value you want to retrieve from the specified resource.

Let us consider an example where we want to retrieve the public IP address of an EC2 instance resource named **MyEC2Instance** using **GetAtt** function.

The CloudFormation template might look like the following:

```
1.  Resources:
2.    MyEC2Instance:
3.      Type: AWS::EC2::Instance
4.      Properties:
5.        ImageId: ami-1234567890
6.        InstanceType: t2.micro
```

Now, if we want to reference the public IP address of this instance in the Output section of the template, we can use **Fn::GetAtt** as follows:

```
1.  Outputs:
2.    EC2InstancePublicIP:
3.      Value: !GetAtt MyEC2Instance.PublicIp
```

In this example:

- ○ **MyEC2Instance** is the logical name of the EC2 instance resource.

- ○ **PublicIp** is the attribute of the EC2 instance resource from which we want to retrieve the public IP address. Here, the **Fn::GetAtt** function allows us to dynamically fetch attributes of resources within the CloudFormation template, enabling us to create dynamic and interconnected infrastructure configurations.

- **Fn::Join function**: The **Fn::Join** function is an intrinsic function in AWS CloudFormation used to concatenate a list of values into a single string with a specified delimiter. This function is particularly useful when you need to construct strings from multiple values or elements within your CloudFormation templates.

The syntax for the same is as follows:

```
1.  Fn::Join: [ delimiter, [ comma-delimited list of values ] ]
```

In the preceding syntax:

- ○ **delimiter** is the first parameter and represents the character or string that will be used to separate the values in the resulting string.

- ○ **[comma-delimited list of values]** is the second parameter and is a list of values that you want to concatenate into a single string. The values are separated by commas and enclosed within square brackets **[ ]**.

Let us take an example snippet to get more understanding on this:

```
1.  Fn::Join: [", ", ["apple", "banana", "orange"]]
```

In this example:

- ○ The **delimiter** is **,** (a comma followed by a space), which will be used to separate the values.

o   The list of values is **["apple", "banana", "orange"]**, where each value represents a fruit.

After using **Fn::Join**, the resulting string will be **apple, banana, orange**, with each fruit separated by a comma and space according to the specified delimiter.

- **Fn::Select function**: The **Fn::Select** function is an intrinsic function in AWS CloudFormation that retrieves a specific element from a list of elements. It allows you to select a single value from an array based on its index position. This function is particularly useful when you need to access specific elements within a list or array in your CloudFormation templates.

The syntax for the same is as follows:

```
1.  Fn::Select: [ Index, listOfObjects ]
```

In the preceding syntax:

o   **Index** parameter specifies the index position of the element to select from the list of elements. Indexing starts from 0, so the first element in the list has an index of 0, the second element has an index of 1, and so on.

o   **listOfObjects** parameter is a list containing the elements from which you want to select a value. The elements can be literals, references to other resources or Parameters, or even other CloudFormation intrinsic functions.

Let us explore an example snippet to gain insight into this:

```
1.  Resources:
2.    MyEC2Instance:
3.      Type: AWS::EC2::Instance
4.      Properties:
5.        ImageId: ami-1234567890
6.        InstanceType: !Select [0, [ "t2.micro", "r5.4xlarge" ]]
```

In the preceding snippet from the **Resources** section of a CloudFormation template, the focus is on setting the **InstanceType** attribute based on the **Fn::Select** query. The **!Select** function selects an element from a list based on its index position. In this case, the index position specified is **0**, indicating that the first item in the list will be selected. The list provided contains two instance types: **t2.micro** and **r5.4xlarge**. Since the index position is **0**, **t2.micro** will be selected as the instance type for the EC2 instance named MyEC2Instance.

- **Fn::GetAZs function**: The **Fn::GetAZs** function is an intrinsic function in AWS CloudFormation used to retrieve the **availability zones (AZs)** for a specified AWS Region. It returns an array of names of all the availability zones available in the specified region in alphabetical order. This function is particularly useful when you need to deploy resources across multiple availability zones within a region for high availability and fault tolerance.

The syntax for the same is as follows:

```
1. Fn::GetAZs: region
```

In the preceding syntax:

- region specifies the AWS Region for which you want to retrieve the availability zones. It can be specified as a parameter, a hard-coded string, or as a reference to a parameter.

So if a CloudFormation stack is created in the us-east-1 region, the **Fn::GetAZs** function is evaluated to the following array:

```
1. ["us-east-1a", "us-east-1b", "us-east-1c", "us-east-1d"]
```

Let us explore the following example snippet to understand this concept better:

```
1. Resources:
2.   MyEC2Instance1:
3.     Type: AWS::EC2::Instance
4.     Properties:
5.       ImageId: ami-1234567890
6.       InstanceType: t2.micro
7.       AvailabilityZone: !Select [0, !GetAZs us-east-1]
```

In the provided example snippet for the **Resources** section, specifically targeting the setup of an EC2 instance, an attribute has been declared under the **Properties** section to ensure that the newly launched EC2 instance is deployed in a predefined availability zone. Let us examine this attribute further to grasp the value it substitutes in this scenario:

```
AvailabilityZone: !Select [0, !GetAZs us-east-1]
```

Here, another intrinsic function, **Fn::Select**, is employed. It assists in choosing the first available availability zone using the placeholder **0** from the array of availability zones returned by the specified query.

- **Fn::Length function**: The **Fn::Length** intrinsic function returns the count of elements within an array or an intrinsic function that returns an array.

The syntaxes for using it is as follows:

```
1. Fn::Length : Array
```

Here, the **Fn::Length** intrinsic function in AWS CloudFormation returns the count of elements within an array or a list. It calculates the length of the specified array and provides the number of elements it contains. Let us explore a different syntax:

```
1. Fn::Length : SomeIntrinsicFunction
```

Here the **Fn::Length** intrinsic function, when used with an intrinsic function as its argument, evaluates the result of that intrinsic function and returns the count of elements within the array it yields.

Let us explore an example snippet to get more insight:

```
1.  Resources:
2.    MyResource:
3.      Type: AWS::SomeResourceType
4.      Properties:
5.        Count: !Fn::Length
6.          - ["apple", "banana", "orange"]
```

Previously, we discussed macros and transforms, where we encountered a scenario involving the declaration of a count macro within a resource section. Instead of explicitly specifying the count within this macro, we can utilize the **Fn::Length** function to dynamically retrieve the count value from the provided query. In this instance, the count is determined to be 3 based on the output generated by the **Fn::Length** query.

- **Fn::Split function**: The **Fn::Split** intrinsic function in AWS CloudFormation is used to split a string into a list of substrings based on a specified delimiter. This function is particularly useful when you need to parse a string and extract individual components from it.

The syntax for the same is as follows:

```
1.  Fn::Split: [ delimiter, source_string ]
```

In the preceding syntax:

- o **delimiter** specifies the character or string that will be used to split the source string into substrings.

- o **source_string** represents the string that you want to split into substrings.

To understand this concept better, let us consider an example snippet where we have a string representing a list of tags separated by commas, and we want to split it into individual tags:

```
1.  TagsString: "tag1,tag2,tag3"
2.  TagsList: !Split [",", !Ref TagsString]
```

In this example:

- o **tag1,tag2,tag3** is the source string representing a list of tags.

- o **,** is the delimiter used to split the source string into substrings.

- o **!Ref TagsString** references the source string.

- o **!Split [",", !Ref TagsString]** is the **Fn::Split** function that splits the source string into substrings based on the specified delimiter.

After evaluation, the value of **TagsList** will be **["tag1", "tag2", "tag3"]**, which is a list of individual tags extracted from the original string.

- **Fn::ToJsonString**: The `Fn::ToJsonString` intrinsic function transforms an object or array into its respective JSON string representation.

The syntax for the same is as follows:

o **Transforming an object**:

```
1. Fn::ToJsonString: Object
```

o **Transforming an array**:

```
1. Fn::ToJsonString: Array
```

In the preceding syntaxes provided, you specify an object or an array as input, and the output will be the corresponding JSON string representation.

Let us now explore an example to understand this in a better way:

```
1. Transform: 'AWS::LanguageExtensions'
2. Resources:
3.   MyBucket:
4.     Type: AWS::S3::Bucket
5.     Properties:
6.       BucketName: !Sub "my-bucket123"
7.
8. Outputs:
9.   JsonOutput:
10.    Value:
11.      Fn::ToJsonString:
12.        key1: hello
13.        key2: !Ref MyBucket
```

In this example:

o The `AWS::LanguageExtensions` transform signifies that the template might include custom language extensions provided by AWS, which may offer enhancements or optimizations to the CloudFormation template syntax or functionality.

o The template creates an S3 bucket named **my-bucket123**.

o It defines an output **JsonOutput** which uses **Fn::ToJsonString** to convert an object with keys **key1** and **key2** into its JSON string representation. **key1** has a static value **hello**, and **key2** references the **MyBucket** resource.

After executing the template, the output would be like:

```
1. {"key1":"hello","key2":"my-bucket123"}
```

- **Fn::ForEach function**: The `Fn::ForEach` intrinsic function in AWS CloudFormation allows you to iterate over a collection and apply the items in the collection to a provided fragment. This powerful function enables a dynamic generation of resources or configurations based on a list of items. It is commonly used within the Conditions, Outputs, and Resources sections of CloudFormation templates.

The syntax for the same is as follows:

```
1. 'Fn::ForEach::LoopName':
2.    - Identifier
3.    - - V1
4.      - V2
5.    - 'OutputKey':
6.        OutputValue
```

In the preceding syntax:

- o **LoopName** serves as an identifier for the loop being created. It is essentially a unique name to distinguish this loop from others if there are multiple nested loops within the template.

- o **Identifier** is the variable that will represent each item in the collection during the iteration. It will take on the values from the collection specified next.

- o **V1** and **V2** are the items within the collection over which the iteration will occur. In this example, the collection consists of two values: **V1** and **V2**.

- o **OutputKey** indicates the key name under which the output will be stored. It is part of the output generated by each iteration of the loop.

- o **OutputValue** is the value associated with the **OutputKey**. It could be any value or expression relevant to the iteration.

> **Note: When utilizing the `Fn::ForEach` intrinsic function within AWS CloudFormation, it is crucial to incorporate the `AWS::LanguageExtensions` transform into your template. This transform enables the usage of advanced features like `Fn::ForEach`, expanding the capabilities of CloudFormation templates beyond their standard functionalities.**

Let us examine an example snippet to enhance our understanding of this concept:

```
1. AWSTemplateFormatVersion: 2010-09-09
2. Transform: 'AWS::LanguageExtensions'
3. Parameters:
4.   pInstanceTypes:
5.     Description: List of EC2 instance types
6.     Type: CommaDelimitedList
```

```
7.  Resources:
8.    'Fn::ForEach::InstanceTypes':
9.      - InstanceType
10.     - !Ref pInstanceTypes
11.     - 'Ec2Instance${InstanceType}':
12.         Type: 'AWS::EC2::Instance'
13.         Properties:
14.           InstanceType: !Ref InstanceType
15.           # Add other properties as needed
```

The preceding example is a snippet illustrating how this implementation operates within the **Resource** section. In the provided example the following mean:

- o **Parameters**: Here, we define a parameter named **pInstanceTypes**. It is a **CommaDelimitedList** type parameter, meaning it allows users to specify a list of values separated by commas. In this context, **pInstanceTypes** represents a list of EC2 instance types that will be used to create EC2 instances.

- o **Fn::ForEach::InstanceTypes** is where we start utilizing the **Fn::ForEach** function. It indicates that we are going to iterate over a collection of instance types specified in the **pInstanceTypes** parameter.

- o **InstanceType** serves as the identifier for each item in the collection during the iteration. In each iteration, **InstanceType** will represent a single instance type from the list.

- o **!Ref pInstanceTypes**: Here, we reference the parameter **pInstanceTypes**, which contains the list of EC2 instance types provided by the user.

- o **Ec2Instance${InstanceType}** is the fragment to which the items from the collection will be applied. It represents the name of the EC2 instance resource to be created for each instance type. **Ec2Instance${InstanceType}** is a dynamic name where **${InstanceType}** is replaced with the actual instance type value during each iteration.

This CloudFormation template, when executed, will create an EC2 instance resource for each instance type specified in the **pInstanceTypes** parameter. It utilizes the **Fn::ForEach** function to dynamically generate resources based on the list of instance types provided by the user.

- **Fn::Base64 function**: The **Fn::Base64** function is used to encode data in Base64 format. This function is commonly used when working with Amazon EC2 instances, as it allows you to pass encoded data into properties like user data, which are often used to bootstrap instances with scripts or configurations.

The syntax for the same is as follows:

```
1. Fn::Base64: valueToEncode
```

Where **valueToEncode** is the value that you want to encode in Base64 format. This can be a string or any other valid CloudFormation expression.

> **Note: When using the short form and immediately including another function in the valueToEncode parameter of Fn::Base64, it is important to ensure that the full function name is used for at least one of the functions. Here are examples of invalid and valid syntax:**

Invalid:

```
1. !Base64 !Sub string
2. !Base64 !Ref logical_ID
```

Valid:

```
1. !Base64
2.    "Fn::Sub": string
3.
4. Fn::Base64:
5.    !Ref logical_ID
```

Let us explore an example for more understanding of this. Here is an example demonstrating how to use **Fn::Base64** to encode a simple shell script and pass it as user data for an EC2 instance:

```
1. Resources:
2.    MyEC2Instance:
3.       Type: AWS::EC2::Instance
4.       Properties:
5.          ImageId: ami-12345678    # Specify your desired AMI ID
6.          InstanceType: t2.
   micro  # Specify your desired instance type
7.          UserData:
8.             Fn::Base64: !Sub |
9.                #!/bin/bash
10.               echo «Hello!» >> /home/ec2-user/user-data-output.txt
```

In this example:

o We are creating an EC2 instance using the **AWS::EC2::Instance** resource type.

o For the **UserData** property, we are using **Fn::Base64** to encode a shell script. This script simply appends a message to a file named **user-data-output.txt** in the **/home/ec2-user/** directory.

When CloudFormation creates the EC2 instance, it will decode the Base64 encoded user data and execute it on the instance during startup. This allows you to perform initialization tasks, install software, or configure the instance as needed.

- Fn::Cidr function: The **Fn::Cidr** function is used to generate a list of Classless Inter-Domain Routing (CIDR) address blocks. This function is commonly used to calculate a range of IP addresses based on a given IP address and prefix length.

The syntax for the same is as follows:

```
1. !Cidr [ ipBlock, count, cidrBits ]
```

In the preceding syntax:

- o **ipBlock**: The base IP address in CIDR notation (For example, 192.0.2.0/24).

- o **count**: The number of CIDR blocks to generate.

- o **cidrBits**: The number of CIDR bits to use for the new blocks (For example, 8, 16, 24).

Let us explore an example snippet to understand the implementation:

```
1.  Resources:
2.    MyVPC:
3.      Type: AWS::EC2::VPC
4.      Properties:
5.        CidrBlock: "10.0.0.0/16"
6.
7.    MySubnets:
8.      Type: AWS::EC2::Subnet
9.      Properties:
10.       VpcId: !Ref MyVPC
11.       CidrBlock: !Select [0, !Fn::Cidr [!Ref MyVPC, 3, 8]]
      # Generate three subnets with /8 CIDR blocks
```

In this example:

- o We define a VPC with the CIDR block **10.0.0.0/16**.

- o We use **Fn::Cidr** to generate a list of three CIDR blocks with a prefix length of /8 based on the VPC CIDR block.

- o The **!Select** function is used to choose the first CIDR block from the generated list, which will be used as the CIDR block for the subnet creation.

This CloudFormation template will create a VPC with the specified CIDR block and then create a subnet within that VPC using the first CIDR block from the list generated by **Fn::Cidr**.

Note: In addition to the previous functions mentioned, there are several other intrinsic functions worth noting:

- Fn::Transform: This function allows for custom processing of templates during stack creation. Detailed coverage of this function has been provided in the previous chapter.

- Fn::FindInMap: This function is used to look up values in a two-level map defined within the CloudFormation template. Comprehensive explanations and examples of its usage have been included in earlier Chapter 4, Parameters, Metadata, Mappings and Conditions.

- Fn::ImportValue: This function enables the importing of values exported from other stacks, facilitating communication between different CloudFormation stacks. Detailed exploration of this function will be provided in subsequent chapters.

Pseudo parameters

Pseudo parameters in AWS CloudFormation are predefined system Parameters that you can reference within your templates. They provide information about the stack, region, and other context-specific details, allowing for dynamic and flexible template creation. Pseudo parameters do not require declarations or definitions; they are automatically available for use within CloudFormation templates.

Types of pseudo parameters

Different types of pseudo parameters are as follows:

- **AWS::AccountId**: Returns the AWS account ID of the account in which the stack is being created. This can be useful for creating resources specific to a particular AWS account. Following is an example syntax for the same:
  - ```
    Resources:
    ```
  - ```
    MyS3Bucket:
    ```
  - ```
    Type: AWS::S3::Bucket
    ```
  - ```
    Properties:
    ```
  - ```
    BucketName: !Join ["-", ["my-bucket", AWS::AccountId]]
    ```

The provided YAML snippet is a CloudFormation template defining an S3 bucket resource named **MyS3Bucket**. In this example, **BucketName** is the property for S3 bucket which specifies the name of the S3 bucket. Here it utilizes the **!Join** function to concatenate strings. The first string is **my-bucket**, and the second part is a dynamic component generated using the **AWS::AccountId** pseudo parameter.
    ```

- **AWS::Region**: Returns the AWS Region in which the stack is being created. This allows for region-specific configurations within your templates. Following is an example syntax for the same:

  ```
  o  Resources:
  o    MyEC2Instance:
  o      Type: AWS::EC2::Instance
  o      Properties:
  o        AvailabilityZone: !Sub "${AWS::Region}a"
  ```

  The provided YAML snippet is a CloudFormation template defining an EC2 instance resource named **MyEC2Instance**. Here **AvailabilityZone** property specifies the AZ in which EC2 instance will be launched. It utilizes the !Sub function along with the pseudo parameter **AWS::Region**. Let us break down the complete query to understand how it works:

  - **!Sub**: This function substitutes variables in a string with their corresponding values. In this case, **${AWS::Region}a** is the string to be substituted.

  - **${AWS::Region}**: This returns the AWS Region in which the stack is being created.

  - **a**: This is a string literal appended to the region name to form the complete availability zone identifier. For example, if the AWS Region is us-east-1, then **${AWS::Region}a** would evaluate to something like us-east-1a, which represents an availability zone within the us-east-1 region.

- **AWS::StackName**: Returns the name of the stack.

  Here, the **StackNameOutput** output will display the name of the stack where the resource is being created or updated using the value obtained from **AWS::StackName**:

  ```
  o  Outputs:
  o    StackNameOutput:
  o      Value: !Sub "${AWS::StackName}"
  ```

- **AWS::StackId**: Returns the stack id for the stack in which the resource is being created.

  In the following configuration, the stack ID is utilized as the name for the S3 bucket using the pseudo parameter, ensuring its uniqueness within the AWS environment:

  ```
  o  Resources:
  o    MyBucket:
  o      Type: AWS::S3::Bucket
  o      Properties:
  o        BucketName:
  o          Fn::Sub: "${AWS::StackId}-my-bucket"
  ```

- **AWS::NotificationARNs**: Returns the list of Amazon Simple Notification Service (SNS) Amazon Resource Names (ARNs) to which your stack related events are published. Look at the following snippet:

```
MyAutoScalingGroup:
    Type: AWS::AutoScaling::AutoScalingGroup
    Properties:
        # Define other properties of the Auto Scaling group
        NotificationConfigurations:
            - TopicARN: !Select [0, !Ref AWS::NotificationARNs]
              NotificationTypes:
                  - autoscaling:EC2_INSTANCE_LAUNCH
                  - autoscaling:EC2_INSTANCE_LAUNCH_ERROR
```

The preceding snippet is a part of the Auto Scaling group (ASG) resource declaration. Here, the **AWS::NotificationARNs** pseudo parameter is automatically populated by CloudFormation with the ARNs of notification targets, such as SNS topics that are subscribed to stack events. Therefore, you do not need to specify its syntax explicitly; you use it as part of the configuration properties of resources that support notifications. Here, **!Ref AWS::NotificationARNs** retrieves the list of ARNs, and **!Select [0, ...]** selects the first ARN from the list. This ARN is then used as the **TopicARN** in the **NotificationConfigurations**.

- **AWS::Partition**: Returns the partition in which the resource is located. The partition identifies the segment of the AWS global infrastructure to which the resource belongs. Here is how it works:

  o For standard AWS Regions, such as us-east-1 or eu-west-1, the partition value returned is simply **aws**. These regions are part of the commercial AWS offering.

  o Resources in the *China* (*Beijing* and *Ningxia*) region have the partition value **aws-cn**.

  o Resources in the AWS GovCloud (US-West) region have the partition value **aws-us-gov**, like:

```
Resources:
    MySNSTopic:
        Type: AWS::SNS::Topic
        Properties:
            DisplayName: !Sub "My Topic (${AWS::Partition})"
```

The preceding code snippet is a segment of an AWS CloudFormation template defining an SNS topic. In this snippet, we utilize the AWS pseudo parameter **AWS::Partition** as a part of the display name for the SNS topic. When the template is executed, it dynamically fetches the relevant information based on the AWS Region and appends it to the actual name of the topic.

For instance, when executed in the us-east-1 region of AWS, the resulting display name would be **My Topic (aws)**. This demonstrates how the template adapts to different regions, providing descriptive display names that incorporate pertinent AWS partition information.

- **AWS::NoValue**: Indicates that a parameter does not have a value. It can be used to conditionally include properties based on the existence of values.

  CloudFormation template snippet:

  ```
  Conditions:
    UseSnapshot: !Equals [ !Ref UseSnapshot, 'true' ]
  Resources:
    MyDBInstance:
      Type: AWS::RDS::DBInstance
      Properties:
        AllocatedStorage: 30
        DBInstanceClass: db.t3.small
        Engine: postgres
        MasterUsername: !Ref AdminUsername
        MasterUserPassword: !Ref AdminPassword
        DBSnapshotIdentifier: !If [ UseSnapshot,
  !Ref DbSnapshot, !Ref 'AWS::NoValue' ]
  ```

  The preceding CloudFormation template snippet introduces a condition called **UseSnapshot**, which checks if the variable **UseSnapshot** is equal to the string **true**. This condition is applied within the **Resources** section to manage the value of the **DBSnapshotIdentifier** property for an RDS DB instance named **MyDBInstance**. If **UseSnapshot** evaluates to **true**, the DB Snapshot specified by the **DbSnapshot** parameter is utilized. Conversely, if **UseSnapshot** is **false**, **AWS::NoValue** is employed, signifying the absence of a DB snapshot. This utilization of **AWS::NoValue** within the template enhances the flexibility of resource configuration in AWS CloudFormation.

- **AWS::URLSuffix**: Retrieves the suffix for the endpoint of the current AWS Region. It returns the domain suffix for the endpoint of AWS services within the current region. For example, in the US East (*N. Virginia*) region, the **AWS::URLSuffix** pseudo parameter would return **amazonaws.com**, while in the *China* (*Beijing*) region, it would return **amazonaws.com.cn**. This pseudo parameter is particularly useful when you need to construct resource ARNs or URLs dynamically within your CloudFormation templates, ensuring that they are region-agnostic and adhere to the appropriate AWS service endpoint for the current region.

  The CloudFormation template snippet:

```
o   Resources:
o     MyBucket:
o       Type: AWS::S3::Bucket
o       Properties:
o         BucketName: !Sub "my-bucket.${AWS::URLSuffix}"
```

In the preceding CloudFormation template snippet, a new S3 bucket resource named **MyBucket** is defined. The bucket's properties include specifying the **BucketName** utilizing the **!Sub** function, which substitutes the placeholder **${AWS::URLSuffix}** with the appropriate URL suffix for the AWS Region where the stack is being deployed. This construct ensures that the bucket name is unique within the specified AWS Region. As a result, the bucket name will be in the format **my-bucket.{region-specific URL suffix}**. For the us-east-1 region, the bucket name will be **my-bucket.amazonaws.com**.

> Note: The bucket names provided in this example are purely for demonstration purposes. The exact bucket names may not be available for use, as they could have already been claimed by other users.

Customizing templates with pseudo parameters

Let us explore the following scenarios accompanied by corresponding CloudFormation templates, showcasing the integration of pseudo parameters and elucidating their substantial benefits:

- **Provisioning an EC2 Instance with a unique account ID tag**: In this scenario, we aim to create a CloudFormation template for provisioning an EC2 instance within an AWS environment. The template will include specifications for creating the EC2 instance and tagging it with a unique identifier based on the AWS account ID. This ensures that each instance is labelled with an account-specific tag, facilitating resource management and identification within the AWS ecosystem. The example template for the same is as follows:

```
o   AWSTemplateFormatVersion: '2010-09-09'
o   Resources:
o     EC2Instance:
o       Type: AWS::EC2::Instance
o       Properties:
o         InstanceType: t2.micro
o         ImageId: ami-0c101f26f147fa7fd
o   # AMI for us-east-1 region
o           Tags:
```

```
o              - Key: AccountID
o                Value: !Sub "${AWS::AccountId}"
```

Next, we will deploy this template using the CloudFormation console and verify the newly provisioned EC2 instance to ensure that the custom tag, generated using the pseudo parameter, has been successfully applied.

The tag section of the newly set up EC2 instance is as follows:

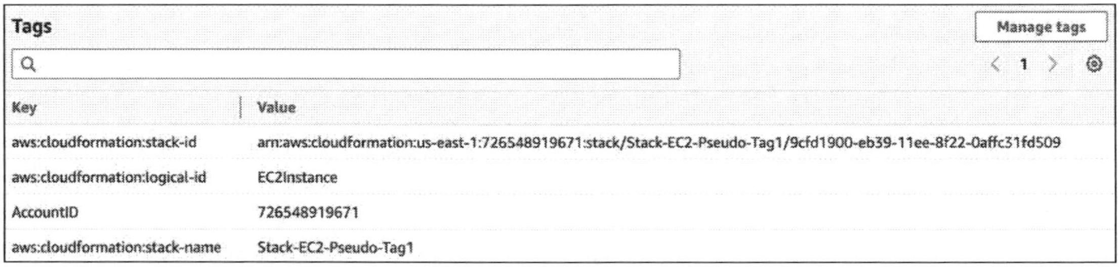

Tags			Manage tags

Key	Value
aws:cloudformation:stack-id	arn:aws:cloudformation:us-east-1:726548919671:stack/Stack-EC2-Pseudo-Tag1/9cfd1900-eb39-11ee-8f22-0affc31fd509
aws:cloudformation:logical-id	EC2Instance
AccountID	726548919671
aws:cloudformation:stack-name	Stack-EC2-Pseudo-Tag1

Figure 6.1: EC2 tags

In the provided figure, it is evident that the newly defined tag AccountID has been successfully added to the resource, consistent with the configuration outlined in our template. Additionally, the tag has been populated with the corresponding AWS account ID value, as intended. This account ID value has been dynamically populated using the pseudo parameter **AWS::AccountId**.

- **Dynamic instance sizing based on region with pseudo parameters**: This scenario illustrates the utilization of AWS CloudFormation pseudo parameters to dynamically adjust the size of EC2 instances based on the region where the stack is deployed. By leveraging pseudo parameters such as **AWS::Region** and conditional logic, the template selects an appropriate instance type, ensuring optimal performance and cost efficiency across different AWS Regions. Through parameterization and condition evaluation, the template enables users to tailor their infrastructure to regional requirements, enhancing flexibility and scalability in their AWS deployments. The example template for the same is as follows:

```
o   AWSTemplateFormatVersion: 2010-09-09
o   Description: >
o     CF template with instance sizing based on the AWS region.
o   Parameters:
o     AMIId:
o       Type: 'AWS::EC2::Image::Id'
o       Description: Enter the ID of the AMI to for the EC2 instance.
o   Conditions:
o     IsUSEast1: !Equals
o       - !Ref 'AWS::Region'
```

```
o        - us-east-1
o    Resources:
o      MyEC2Instance:
o        Type: 'AWS::EC2::Instance'
o        Properties:
o          InstanceType: !If
o            - IsUSEast1
o            - t2.micro
o            - t2.small
o          ImageId: !Ref AMIId
```

Next, we will attempt to deploy the template in the us-west-2 region instead of **us-east-1**. We will provide an appropriate AMI ID as a parameter specifically tailored for the us-west-2 region. Upon stack creation, the template's Conditions will be evaluated, leading to the selection of **t2.small** instance type instead of **t2.micro**, as the latter is not applicable for the us-west-2 region. Finally, we will inspect the newly provisioned EC2 instance to confirm its size.

Please refer to the following figure of the EC2 console page to validate the same:

Figure 6.2: EC2 sizing

In this observation, the size of the newly provisioned EC2 instance is identified as **t2.small**, aligning with the condition evaluation tailored for the us-west-2 (Oregon) region. This observation serves as confirmation of the validation process.

- **Customizing SNS topic names**: In this scenario, we are defining an AWS CloudFormation template to create an SNS topic resource. The SNS topic is configured with a display name that includes the name of the CloudFormation stack it belongs to. This ensures clarity and context when identifying the SNS topic within the AWS environment. The example template for the same is as follows:

```
o    AWSTemplateFormatVersion: '2010-09-09'
o    Resources:
o      MySNSTopic:
o        Type: AWS::SNS::Topic
```

```
o        Properties:
o            DisplayName: !Sub "Stack-Events-${AWS::StackName}"
```

Our stack is named **Stack-SNS-Pseudo**. A figure showing the newly created SNS topic is as follows:

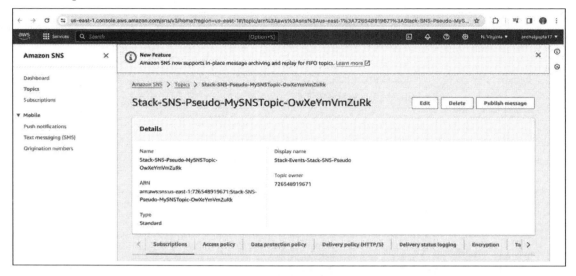

Figure 6.3: SNS topic setup

We notice that the Display name is **Stack-Events-Stack-SNS-Pseudo**, with Stack-SNS-Pseudo representing the stack name. This has been appended with the predefined prefix Stack-Events as specified in our template, thereby confirming the usage of the pseudo parameter **AWS::StackName**.

Conclusion

In conclusion, this chapter has provided a comprehensive understanding of intrinsic functions and pseudo parameters, illuminating their diverse applications in template customization. We have explored various types of intrinsic functions and their usage, as well as the importance of pseudo parameters in tailoring templates to specific needs. In the next chapter, we move onto advanced template integration with AWS Secrets Manager, encompassing creation policies, helper scripts, wait Conditions, and EC2 bootstrapping. Armed with this knowledge, we are primed to optimize our deployment processes, enhance infrastructure manageability, and scale our solutions effectively within the AWS ecosystem. This foundational understanding will serve as a springboard for exploring more advanced AWS template management techniques.

Multiple choice questions

1. **Which of the following is not a type of intrinsic function in AWS CloudFormation?**

    a. Fn::Sub

    b. Fn::If

    c. Fn::Random

    d. Fn::Join

2. **Which pseudo parameter provides the AWS Region in which the stack is being created?**

    a. AWS::Region

    b. AWS::AccountId

    c. AWS::StackName

    d. AWS::Partition

3. **How are intrinsic functions typically represented within CloudFormation templates?**

    a. ${}

    b. @@

    c. $5

    d. Fn::

4. **Which intrinsic function would you use to concatenate multiple strings in a CloudFormation template?**

    a. Fn::Sub

    b. Fn::If

    c. Fn::Random

    d. Fn::Join

5. **What is the primary purpose of using the Fn::If intrinsic function?**

    a. To define Conditions for resource creation based on Parameters

    b. To perform mathematical operations within the template

    c. To create pseudo parameters

    d. To define environment variables for resources

Answers

1. c
2. a
3. d
4. d
5. a

Join our book's Discord space

Join the book's Discord Workspace for Latest updates, Offers, Tech happenings around the world, New Release and Sessions with the Authors:

https://discord.bpbonline.com

Enhancing Amazon Web Services CloudFormation

Introduction

In this chapter, we embark on an exploration of advanced concepts and techniques to enhance your AWS CloudFormation templates. Our journey begins with an examination of integrating AWS Secrets Manager, demonstrating how to adeptly handle sensitive data and configurations with utmost security. Furthermore, we will explore the intricacies of creation policies, enabling us to meticulously fine-tune resource creation. We will unravel the potential of helper scripts to tailor resource behaviour and harness the utility of Wait conditions in orchestrating resource provisioning.

The apex of our exploration is a comprehensive study of EC2 bootstrapping, empowering us with the expertise to efficiently configure and customize EC2 instances throughout the stack creation process. These sophisticated methodologies pave the path for meticulously crafted and resilient AWS infrastructure deployments.

Structure

The chapter covers the following topics:

- Integration of AWS Secrets Manager
- CreationPolicy
- Helper scripts

- Wait Conditions
- EC2 bootstrapping

Objectives

This chapter aims to provide readers with an in-depth understanding of advanced concepts and techniques for optimizing AWS CloudFormation templates. By exploring the integration of AWS Secrets Manager, readers will learn how to securely manage sensitive data and configurations within their templates. Additionally, they will gain insight into the implementation of creation policies to fine-tune resource management, the utilization of helper scripts for customizing resource behaviour, and the orchestration of resource provisioning using Wait Conditions. Furthermore, readers will undergo a comprehensive examination of EC2 bootstrapping, acquiring the skills necessary to efficiently configure and customize EC2 instances during stack creation. By mastering these advanced concepts, readers will create highly tailored and secure AWS infrastructure deployments, enhancing their proficiency in managing complex cloud environments.

Integration of AWS Secrets Manager

AWS Secrets Manager is a service designed to simplify the management of credentials, API keys, and other sensitive information used by applications and services within the AWS ecosystem. Integrating AWS Secrets Manager with AWS CloudFormation provides a streamlined approach to securely manage and access secrets within your infrastructure deployments.

To facilitate this integration, AWS Secrets Manager offers four distinct resource types specifically designed for use within CloudFormation templates. The detailed explanation of each is as follows:

- **AWS::SecretsManager::ResourcePolicy**: This resource type empowers users to define resource-based access policies for secrets stored in AWS Secrets Manager. These policies dictate who can access the secrets and the actions they are authorized to perform. By crafting granular permissions for IAM principals and AWS services, users can enforce strict access controls, enhancing the security posture of their secrets.

  The syntax for the same is as follows:

```
1. Type: AWS::SecretsManager::ResourcePolicy
2. Properties:
3.    BlockPublicPolicy: Boolean
4.    ResourcePolicy: Json
5.    SecretId: String
```

  Let us break down the preceding defined syntax for more understanding:

o The **AWS::SecretsManager::ResourcePolicy** syntax within an AWS CloudFormation template signifies the declaration of a resource policy specifically tailored for AWS Secrets Manager. Within this policy, various properties are defined to configure its behaviour.

o The **BlockPublicPolicy** property, represented as a **Boolean** value, determines whether public access to the secret should be blocked (true) or permitted (false). This setting is pivotal for controlling the level of access to the secret and safeguarding sensitive information from unauthorized exposure.

o The **ResourcePolicy** property holds a JSON formatted resource policy that outlines permissions governing access to the secret. This policy delineates which IAM principals or AWS services are granted access and specifies the actions they are authorized to perform on the secret. Adhering to AWS IAM policy syntax, this configuration plays a crucial role in enforcing granular access controls and maintaining the secret's security.

o Furthermore, the **SecretId** property identifies the specific secret to which the resource policy applies, utilizing the ARN of the secret as its value. This linkage ensures that the resource policy is appropriately associated with the intended secret, orchestrating the implementation of access controls effectively.

An example snippet using the preceding defined syntax:

```
1.  Resources:
2.    MyCustomSecretResourcePolicy:
3.      Type: AWS::SecretsManager::ResourcePolicy
4.      Properties:
5.        BlockPublicPolicy: true
6.        SecretId: !Ref MyCustomSecret
7.        ResourcePolicy:
8.          Version: '2012-10-17'
9.          Statement:
10.           - Resource: "*"
11.             Action: secretsmanager:GetSecretValue
12.             Effect: Allow
13.             Principal:
14.               AWS: arn:aws:iam::123456789012:user/Bob
```

In this CloudFormation example, we define a resource policy for a custom secret named **MyCustomSecretResourcePolicy**. The policy is designed to block public access to the secret by setting **BlockPublicPolicy** to **true**. The **SecretId** property references the **MyCustomSecret** resource.

The resource policy allows the **secretsmanager:GetSecretValue** action for the IAM user Bob, restricting access solely to this user. This configuration ensures secure management of sensitive information while granting specific access permissions within the AWS ecosystem.

- **AWS::SecretsManager::RotationSchedule**: With this resource type, users can automate the rotation of secrets stored in AWS Secrets Manager. Rotation schedules specify when and how frequently AWS Secrets Manager should automatically rotate the secret value, reducing manual intervention and bolstering security by regularly updating credentials.

To enable rotation functionality, AWS Lambda service is essential. We have two options: either create a new rotation Lambda function from the available Secrets Manager rotation function templates, or utilize an existing rotation function.

The syntax for the same is as follows:

```
1.    Type: AWS::SecretsManager::RotationSchedule
2.  Properties:
3.    HostedRotationLambda:
4.      HostedRotationLambda
5.    RotateImmediatelyOnUpdate: Boolean
6.    RotationLambdaARN: String
7.    RotationRules:
8.      RotationRules
9.    SecretId: String
```

Let us break down the preceding defined syntax for more understanding:

- The **AWS::SecretsManager::RotationSchedule** syntax within a template denotes the setup of a rotation schedule for managing secret rotation in AWS Secrets Manager. This declaration outlines essential properties such as the Lambda function responsible for rotation, rules determining rotation frequency, and the target secret ID.

- The **HostedRotationLambda** property identifies the Lambda function tasked with executing rotation logic. Users can either input an existing Lambda ARN to utilize an established rotation function or create a new Lambda rotation function from one of Secrets Manager's rotation function templates.

- The **RotateImmediatelyOnUpdate Boolean** property determines whether the rotation should occur immediately or wait until the next scheduled rotation window.

- The **RotationLambdaARN** property defines the ARN of the Lambda function that manages secret rotation. To reference a rotation function within the same template, employ the Ref function.

o The **RotationRules** property further elaborates on the rotation rules to be applied.

o The **SecretId** attribute specifies the ID of the secret to which the rotation schedule applies. We can either provide the ARN or the name of the secret to rotate.

Here is a snippet exemplifying the preceding syntax:

```
1.  Resources:
2.     MyCustomRotationSchedule:
3.        Type: AWS::SecretsManager::RotationSchedule
4.        DependsOn: MyCustomRotationLambda
5.        Properties:
6.           SecretId: !Ref MySecureSecret
7.           RotationLambdaARN: !GetAtt MyCustomRotationLambda.
     Arn
8.           RotationRules:
9.              Duration: 3h
10.             ScheduleExpression: 'cron(0 2 * * ? *)'
```

The snippet defines a rotation schedule resource named **MyCustomRotationSchedule**, reliant on **MyCustomRotationLambda**. It orchestrates the rotation of the **MySecureSecret** at a three-hour interval, following a daily **cron** schedule expression set for 2:00 AM. This configuration aut+omates the periodic rotation of secrets, enhancing security and compliance within the AWS environment.

- **AWS::SecretsManager::Secret**: The secret resource type allows users to define secrets directly within their CloudFormation templates. This includes sensitive data like passwords, API keys, and database connection strings. Secrets stored in AWS Secrets Manager are encrypted at rest and in transit, ensuring robust data protection measures.

The syntax for the same is as follows:

```
1.  Type: AWS::SecretsManager::Secret
2.  Properties:
3.    Description: String
4.    GenerateSecretString:
5.      GenerateSecretString
6.    KmsKeyId: String
7.    Name: String
8.    ReplicaRegions:
9.      - ReplicaRegion
10.   SecretString:
```

```
11.      String
12.   Tags:
13.      - Tag
```

Let us break down the preceding syntax for more understanding:

o   The **AWS::SecretsManager::Secret** specifies the resource type within the AWS CloudFormation template. In this case, it indicates that we are defining a secret within AWS Secrets Manager.

o   The **GenerateSecretString** defines a structure to generate a password for encryption and storage within the secret.

o   The **KmsKeyId** property specifies the AWS **Key Management Service (KMS)** key ID to use for encrypting the secret. It is a string value representing the ARN of the KMS key. If not specified, then Secrets Manager uses the key **aws/secretsmanager.**

o   The **Name** property specifies the name of the secret. It is a string value that uniquely identifies the secret within AWS Secrets Manager.

o   The **ReplicaRegions** property specifies a region and the **KmsKeyId** for a replica set.

o   The **SecretString** property indicates the plaintext value of the secret, presented as a string representing the confidential data. For structuring the secret value, it is advisable to employ a JSON format consisting of key/value pairs. To generate a randomized password, opt for **GenerateSecretString**. In the absence of both **GenerateSecretString** and **SecretString**, an empty secret is formed, resulting in the creation of a new secret version upon modification.

o   The **Tags** property specifies tags to associate with the secret.

A snippet exemplifying the syntax described is as follows:

```
1. Resources:
2.   MyNewSecret:
3.     Type: 'AWS::SecretsManager::Secret'
4.     Properties:
5.       Name: MySecret
6.       Description: "secret contains a dynamically
   generated pwd."
7.       GenerateSecretString:
8.         SecretStringTemplate: '{"username": "john"}'
9.         GenerateStringKey: "Welcome123"
10.        PasswordLength: 20
11.        ExcludeCharacters: '"@&$'
```

```
12.        Tags:
13.        -
14.            Key: ApplicationName
15.            Value: Calculator
```

The provided snippet defines an AWS Secrets Manager entity intended to manage sensitive information. Referred to as **MySecret**, this secret holds a dynamically generated password, generated to be **20** characters in length and excluding specific characters like **"@&$** for enhanced security. The password key, **Welcome123**, serves as the identifier for the generated password within the secret. Additionally, the secret is associated with a tag labelled **ApplicationName**, set with the value **Calculator**, facilitating organizational and management tasks within the AWS ecosystem.

• **AWS::SecretsManager::SecretTargetAttachment**: This resource type facilitates the attachment of secrets stored in AWS Secrets Manager to the associated database by adding the database connection information to the secret JSON.

The syntax for the same is as follows:

```
1. Type: AWS::SecretsManager::SecretTargetAttachment
2. Properties:
3.   SecretId: String
4.   TargetId: String
5.   TargetType: String
```

Let us break down the preceding defined syntax for more understanding:

o The **AWS::SecretsManager::SecretTargetAttachment** specifies the resource type that defines the attachment of the secrets with the necessary database.

o **SecretId** specifies the ID of the secret to be attached. This ID is a string representing the ARN of the secret.

o **TargetId** specifies the ID of the database or the cluster.

o The **TargetType** property specifies the type of service or database linked to the secret. This information guides the Secrets Manager on how to update the secret with the specific details of the associated service or database. It is essential to ensure that this value corresponds to one of the following predefined options provided:

  ▪ **AWS::RDS::DBInstance**
  ▪ **AWS::RDS::DBCluster**
  ▪ **AWS::Redshift::Cluster**
  ▪ **AWS::DocDB::DBInstance**
  ▪ **AWS::DocDB::DBCluster**

Here is a template exemplifying the preceding syntax:

```
1.   Resources:
2.     RDSInstanceSecret:
3.       Type: AWS::SecretsManager::Secret
4.       Properties:
5.         Name: mysecret
6.         GenerateSecretString:
7.           SecretStringTemplate:
     !Sub '{"username":"root", "dbname":"db"}'
8.           GenerateStringKey: password
9.           PasswordLength: 16
10.          ExcludeCharacters: '"@/\'
11.    RDSInstance:
12.      Type: AWS::RDS::DBInstance
13.      DependsOn: RDSInstanceSecret
14.      Properties:
15.        DBInstanceClass: db.m5.large
16.        AllocatedStorage: 20
17.        DBName: !Join
18.          - ''
19.          - - '{{resolve:secretsmanager:'
20.            - !Ref RDSInstanceSecret
21.            - ':SecretString:dbname}}'
22.        Engine: mysql
23.        MasterUserPassword: !Join
24.          - ''
25.          - - '{{resolve:secretsmanager:'
26.            - !Ref RDSInstanceSecret
27.            - ':SecretString:password}}'
28.        MasterUsername: !Join
29.          - ''
30.          - - '{{resolve:secretsmanager:'
31.            - !Ref RDSInstanceSecret
32.            - ':SecretString:username}}'
33.    SecretRdsAttachment:
34.      Type: AWS::SecretsManager::SecretTargetAttachment
35.      Properties:
36.        SecretId: !Ref RDSInstanceSecret
37.        TargetId: !Ref RDSInstance
38.        TargetType: AWS::RDS::DBInstance
```

This template is a configuration written in AWS CloudFormation syntax. It defines AWS resources such as a Secrets Manager secret (**RDSInstanceSecret**), an RDS database instance (**RDSInstance**), and an attachment between the secret and the RDS instance (**SecretRdsAttachment**). Here is a breakdown of each section:

o **RDSInstanceSecret**: Defines an AWS Secrets Manager secret named **mysecret**. It specifies the secret's properties such as its name, how to generate the secret string, and constraints like the password length and excluded characters.

o **RDSInstance**: Defines an AWS RDS DB instance. It depends on the **RDSInstanceSecret** resource, meaning it will only be created after the secret is created. It specifies properties of the RDS instance, like its instance class, allocated storage, database name, engine, master user password, and username. The database name, master user password, and username are retrieved from the **RDSInstanceSecret** using **!Join** and **!Ref** functions, along with the **resolve:secretsmanager** directive.

o **SecretRdsAttachment**: Defines an attachment between the **RDSInstanceSecret** and the **RDSInstance**. This attachment allows the RDS instance to access the secrets stored in the Secrets Manager. It specifies the **SecretId** (the **RDSInstanceSecret**) and the **TargetId** (the **RDSInstance**), along with the **TargetType**.

Overall, this CloudFormation template sets up an RDS instance with its master user credentials stored securely in AWS Secrets Manager, ensuring sensitive information like passwords are managed safely.

CreationPolicy

The CreationPolicy attribute in AWS CloudFormation allows you to control the stack creation process by delaying the completion of resource creation until certain conditions are met. This ensures that resources are fully configured and operational before the stack creation process proceeds.

Workings of CreationPolicy

CreationPolicy prevents a resource's status from transitioning to create complete until AWS CloudFormation receives a specified number of success signals, or the timeout period is exceeded. These signals indicate that the resource is ready for use. CloudFormation tracks these signals through stack events, providing visibility into the creation progress.

Currently, CreationPolicy is supported for the following CloudFormation resources:

• **AWS::AppStream::Fleet**

- **AWS::AutoScaling::AutoScalingGroup**
- **AWS::EC2::Instance**
- **AWS::CloudFormation::WaitCondition**

Implementation example

Let us consider the scenario of deploying applications on an Amazon EC2 instance using AWS CloudFormation. You can add a CreationPolicy attribute to the EC2 instance resource properties and use the **cfn-signal** helper script to send a success signal after the applications are installed and configured.

Here is a high-level overview of the process:

- Include the CreationPolicy attribute in the resource definition.
- Install and configure the applications within the EC2 instance's user data.
- Use the **cfn-signal** helper script to send a success signal to CloudFormation once the applications are ready.

Note: We will explore the **cfn-signal** helper script in detail in the upcoming section. For now, it is important to understand its role: the **cfn-signal** script notifies CloudFormation of the successful creation or update of Amazon EC2 instances. In situations where software applications are installed and configured on, **cfn-signal** facilitates informing CloudFormation when these applications are prepared for use.

Here is the example template showcasing how CreationPolicy is integrated:

```
1.  Resources:
2.    MyEC2Instance:
3.      Type: AWS::EC2::Instance
4.      Properties:
5.        ImageId: ami-12345678
6.        InstanceType: t2.micro
7.        UserData:
8.          Fn::Base64: |
9.            #!/bin/bash
10.            # Install and configure applications
11.            # Send success signal after applications
    are installed and configured
12.            /opt/aws/bin/cfn-signal -e $? --stack ${AWS::StackName}
    --resource MyEC2Instance
13.      CreationPolicy:
14.        ResourceSignal:
15.          Count: 1
16.          Timeout: PT5M
```

In this example, we are creating an EC2 instance named **MyEC2Instance**. The **UserData** section contains a bash script that installs and configures applications. Once the setup is complete, the **cfn-signal** script sends a success signal to CloudFormation. This topic for **cfn-signal** will be discussed further in an upcoming section.

Now, let us break down the CreationPolicy syntax used in the provided example:

- **CreationPolicy**: This is the top-level attribute within the resource definition where you specify the creation policy settings. Let us explore the child attributes:

  - **ResourceSignal**: This sub-attribute defines the Conditions for signaling CloudFormation that the resource creation is complete.

  - **Count**: Specifies the number of success signals that CloudFormation must receive before considering the resource creation complete. In this example, **Count: 1** means that CloudFormation waits for one success signal.

  - **Timeout**: Specifies the timeout period for waiting for the specified number of success signals. If the required number of signals is not received within this time, CloudFormation marks the resource creation as failed. Here, **Timeout: PT5M** indicates a timeout period of 5 minutes (PT stands for period of time).

Syntax for CreationPolicy

Now, let us explore the syntax for defining CreationPolicy for the previously mentioned resources.

- **AWS::AppStream::Fleet**:

```
o  CreationPolicy:
o     StartFleet:
o        Type: Boolean
```

Here, the **CreationPolicy** attribute, specifically **StartFleet**, is utilized to manage the startup behavior of an AWS AppStream fleet during stack creation in AWS CloudFormation. It is a Boolean attribute, meaning it can either be set to true or false:

  - **When StartFleet is set to true**: CloudFormation instructs AppStream to start the fleet as soon as it is created. This ensures that the fleet is immediately available for use once the stack creation is complete.

  - **When StartFleet is set to false**: CloudFormation creates the fleet but does not start it automatically. You would need to manually start the fleet after the stack creation process completes, either through the AWS Management Console, AWS CLI, or SDKs.

This attribute provides flexibility in managing the lifecycle of AppStream fleets within CloudFormation stacks, allowing you to control when the fleet becomes operational based on your deployment requirements.

- **AWS::AutoScaling::AutoScalingGroup**:
    - `CreationPolicy:`
    - `    AutoScalingCreationPolicy:`
    - `        MinSuccessfulInstancesPercent: Integer`
    - `    ResourceSignal:`
    - `        Count: Integer`
    - `        Timeout: String`

This **CreationPolicy** snippet is used to configure resource creation behavior in AWS CloudFormation, specifically for auto scaling groups. Let us have a look at its attributes:

- **MinSuccessfulInstancesPercent**: This attribute determines the percentage of instances that must successfully signal completion before CloudFormation considers the auto scaling group creation successful. For example, setting it to 50 means that at least 50% of the instances must signal success for the creation to proceed.

- **Count**: Specifies the number of success signals CloudFormation must receive from the resources before considering the creation process successful. For instance, if set to 1, CloudFormation waits for a single success signal.

- **Timeout**: Defines the maximum time CloudFormation waits for the specified number of success signals. If the signals are not received within this time, CloudFormation marks the resource creation as failed.

> Note: We have previously covered the **CreationPolicy** for the EC2 instance resource in a previous example. Therefore, we would not reiterate the syntax here. Additionally, the **AWS::CloudFormation::WaitCondition** resource will be discussed in the forthcoming section.

Helper scripts

AWS CloudFormation provides a suite of Python helper scripts that streamline the installation of software and management of services on Amazon EC2 instances within your stacks. These scripts facilitate various tasks during the stack creation, update, and deletion processes. Let us explore the different categories of CloudFormation helper scripts, along with their usage and considerations:

- **cfn-init**:
    - **Purpose**: Used to retrieve and interpret resource Metadata, install packages, create files, and start services on EC2 instances.

- o **Usage**: Integrated directly into your CloudFormation template to execute initialization tasks on EC2 instances.

- **cfn-signal**:
  - o **Purpose**: Signals CloudFormation with a **CreationPolicy** or **WaitCondition**, enabling synchronization with other resources in the stack when a prerequisite resource or application is ready.
  - o **Usage**: Typically called within **UserData** scripts to indicate the successful completion of setup tasks.

- **cfn-get-metadata**:
  - o **Purpose**: Retrieves Metadata for a specific resource or path from CloudFormation, allowing dynamic fetching of resource attributes.
  - o **Usage**: Utilized within **UserData** scripts or other helper scripts to access Metadata relevant to resource configuration.

- **cfn-hup**:
  - o **Purpose**: Monitors for updates to Metadata and triggers custom hooks when changes are detected, facilitating automatic updates and configuration refreshes.
  - o **Usage**: Configured to run as a service on EC2 instances, ensuring that instances remain up-to-date with any changes in the CloudFormation stack.

Installation and usage considerations

Let us now explore some key points regarding the installation and usage of helper scripts:

- **Preinstalled on Amazon Linux AMI**: The CloudFormation helper scripts come preinstalled on Amazon Linux AMI images with bootstrap scripts installed, located in **/opt/aws/bin**.

- **Downloading for other platforms**: For non-Amazon Linux distributions and Microsoft Windows platforms, the **aws-cfn-bootstrap** package can be downloaded and installed manually.

- **Permissions**: By default, helper scripts do not require credentials, but if specified, consider using only one of the available options (**--role**, **--credential-file**, **--access-key** with **--secret-key**).

- **Updating scripts**: Ensure that EC2 instances are using the latest version of the scripts to leverage any improvements or fixes. This can be achieved by including a command to install the latest version (**yum install -y aws-cfn-bootstrap**) in the **UserData** property of your CloudFormation template.

These CloudFormation helper scripts enhance automation and customization capabilities, enabling smoother and more efficient stack deployments and management.

Example

Let us revisit the example we explored in the CreationPolicy section. Here is the template snippet:

```
1.  MyEC2Instance:
2.      Type: AWS::EC2::Instance
3.      Properties:
4.        ImageId: ami-12345678
5.        InstanceType: t2.micro
6.        UserData:
7.          Fn::Base64: |
8.            #!/bin/bash
9.            # Install and configure applications
10.           # Send success signal after applications
   are installed and configured
11.           /opt/aws/bin/cfn-
   signal -e $? --stack ${AWS::StackName} --resource MyEC2Instance
```

In the provided template snippet, the **cfn-signal** command is used within the **UserData** section of an EC2 instance resource definition. Let us break down how it works:

- **Purpose**: The **cfn-signal** command sends a signal to AWS CloudFormation, indicating the successful completion of certain tasks or initialization steps on the EC2 instance.

- **Usage**: It is typically included in the **UserData** section, which allows you to run shell commands or scripts during the bootstrapping process of the EC2 instance.

- **Arguments**:

  o **-e $?**: Specifies the exit code of the signal. Dynamically captures the exit status of the preceding command, ensuring that the signaling accurately reflects whether the preceding command succeeded or failed.

  o **--stack ${AWS::StackName}**: Specifies the name of the CloudFormation stack to which the instance belongs.

  o **--resource MyEC2Instance**: Specifies the logical ID of the resource within the stack. In this case, it is an EC2 instance named MyEC2Instance.

- **Effect**: When CloudFormation encounters this **cfn-signal** command during stack creation or update, it waits for the signal to be sent before proceeding. This ensures that CloudFormation can track the progress of the EC2 instance setup and configuration.

To summarize, the **cfn-signal** command in this template snippet informs AWS CloudFormation that the EC2 instance setup and application configuration tasks have finished successfully, enabling CloudFormation to proceed with the stack creation process. Likewise, other helper scripts can be utilized as required. For further information on each of these scripts, please refer to the following page:

https://docs.aws.amazon.com/AWSCloudFormation/latest/UserGuide/cfn-helper-scripts-reference.html

Wait Conditions

In AWS CloudFormation, Wait Conditions are powerful mechanisms used to coordinate the execution of stacks. They allow you to pause the stack creation process until a certain Condition is met, typically signalling the successful completion of a task or a specific state in your AWS resources. These Conditions are often used in scenarios where resource provisioning or configuration requires some time to complete, such as deploying an EC2 instance or setting up a database.

Its workings

Integrating WaitCondition into your CloudFormation template requires the setup of CloudFormation helper scripts, commonly known as **cfn helper scripts** (which we have discussed in the last section), on your instances. These cfn helper scripts are essential for sending success signals to the WaitCondition. To ensure smooth operation, it is essential to have these cfn helper scripts preconfigured on your Amazon EC2 instance. If they are not already set up, you can easily include them as part of your UserData. This ensures that the necessary scripts are available and operational during the instance initialization process, enabling seamless interaction with WaitCondition and other CloudFormation features.

Once a WaitCondition resource is instantiated, a timer begins. It transitions to the CREATE_COMPLETE state upon receiving the required number of success signals, which are sent by the cfn helper scripts. However, if the signals are not received within the specified timeout period, the WaitCondition enters the CREATE_FAILED state, prompting a rollback of the stack creation process. This mechanism safeguards against potential hangs or incomplete setups, ensuring stack integrity during creation.

Syntax

The syntax for how to declare the **WaitCondition** in the template is as follows:

```
1.  Type: AWS::CloudFormation::WaitCondition
2.  Properties:
3.    Count: Integer
4.    Handle: String
5.    Timeout: String
```

Now, let us explore the breakdown of the preceding syntax:

- **Type: AWS::CloudFormation::WaitCondition**: This line specifies the type of resource being defined, which is a WaitCondition.

- **Count: Integer**: This property attribute specifies the number of success signals that the WaitCondition must receive before it transitions to the CREATE_COMPLETE state. The value of **Count** is an **Integer**. If the Wait Condition does not receive the specified number of success signals before the **Timeout** period expires, CloudFormation assumes that the Wait Condition has failed and rolls the stack back.

- **Handle: String**: This attribute refers to the Wait Condition handle utilized for signaling this specific Wait Condition. To incorporate a Wait Condition in a stack, it is necessary to declare an **AWS::CloudFormation::WaitConditionHandle** resource in the stack's template. Although a Wait Condition handle has no properties, referencing a **WaitConditionHandle** resource resolves to a pre-signed URL, enabling signaling of success or failure to the **WaitCondition**. The type for declaration of Wait condition handle resource in the template is as follows:

    o Type: AWS::CloudFormation::WaitConditionHandle

- **Timeout: String**: This property specifies the maximum amount of time that the WaitCondition will wait for the required number of success signals before timing out. The maximum duration allowed for this property is 12 hours (43200 seconds). Upon receiving a positive signal before reaching the timeout value, the timer halts automatically, initiating the execution of the template.

Example

Let us dive into an example to gain a deeper understanding of the concept. The following template is employed to launch an EC2 instance, with the objective of updating the installed packages using the yum update command. After the update process is completed, a success signal is dispatched via the **cfn-signal** helper script to the handle, initiating the **WaitCondition** for the stack to proceed with further execution:

```
1. AWSTemplateFormatVersion: '2010-09-09'
2. Resources:
3.   MyEC2Instance:
4.     Type: AWS::EC2::Instance
5.     Properties:
6.       ImageId: ami-04e5276ebb8451442
7.       InstanceType: t2.micro
8.       UserData: !Base64
9.         Fn::Join:
10.          - ''
```

```
11.          - - |
12.             #!/bin/bash
13.          - |
14.             yum update -y
15.          - |
16.             # Signal the status from cfn-init
17.          - '/opt/aws/bin/cfn-signal -e 0 -r "Success" '
18.          - !Ref WaitHandle
19.          - |

20.          <
21.      Tags:
22.        - Key: Name
23.          Value: TestInstance
24.      NetworkInterfaces:
25.        - DeleteOnTermination: 'true'
26.          Description: Primary interface
27.          DeviceIndex: 0
28.          AssociatePublicIpAddress: 'true'
29.  WaitHandle:
30.    Type: AWS::CloudFormation::WaitConditionHandle
31.  WaitCondition:
32.    Type: AWS::CloudFormation::WaitCondition
33.    DependsOn: MyEC2Instance
34.    Properties:
35.      Handle: !Ref WaitHandle
36.      Timeout: '180'
```

Let us break down this template for more understanding:

- **EC2 Instance (MyEC2Instance)**: This section defines an EC2 instance resource named **MyEC2Instance**. The **UserData** property contains a script that will be executed when the instance starts. In this case, it is a bash script. Inside the script, **yum update -y** is used to update the installed packages on the EC2 instance.

  After the update, **cfn-signal** command is used to send a signal to CloudFormation. This signal includes the exit status of the yum update command (**$?**) and information about the stack (**AWS::StackName**) and the resource (**MyWaitConditionHandle**) to signal.

- **Wait condition handle (MyWaitConditionHandle)**: This section defines a **WaitConditionHandle** resource named **MyWaitConditionHandle**. It is used to receive signals from the **cfn-signal** command in the **UserData** script of the EC2 instance.

- **WaitCondition** (**MyWaitCondition**): This section defines a **WaitCondition** resource named **MyWaitCondition**. It depends on MyEC2Instance, ensuring that the EC2 instance is created before the Wait Condition is evaluated.

- The **Handle** property references the **MyWaitConditionHandle** resource, indicating where to send the success signal.

- The **Timeout** property specifies the maximum time (in seconds) to wait for the success signal before timing out (in this case, 600 seconds or 10 minutes).

> **Note: Although the WaitCondition CloudFormation resource may resemble the DependsOn attribute, they serve distinct purposes. DependsOn dictates the order of resource creation in your CloudFormation stack, ensuring that one resource is created after another. However, it does not wait for signals indicating success or failure from AWS resources before proceeding. Conversely, WaitCondition pauses the execution of the CloudFormation template until success signals are received from AWS resources. Despite their differences, WaitCondition and DependsOn can collaborate when there is a need for resource creation dependency.**

EC2 bootstrapping

EC2 bootstrapping refers to the process of customizing and configuring EC2 instances during their initialization phase. While we have encountered EC2 bootstrapping in earlier examples and references, let us dive deeper into how it is used and declared within the EC2 instance resource section. This process typically involves installing software, applying configurations, and executing scripts to prepare the instances for their intended use. AWS CloudFormation provides a convenient way to automate EC2 bootstrapping as part of your infrastructure deployment.

In CloudFormation templates, EC2 instances are defined using the **AWS::EC2::Instance** resource type. Within the properties of the instance resource, the **UserData** field allows you to specify a script, or commands executed when the instance is launched. This **UserData** field is where you can perform EC2 bootstrapping tasks.

For example, you can use **UserData** to execute shell scripts that install software packages, configure applications, or set up environment variables. You can also use it to download and execute scripts from remote locations, such as Amazon S3 or a version control system or from the internet.

Here is a basic example of EC2 bootstrapping using CloudFormation:

```
1. Resources:
2.    MyEC2Instance:
3.      Type: AWS::EC2::Instance
4.      Properties:
5.        ImageId: ami-12345678
```

```
6.         InstanceType: t2.micro
7.         UserData:
8.           Fn::Base64:
9.             Fn::Join:
10.               - ''
11.               - - "#!/bin/bash -xe\n"
12.                 - "yum update -y\n"
13.                 - "yum install -y httpd\n"
14.                 - "service httpd start\n"
```

In this example, the **UserData** field contains a script that updates the package repository (**yum update -y**), installs the Apache web server (**yum install -y httpd**), and starts the Apache service (**service httpd start**). In this example, we are using the **Fn::Base64** function to encode the user data script and **Fn::Join** function to concatenate the script lines. This script will be executed automatically when the EC2 instance is launched using this template.

Benefits of EC2 bootstrapping

Now, let us explore some of the advantages gained through EC2 bootstrapping:

- **Consistency**: EC2 bootstrapping ensures consistency across deployments by automating the execution of standardized configuration steps. This reduces the risk of human error and ensures that each instance is configured identically.

- **Efficiency**: By automating the initialization process, EC2 bootstrapping saves time and effort compared to manual configuration. It allows you to launch and configure multiple instances simultaneously, streamlining the deployment process.

- **Flexibility**: EC2 bootstrapping enables you to customize the configuration of instances based on your specific requirements. You can include custom scripts, install additional software packages, and configure settings tailored to your application's needs.

- **Scalability**: EC2 bootstrapping facilitates the rapid scaling of infrastructure by automating the setup of new instances. This allows you to quickly add capacity in response to changing demand without manual intervention.

- **Version control**: By defining the configuration steps within the CloudFormation template, EC2 bootstrapping enables version control and change management. You can track and manage changes to the configuration over time, ensuring consistency and compliance.

Conclusion

In conclusion, this chapter has covered several key aspects of AWS CloudFormation deployment and management. We explored the integration of AWS Secrets Manager for securely storing and accessing sensitive information. Additionally, we discussed creation policy, helper scripts, Wait Conditions, and EC2 bootstrapping, which are fundamental techniques for orchestrating resource creation and initialization within CloudFormation templates.

Moving forward, the next chapter will continue to expand our understanding of CloudFormation with a focus on advanced topics. We will explore resource import, circular dependencies, and custom resources and implementation, providing insights into strategies for managing complex dependencies and custom logic within CloudFormation stacks. Furthermore, we will explore the deployment of stacks using the AWS CLI and the utilization of VPC endpoints for the CloudFormation service, offering comprehensive insights into advanced CloudFormation usage and deployment techniques.

Multiple choice questions

1. **Which AWS service provides a secure and centralized solution for storing and managing sensitive information such as passwords, API keys, and encryption keys, and can be seamlessly integrated with AWS CloudFormation?**

    a. AWS Key Management Service (KMS)

    b. AWS Systems Manager

    c. AWS Secrets Manager

    d. AWS IAM

2. **How does EC2 bootstrapping benefit AWS CloudFormation deployments?**

    a. Enhances security.

    b. Automates instance setup.

    c. Optimizes resource usage.

    d. Monitors performance metrics.

3. **What is the primary function of Wait Conditions in AWS CloudFormation?**

    a. To specify the order in which resources are created.

    b. To define policies for managing resource creation retries and timeouts.

    c. To wait for success signals from AWS resources before proceeding.

    d. To execute custom scripts during resource creation.

4. **Which CloudFormation resource type is used to specify the maximum time to wait for a specified Condition to be met during stack creation?**

   a. AWS::CloudFormation::WaitCondition

   b. AWS::EC2::Instance

   c. AWS::IAM::Role

   d. AWS::S3::Bucket

5. **What is the purpose of the cfn-signal command in AWS CloudFormation?**

   a. To send success or failure signals to WaitConditions.

   b. To initialize EC2 instances with configuration data.

   c. To monitor stack events and update Metadata.

   d. To retrieve Metadata from AWS resources.

Answers

1. c

2. b

3. c

4. a

5. a

Join our book's Discord space

Join the book's Discord Workspace for Latest updates, Offers, Tech happenings around the world, New Release and Sessions with the Authors:

https://discord.bpbonline.com

CHAPTER 8
Advanced CloudFormation, Custom Deployment and VPC Endpoint

Introduction

This chapter is designed to guide you through increasingly complex features and techniques of AWS CloudFormation, shedding light on how to manage intricate deployment scenarios effectively.

We begin by exploring one of the important intrinsic functions, that is, *Fn::ImportValue*, which is used to import the output value from another stack to your current stack. Following this, we will explore the scenarios of *Circular dependencies*, an issue that can complicate the deployment process when resources depend on each other cyclically. We will provide strategies for detecting, resolving, and preventing such dependencies to ensure seamless stack updates and management.

The chapter progresses to discuss *Custom resources and implementation*. Here, we extend beyond the default set of resources provided by AWS, employing custom resources to cover scenarios where native support is absent. Next, we cover the section *Deploying stack using AWS CLI*. Although the AWS Management Console is commonly used, the AWS **command line interface (CLI)** presents a more flexible and powerful alternative for the automation and scripting of CloudFormation operations. Detailed steps on how to deploy, update, and manage stacks via the AWS CLI will be provided to ensure you can leverage this tool effectively.

Lastly, the chapter will conclude with a discussion on setting up a *VPC endpoint for the CloudFormation service*. This setup is vital for enhancing the security posture of your CloudFormation operations, enabling your stacks to communicate within AWS without traversing the public internet.

Structure

The chapter covers the following topics:

- Fn::ImportValue
- Circular dependencies
- Custom resources and implementation
- Deploying stacks using AWS command line interface
- Virtual Private Cloud endpoint for CloudFormation service

Objectives

The primary objective of this chapter is to equip readers with advanced skills and a comprehensive understanding of AWS CloudFormation, particularly in scenarios that involve complex deployments and enhancements in security and management. By examining topics such as Fn::ImportValue, circular dependencies, custom resources, CLI deployment techniques, and VPC endpoints, the chapter aims to deepen the reader's proficiency in managing and automating AWS resources effectively. Upon completion, readers should be able to confidently import existing resources into CloudFormation, resolve and prevent circular dependencies, utilize custom resources for non-native functionality, deploy and manage stacks using the AWS CLI, and secure CloudFormation operations using VPC endpoints. This knowledge will prepare readers to handle advanced Cloud infrastructure challenges and optimize their AWS environments for better performance, reliability, and security.

Fn::ImportValue

`Fn::ImportValue` is a pivotal intrinsic function in AWS CloudFormation that facilitates the sharing of values across different stacks. This function allows a CloudFormation stack to import output values exported by another stack, providing a mechanism for sharing resources and configurations in a controlled manner across your AWS environment. Understanding the nuances of `Fn::ImportValue` can greatly enhance your ability to design interconnected and efficient cloud architectures.

Basic concepts and syntax

The `Fn::ImportValue` function imports a value that has been exported from another stack using the **Outputs** section of that stack's CloudFormation template. This function is primarily used when you need to share common resources or configurations, such as VPC IDs, subnet IDs, security group IDs, ARNs of IAM roles, or any custom configuration strings across multiple stacks.

The syntax for **Fn::ImportValue** is straightforward where **ExportName** is a placeholder for the name given to the output value in the exporting stack. The syntax is as follows:

```
1. ValueToImport: !ImportValue ExportName
```

Creating exports in a stack

Before you can import a value, it must be explicitly exported from another stack. Here is how you define an export within an AWS CloudFormation template:

```
1. Outputs:
2.   SomeOutputValue:
3.     Description: A description of what this output is used for
4.     Value: !Ref SomeResource
5.     Export:
6.       Name: UniqueExportName
```

In the preceding syntax, we have the following:

- **SomeOutputValue**: This is the logical ID of the output within the CloudFormation template.

- **Value**: This is the actual data that you want to export. It could be a direct reference to a resource's attribute, or a value derived from intrinsic functions.

- **UniqueExportName**: This is the identifier that other stacks will use to import this value. It must be unique within the region.

Now, once an output is exported from a stack, it can be referenced in other stacks using the **Fn::ImportValue**. Kindly refer to following example syntax:

```
1. Resources:
2.   SomeResource:
3.     Type: AWS::EC2::Instance
4.     Properties:
5.       SubnetId: !ImportValue SubnetIDExportedFromAnotherStack
```

To fully understand the **Fn::ImportValue** functionality within AWS CloudFormation, let us explore a detailed example that involves the following two separate stacks:

- **VPC stack**: This stack will create a VPC along with its associated resources and will export necessary values, like the VPC ID and a subnet ID.

- **EC2 stack**: This stack will import the exported VPC ID and subnet ID from the VPC stack to launch an EC2 instance within the same VPC.

VPC stack (stack A): We will set up a VPC along with all necessary components with a single private and public subnet and export the VPC ID and the respective subnet IDs. The template that we will use to achieve the same is as follows:

```
1.  AWSTemplateFormatVersion: '2010-09-09'
2.  Description: VPC Stack with all networking components and exports
3.
4.  Resources:
5.    MyVPC:
6.      Type: AWS::EC2::VPC
7.      Properties:
8.        CidrBlock: 10.0.0.0/16
9.        EnableDnsSupport: true
10.       EnableDnsHostnames: true
11.
12.   InternetGateway:
13.     Type: AWS::EC2::InternetGateway
14.
15.   VPCGatewayAttachment:
16.     Type: AWS::EC2::VPCGatewayAttachment
17.     Properties:
18.       VpcId: !Ref MyVPC
19.       InternetGatewayId: !Ref InternetGateway
20.
21.   PublicSubnet:
22.     Type: AWS::EC2::Subnet
23.     Properties:
24.       VpcId: !Ref MyVPC
25.       CidrBlock: 10.0.1.0/24
26.       MapPublicIpOnLaunch: true
27.
28.   PrivateSubnet:
29.     Type: AWS::EC2::Subnet
30.     Properties:
31.       VpcId: !Ref MyVPC
32.       CidrBlock: 10.0.2.0/24
33.
34.   PublicRouteTable:
35.     Type: AWS::EC2::RouteTable
36.     Properties:
37.       VpcId: !Ref MyVPC
```

```
38.
39.    PublicRoute:
40.      Type: AWS::EC2::Route
41.      Properties:
42.        RouteTableId: !Ref PublicRouteTable
43.        DestinationCidrBlock: 0.0.0.0/0
44.        GatewayId: !Ref InternetGateway
45.
46.    PublicSubnetRouteTableAssociation:
47.      Type: AWS::EC2::SubnetRouteTableAssociation
48.      Properties:
49.        SubnetId: !Ref PublicSubnet
50.        RouteTableId: !Ref PublicRouteTable
51.
52. Outputs:
53.    ExportedVPCID:
54.      Description: The ID of the VPC
55.      Value: !Ref MyVPC
56.      Export:
57.        Name: !Sub ${AWS::StackName}-VPCID
58.
59.    ExportedPublicSubnetID:
60.      Description: The ID of the Public Subnet
61.      Value: !Ref PublicSubnet
62.      Export:
63.        Name: !Sub ${AWS::StackName}-PublicSubnetID
64.
65.    ExportedPrivateSubnetID:
66.      Description: The ID of the Private Subnet
67.      Value: !Ref PrivateSubnet
68.      Export:
69.        Name: !Sub ${AWS::StackName}-PrivateSubnetID
```

In the preceding CloudFormation template, three key output values—VPC ID, public subnet ID, and private subnet ID—are defined and configured for export. These output values are integral components of the networking infrastructure created by the stack, and by marking them for export, they are made available for use in other CloudFormation stacks. This capability is crucial for creating modular, interconnected AWS environments, where resources created in one stack need to be referenced and utilized in another.

Following is the figure showcasing the output section for the VPC stack which we created using the preceding template:

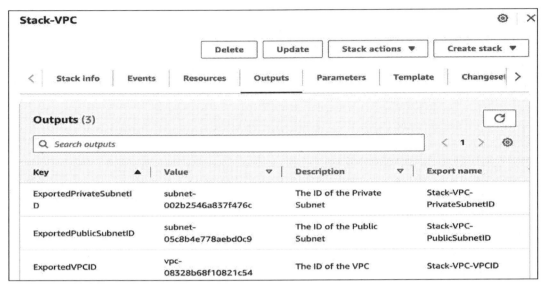

Figure 8.1: VPC stack Outputs section

In the preceding figure, we noted that each essential networking component, such as the VPC, public subnet, and private subnet, is assigned a unique export name. This unique naming is achieved by appending specific identifiers (For example, **-VPCID**, **-PublicSubnetID**, **-PrivateSubnetID**) to the stack's name, creating distinct and recognizable export names for each resource.

Let us now turn our attention to stack B, where we will configure an EC2 instance utilizing the exported values discussed previously. This approach will demonstrate how to effectively leverage the foundational networking components created in *stack A*, ensuring that our EC2 instance is seamlessly integrated into the established VPC and subnet infrastructure.

The template for the deployment of stack B is as follows:

```
1. AWSTemplateFormatVersion: '2010-09-09'
2. Description: Launch an EC2 instance using directly
   imported VPC and Subnet IDs
3.   from another stack
4.
5. Parameters:
6.   KeyName:
7.     Type: AWS::EC2::KeyPair::KeyName
8.     Description: Name of an existing EC2 KeyPair
   to enable SSH access to the instance
9.
10. Resources:
```

```
11.   MySecurityGroup:
12.     Type: AWS::EC2::SecurityGroup
13.     Properties:
14.       GroupDescription: Security group for my instance
15.       VpcId: !ImportValue Stack-VPC-VPCID # Direct reference
16.       SecurityGroupIngress:
17.         - IpProtocol: tcp
18.           FromPort: 22
19.           ToPort: 22
20.           CidrIp: 0.0.0.0/0
21.         - IpProtocol: tcp
22.           FromPort: 80
23.           ToPort: 80
24.           CidrIp: 0.0.0.0/0
25.
26.   MyEC2Instance:
27.     Type: AWS::EC2::Instance
28.     Properties:
29.       InstanceType: t2.micro
30.       ImageId: ami-07caf09b362be10b8
31.       SubnetId: !ImportValue Stack-VPC-PublicSubnetID
   # Direct reference
32.
33.       SecurityGroupIds:
34.         - !Ref MySecurityGroup
35.       KeyName: !Ref KeyName
36.
37. Outputs:
38.   InstanceId:
39.     Description: The ID of the created EC2 instance
40.     Value: !Ref MyEC2Instance
```

In the template provided, we are utilizing the **Fn::importvalue** function to directly reference the necessary VPC ID and subnet ID from the previously exported values. Let us deploy the template quickly to confirm its correctness. The figure showcasing the CloudFormation console page for the template execution is as follows:

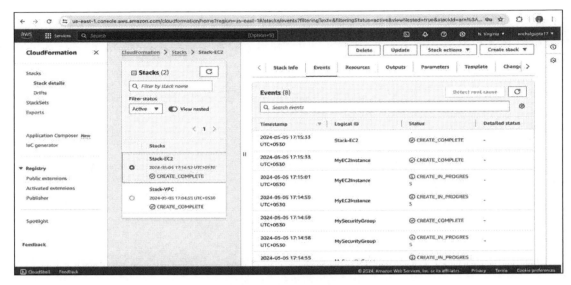

Figure 8.2: EC2 stack execution status

We can see that the stack setup was completed successfully, indicating that it successfully utilized the exported values from the VPC stack to configure the necessary parameters for creating the EC2 instance.

Circular dependencies

Circular dependencies in AWS CloudFormation occur when resources in a stack depend on each other in such a way that it creates a loop, preventing the stack from resolving the order in which resources should be created, updated, or deleted. This situation often leads to a failure in deploying the stack, as CloudFormation cannot determine a starting point or a clear sequence of operations.

Note: When deleting such stacks, always ensure that the stack importing variables from another is deleted first.

Common causes

Let us now understand some of the common reasons for the occurrence of circular dependencies. They are as follows:

- **Resource references**: The most typical cause is improperly configured resource attributes that reference each other. For example, a security group depending on an instance that, in turn, relies on the same security group for its configuration.

- **Implicit dependencies**: These are not directly stated in the CloudFormation template but are inferred by CloudFormation based on the properties that resources use. For instance, an EC2 instance using a specific subnet implicitly creates a dependency on the corresponding VPC and subnet.

- **Exported stack outputs**: Using exported outputs can lead to circular dependencies between stacks. For example, if stack A exports a value that stack B uses and stack B simultaneously exports a value used by stack A.

Identifying circular dependencies

CloudFormation usually identifies circular dependencies during the creation or updating of a stack and returns an error message. These messages typically indicate which resources are involved in the loop, although deciphering the exact cause may require careful examination of the template.

To illustrate how circular dependencies are identified in the AWS CloudFormation console, let us walk through a simplified example involving two AWS resources: an EC2 instance and a security group. This example will demonstrate how a circular dependency can be inadvertently created and how CloudFormation detects and reports it:

- **Scenario: EC2 instance and security group**

  Suppose we have a CloudFormation template with the following elements:

  o **EC2 instance**: This requires a security group to define its network access.

  o **Security group**: This security group is set to allow inbound traffic from the IP address of the EC2 instance itself.

  o An example template for this scenario is as follows:

```
1.  Resources:
2.    MyInstance:
3.      Type: AWS::EC2::Instance
4.      Properties:
5.        ImageId: ami-07caf09b362be10b8
6.        InstanceType: t2.micro
7.        SecurityGroups:
8.          - Ref: InstanceSecurityGroup
9.
10.   InstanceSecurityGroup:
11.     Type: AWS::EC2::SecurityGroup
12.     Properties:
13.       GroupDescription: "Security group for instance"
14.       SecurityGroupIngress:
15.         - IpProtocol: tcp
16.           FromPort: 22
```

```
17.          ToPort: 22
18.          CidrIp: !GetAtt MyInstance.PrivateIp
```

If we now attempt to deploy the preceding template using the CloudFormation console, we will encounter an error message due to circular dependencies, as shown in the following figure:

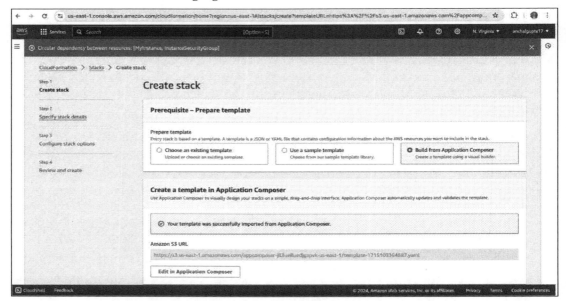

Figure 8.3: Error screen for circular dependencies

The error shown in the preceding figure arises because the creation of the EC2 instance depends on the security group, while the creation of the security group is dependent on the EC2 instance. This mutual dependency leads to an error for circular dependencies.

Resolution of dependency issues

We will now explore how to resolve dependency issues. There could be multiple approaches to consider, depending on the specific requirements. For the previously discussed scenario, we can consider the following approach:

- **Approach**: Remove direct reference. We can modify the security group rule to not directly depend on the EC2 instance's IP address. Instead, we can use a broader CIDR range or specific allowed IPs that do not require a direct attribute call to the EC2 instance. This is the simplest solution, but it may not meet the security requirements if restricting access to the EC2 instance is necessary. An example syntax for the same is as follows:

```
1. Resources:
2.    InstanceSecurityGroup:
```

```
3.    Type: AWS::EC2::SecurityGroup
4.    Properties:
5.      GroupDescription: "Security group for instance"
6.      SecurityGroupIngress:
7.      - IpProtocol: tcp
8.        FromPort: 22
9.        ToPort: 22
10.       CidrIp: "0.0.0.0/0"  # Example only,
    ideally specify more restrictive CIDR blocks
```

Now, if we update our original template with the corrected section and then execute it again, we should no longer encounter the circular dependency error. The following figure showcases the output after making these changes:

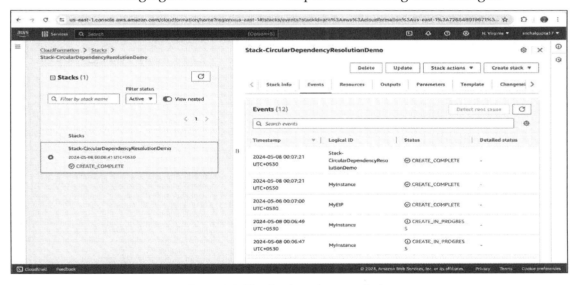

Figure 8.4: Circular dependency resolution

Custom resources and implementation

Custom resources in AWS CloudFormation are a powerful feature that extends its functionality beyond the built-in types. They allow you to integrate custom provisioning logic into your templates, which is executed whenever you create, update (provided there are changes to the custom resource), or delete stacks. This feature is particularly useful for including resources that are not available as standard AWS CloudFormation resource types. By using custom resources, you can incorporate these external resources and manage all related resources within a single stack, ensuring a cohesive and streamlined infrastructure management experience. Custom resources enable you to write custom provisioning logic in templates that CloudFormation does not support out of the box.

Syntax for the custom resource type

Custom resources are implemented by defining a CloudFormation resource with the type **AWS::CloudFormation::CustomResource** or **Custom::MyResourceType**. A typical syntax for the declaration of such a resource looks like the following:

```
1.  Resources:
2.    MyCustomResource:
3.      Type: Custom::ThirdPartyResource
4.      Properties:
5.        ServiceToken: arn:aws:lambda:region:account-
   id:function:function-name
6.        Property1: Value1
7.        Property2: Value2
```

Now, let us understand the essential component used in the preceding syntax. The components are as follows:

- **Service token**: This is an identifier that CloudFormation uses to send notifications to a target (Lambda function or SNS topic), which triggers the code to manage the resource. The service token is specified in the template. It must be from the same region in which you are creating the stack.

> **Note: Only ServiceToken is defined by AWS for a custom resource. The others are defined by the service providers.**

- **Property1 and Property2**: These are placeholders for user defined properties that you can specify in your CloudFormation template. These properties are passed to the service (such as an AWS Lambda function) that handles the custom resource and are used to configure or influence the behavior of that resource.

Let us explore an example to understand the implementation of the previously defined concept. The following is an example of an AWS CloudFormation template that defines a different custom resource along with its associated properties and outputs. This template could be used to manage a hypothetical external **Domain Name System (DNS)** record configuration via a custom resource, which is facilitated by an AWS Lambda function:

```
1.  AWSTemplateFormatVersion: 2010-09-09
2.  Description: A
      template to manage external DNS records via a custom resource.
3.
4.  Resources:
5.    DnsRecordManager:
6.      Type: 'Custom::DNSRecord'
```

```
7.        Properties:
8.          ServiceToken: 'arn:aws:lambda:us-west-
   2:12345EXAMPLE:function:ManageDNS'
9.          RecordName: 'example.com'
10.         RecordType: 'A'
11.         RecordValue: '192.168.1.1'
12.         TTL: '300'
13.
14. Outputs:
15.   DNSOperationResult:
16.     Description: "The result of the DNS record operation."
17.     Value: !GetAtt DnsRecordManager.OperationStatus
18.
19.   DNSRecordInfo:
20.     Description: "Details about the DNS record that was managed."
21.     Value: !GetAtt DnsRecordManager.RecordDetails
```

This template is useful for scenarios where the DNS records need to be dynamically managed as part of infrastructure deployments but are hosted outside of AWS-managed DNS services like Route 53. The custom resource, handled by a Lambda function, offers flexibility to integrate with various external DNS service providers. Let us break down the template to understand its different components, which are as follows:

- **Type**: `Custom::DNSRecord`. This indicates that the resource is a custom type. `Custom::DNSRecord` is a label that will be used by the Lambda function to recognize the requests it needs to handle.

- **Properties**:

  o **ServiceToken**: This is the ARN of the AWS Lambda function (**ManageDNS**) that CloudFormation will invoke for creating, updating, or deleting the DNS record. This function needs to be pre-configured to handle these operations.

  o **RecordName**: Specifies the DNS record name to be managed.

  o **RecordType**: The type of DNS record. For example, A, AAAA, TXT, etc.

  o **RecordValue**: The value for the DNS record, such as an IP address for A records.

  o **TTL**: Time-to-live for the DNS record, indicating how long it should be cached by resolvers.

- **Outputs section**:
  - **DNSOperationResult**: Uses the **!GetAtt** function to retrieve the **OperationStatus** attribute from the **DnsRecordManager** resource. This status could indicate whether the DNS record was successfully created, updated, or deleted.

  - **DNSRecordInfo**: Retrieves detailed information about the DNS record, such as its full configuration details from the **DnsRecordManager** resource.

This template thus demonstrates the practical application of custom resources in AWS CloudFormation, enabling comprehensive infrastructure management, including components not natively supported within the AWS ecosystem.

Deploying stacks using AWS Command Line Interface

Deploying AWS CloudFormation stacks via the AWS CLI is a powerful approach for automating and managing infrastructure deployments directly from your terminal or scripts. This method offers flexibility, precision, and the ability to integrate with other tools and systems.

Overview

AWS CLI provides commands for AWS CloudFormation that allow you to create, update, delete, and query the status of the stacks. It interacts with AWS services based on command inputs and manages resources as specified in your CloudFormation templates.

Prerequisites

Before you start deploying stacks using AWS CLI, ensure the following:

- **AWS CLI is installed**: You must have the AWS CLI installed on your machine. You can download it from the AWS CLI website.

- **Configured AWS credentials**: Configure your AWS credentials (AWS access key ID and secret access key) either through the AWS CLI with AWS configure or by setting them in your environment variables.

- **CloudFormation template**: Have your CloudFormation template ready in either JSON or YAML format. This file will describe all the AWS resources you wish to provision.

Basic commands

Let us look at some of the basic commands that can be executed on the AWS CLI for stack creation and management:

- **Create stack**: Let us assume our template file name is **mytemplate.yaml**. The command which can be used to create the stack out of this template is as follows:

  - ```
    aws cloudformation create-stack --stack-
    name MyStack --template-body file://mytemplate.yaml
    ```

- **Update stack**: This command updates an existing stack named **MyStack** with the changes defined in the updated template file. The syntax for the same is as follows:

  - ```
    aws cloudformation update-stack --stack-
    name MyStack --template-body file://mytemplate.yaml
    ```

- **Delete stack**: The following command deletes the stack named **MyStack**. All resources defined in the stack will be terminated and deleted:

  - ```
    aws cloudformation delete-stack --stack-name MyStack
    ```

- **Describe stack**: The following command provides detailed information about the specified stack, including status, parameters, and outputs:

  - ```
    aws cloudformation describe-stack --stack-name MyStack
    ```

> **Note: For a comprehensive understanding of AWS CLI commands for AWS CloudFormation beyond the basics, refer to the following official AWS CLI CloudFormation documentation page:**

https://docs.aws.amazon.com/cli/latest/reference/cloudformation/

> **This documentation offers detailed insights into advanced commands, options, and features, empowering you to optimize your infrastructure deployment and management workflows. Explore the documentation to discover advanced functionalities such as change sets, stack policies, stack sets, and more, enabling you to leverage the full potential of AWS CloudFormation for your AWS environment.**

Let us dive deep into a scenario demonstrating the deployment of a sample stack using the AWS CLI. In this stack, we will utilize a parameter file to showcase how parameters can be passed directly into the template.

Example

We will set up a simple S3 bucket using the CloudFormation template which we will deploy using AWS CLI. Following is the template structure along with a separate parameter file.

Template:
```
1. AWSTemplateFormatVersion: '2010-09-09'
```

```
2. Description: Create an S3 bucket
3.
4. Parameters:
5.   BucketName:
6.     Type: String
7.     Description: Name for the S3 bucket
8.
9. Resources:
10.   MyS3Bucket:
11.     Type: 'AWS::S3::Bucket'
12.     Properties:
13.       BucketName: !Ref BucketName
```

Parameter file:

```
1. [
2.   {
3.     "ParameterKey": "BucketName",
4.     "ParameterValue": "demo-awscli-s3-2024-bucket"
5.   }
6. ]
```

We will now proceed to deploy the template and parameter file mentioned earlier through the AWS CLI. This process entails leveraging the AWS CLI to efficiently implement the specified template and parameter file. Let us navigate through each stage systematically to ensure a successful deployment.

Deployment steps

Let us now take a look at the deployment steps for the stack using AWS CLI:

1. Login to the AWS console from command line using the access key ID and secret access key of the respective IAM user:

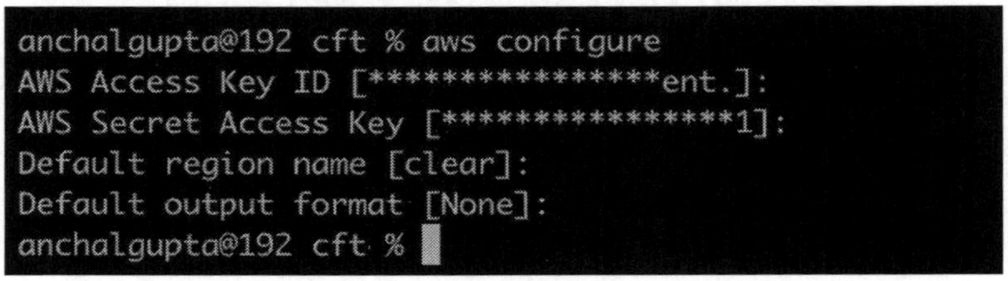

```
anchalgupta@192 cft % aws configure
AWS Access Key ID [****************ent.]:
AWS Secret Access Key [****************1]:
Default region name [clear]:
Default output format [None]:
anchalgupta@192 cft %
```

Figure 8.5: AWS configure setup

We just need to input our access key ID and secret access key, along with the **region name**. As for the **output format**, we can either leave it blank or specify a preferred format, such as JSON or YAML. By default, the format is JSON.

2. After successfully completing the previous step, we are ready to deploy the stack using the template and parameter file. Next, we will swiftly navigate to the designated folder where the necessary files are stored. Kindly refer to the following figure for the same:

```
anchalgupta@192 cft % ls
Template_S3.yaml        parameter.json
anchalgupta@192 cft %
```

Figure 8.6: Folder content

3. Let us proceed to execute the stack using the command we previously discussed:

Figure 8.7: Stack creation using CLI

In the preceding figure, upon executing the **create-stack** command, we promptly received an output response containing the **StackId**. This indicates that the stack execution process has commenced in the CloudFormation console's backend. To validate this, we will quickly navigate back to the CloudFormation console to verify the same.

4. The following figure showcases the **CloudFormation** console to validate the stack:

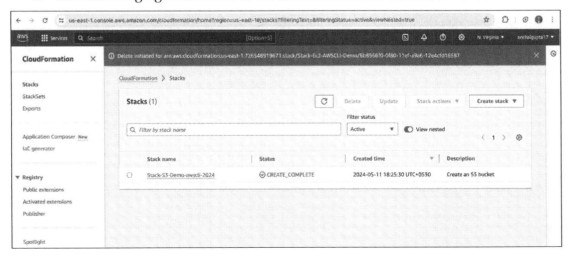

Figure 8.8: CloudFormation Console

We can observe that the stack name matches the one provided in the command line. This confirms successful validation for the stack creation process using the AWS CLI.

Virtual Private Cloud endpoint for CloudFormation service

A VPC endpoint for the CloudFormation service allows you to privately access CloudFormation APIs from within your VPC without needing an internet gateway, **Network Address Translation (NAT)** device, VPN connection, or AWS Direct Connect connection. This enhances security and reduces latency by keeping traffic between your VPC and CloudFormation service within the AWS network.

Configuration

To create a VPC endpoint for the CloudFormation service, you can perform the following steps:

1. **Access Management Console**: Navigate to the AWS Management Console and access the VPC dashboard.

2. **Create a VPC endpoint**:
   a. Click on Endpoints in the VPC dashboard.
   b. Choose Create Endpoint and select **AWS services** as the service category.
   c. In the service name, search for `com.amazonaws.<region>.cloudformation` (replace `<region>` with your AWS Region).
   d. Select the VPC where you want to create the endpoint. Refer to the following screenshots for more detail:

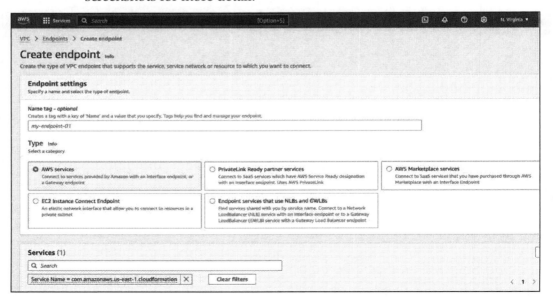

Figure 8.9: VPC endpoint setup (part 1)

To view further, refer to the following figure

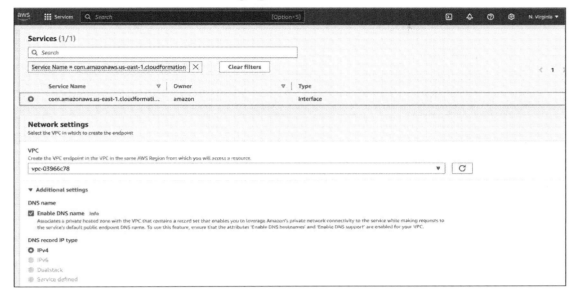

Figure 8.10: VPC endpoint setup (part 2)

3. **Security settings**:

   a. Configure security settings for the endpoint. You can choose to enable private DNS for the endpoint, allowing your instances to use custom DNS names to access the CloudFormation service.

   b. Define the policies that control access to the endpoint. You can attach IAM policies to control which users or roles can access the CloudFormation service through the endpoint. Refer to the following screenshot:

Figure 8.11: VPC endpoint setup (part 3)

An example of an endpoint policy for CloudFormation service is as follows:

```
1. {
2.    "Statement": [
3.      {
4.        "Action": "cloudformation:*",
5.        "Effect": "Allow",
6.        "Principal": "*",
7.        "Resource": "*"
8.      },
9.      {
10.        "Action": "cloudformation:DeleteStack",
11.        "Effect": "Deny",
12.        "Principal": "*",
13.        "Resource": "*"
14.      }
15.    ]
16. }
```

In the provided example, all users are restricted from deleting the stacks via the VPC endpoint while retaining full access to all other actions within the CloudFormation service.

Conclusion

In summary, this chapter has explored advanced AWS CloudFormation topics, including Fn::ImportValue, circular dependencies, custom resources, deploying stacks with AWS CLI, and implementing VPC endpoint for CloudFormation service. These discussions have equipped readers with the knowledge to handle complex deployments efficiently while ensuring security and modularity. In the next chapter, we will explore CloudFormation Designer, offering insights into visually designing and managing CloudFormation templates. You will learn how to visually design, edit, and visualize your infrastructure as code, streamlining the development and maintenance of complex AWS environments.

Multiple choice questions

1. **What is the purpose of the Fn::ImportValue function in AWS CloudFormation?**

   a. It imports values from S3 buckets into CloudFormation templates.

   b. It imports values from one stack into another stack.

   c. It imports values from IAM roles into CloudFormation templates.

   d. It imports values from DynamoDB tables into CloudFormation templates.

2. **What is a circular dependency in AWS CloudFormation?**

    a. It occurs when there is a circular reference between two resources or stacks.

    b. It happens when a stack is dependent on another stack in a linear sequence.

    c. It refers to the dependency between CloudFormation stacks and IAM policies.

    d. It is a dependency issue between CloudFormation templates and Lambda functions.

3. **Which AWS CLI command is used to deploy a CloudFormation stack?**

    a. aws cloudformation deploy-stack

    b. aws cloudformation create-stack

    c. aws deploy cloudformation stack

    d. aws cloudformation deploy

4. **How does using a VPC endpoint for the CloudFormation service affect stack creation time?**

    a. It accelerates stack creation by bypassing the public internet.

    b. It increases stack creation time due to additional VPC routing.

    c. It has no impact on stack creation time.

    d. It depends on the size and complexity of the stack.

Answers

1. b

2. a

3. b

4. a

Join our book's Discord space

Join the book's Discord Workspace for Latest updates, Offers, Tech happenings around the world, New Release and Sessions with the Authors:

https://discord.bpbonline.com

CHAPTER 9

Harnessing the Power of CloudFormation Designer

Introduction

This chapter explores the essential aspects of AWS CloudFormation Designer, a visual tool that simplifies the creation and management of AWS CloudFormation templates. We will start with an overview to understand the purpose and significance of AWS CloudFormation Designer. As we explore working with stacks, we will cover the core features of stack management, from creation to deletion, all within the intuitive Designer interface.

Next, we will understand how visual modeling helps to visually represent AWS resources, their connections, and dependencies, providing a more intuitive understanding of your infrastructure code. The chapter also guides us through the practical aspects of importing and exporting templates, facilitating seamless integration with existing projects. Additionally, we will gain insights into best practices for effective template design and maintenance.

By the end of this chapter, you will have a solid foundation in AWS CloudFormation Designer, enabling you to create, manage, and optimize templates with ease and efficiency. This knowledge empowers you to harness the power of visual modeling for your infrastructure as code projects.

Structure

The chapter covers the following topics:

- Introduction to CloudFormation Designer
- Working with stacks
- Visual modelling
- Template import and export
- Best practices

Objectives

The objective of this chapter is to equip you with a comprehensive understanding of AWS CloudFormation Designer, a powerful visual tool for creating and managing AWS CloudFormation templates. By the end of this chapter, you will understand the purpose and significance of AWS CloudFormation Designer, master the core features of stack management within the Designer interface, and learn to visually model AWS resources, their connections, and dependencies. Additionally, you will gain practical skills in importing and exporting templates for seamless project integration and acquire best practices for effective template design and maintenance. This foundation will enable you to efficiently create, manage, and optimize AWS CloudFormation templates, leveraging visual modeling to enhance your infrastructure as code projects.

Introduction to CloudFormation Designer

AWS CloudFormation Designer is a powerful visual tool within the AWS CloudFormation service, designed to simplify the process of creating and managing AWS CloudFormation templates. This tool provides a user friendly, drag and drop interface that allows you to visually construct and modify your cloud infrastructure templates, making it easier to conceptualize and manage complex AWS environments.

Purpose and significance

The primary purpose of CloudFormation Designer is to offer an intuitive and visual approach to defining AWS infrastructure as code. Unlike traditional methods that require you to write JSON or YAML templates manually, CloudFormation Designer provides a graphical interface where you can visually drag and drop AWS resources onto a canvas. This not only speeds up the process of template creation but also reduces the likelihood of errors that can occur with manual coding. The visual representation helps you better understand the relationships and dependencies between various AWS resources, ensuring that your infrastructure is designed correctly and efficiently from the outset.

Key features and benefits

Let us take a look at some of the key features and benefits of this tool:

- **Visual representation**: CloudFormation Designer allows you to see a visual representation of your AWS resources and their relationships. This visual overview helps in comprehending the architecture at a glance, which is particularly beneficial for complex environments.

- **Drag and drop interface**: The intuitive drag and drop interface simplifies the process of adding and configuring AWS resources. You can easily select resources from the side panel and place them onto the design canvas, adjusting configurations through user friendly property dialogs.

- **Automatic dependency handling**: CloudFormation Designer automatically manages the dependencies between resources. When you add resources that depend on each other, the tool ensures that these dependencies are correctly defined in the template, saving you from manually coding dependency relationships.

- **Template editing**: You can seamlessly switch between the visual interface and the template editor. This allows you to make direct modifications to the underlying JSON or YAML code if needed, providing flexibility for advanced users who prefer to fine-tune their templates manually.

- **Resource grouping**: The tool supports resource grouping, which helps in organizing related resources together. This makes it easier to manage and navigate large templates by logically grouping components, enhancing clarity and maintainability.

- **Real-time validation**: CloudFormation Designer includes real-time validation features that check for common template errors as you build your infrastructure. This proactive error detection helps prevent issues during stack creation and deployment.

Visual interface

To navigate to the CloudFormation Designer page, perform the following steps:

1. Search for it in the search box on the AWS console page. A graphical representation of this process is shown in the following figure:

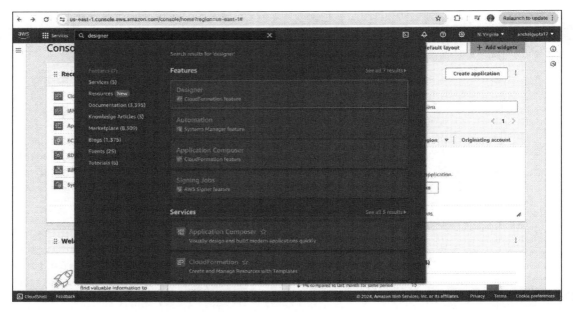

Figure 9.1: CloudFormation Designer page

After clicking on the **Designer** option, it will take us to the console for the designer.

2. After clicking on the **Designer** option, you will be taken to the Designer console. An example representation for the same is as follows:

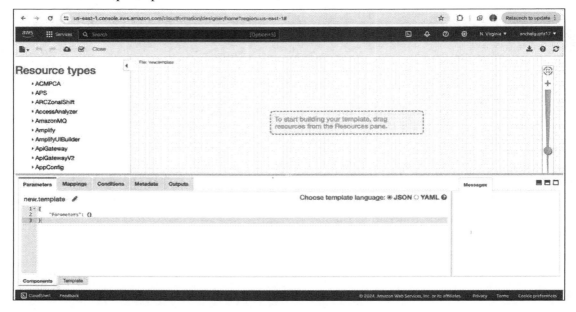

Figure 9.2: CloudFormation Designer console page

The console page of the CloudFormation Designer includes several options and tabs that help you work with your CloudFormation templates more efficiently. Here is an overview of the different options and tabs available:

- **Navigation pane**: On the left side of the console, you will find the navigation pane, which includes the **Resource types**. This tab lists all the AWS resource types you can include in your template. You can drag and drop these resources into the design canvas to add them to your template.

- **Design canvas**: The main area of the console is the design canvas. This is where you visually arrange and connect resources. Key features include the following:

  o **Drag and drop interface**: Easily add resources to your template by dragging them from the **Resource types** tab onto the canvas.

  o **Connect resources**: Draw lines between resources to define relationships (for example, dependencies).

  o **Zoom and pan controls**: Adjust your view of the canvas for easier navigation and detailed design work.

- **Properties pane**: When you select a resource on the design canvas, the **Properties** pane appears on the console. This pane allows you to configure the properties of the selected resource. It includes the following:

  o **Properties**: Properties specific to the type of resource selected. For example, an EC2 instance will have different configurable properties compared to an S3 bucket.

  o **Metadata**: Option to add Metadata to your resources.

  o **Deletion policy**: Specifies the actions to take on a resource when its stack is Deleted, such as retaining, deleting, or creating a snapshot of the resource.

  o **DependsOn**: Specifies that the creation or deletion of a resource follows another resource's creation or deletion.

  o **Condition**: It allows you to define Conditions that determine whether certain resources are created or configured in a stack.

A sample figure of this section for one of the selected resource type is as follows:

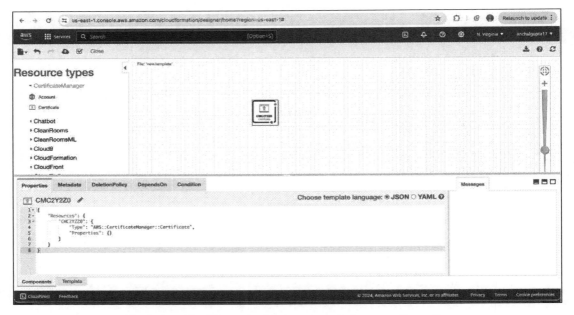

Figure 9.3: CloudFormation Designer console for properties section

- **Template tab**: Located below the design canvas, this tab displays the JSON or YAML code for the template you are working on. Kindly refer to the following figure:

Figure 9.4: Template section

- **Parameters, Mappings, and Outputs tab**: Next to the template tab, you will find additional tabs that help in defining other aspects of your CloudFormation template:

    o **Parameters**: Define input Parameters that can be passed to the template at runtime. These Parameters can be used to customize the stack without changing the template.

    o **Mappings**: Define fixed values can be used to look up for a given input, similar to a table lookup.

    o **Outputs**: Specify the Outputs of the CloudFormation stack. Outputs can include resource attributes that might be needed after the stack is created, such as the endpoint of an Amazon RDS database.

- **Toolbar**: Above the design canvas, the toolbar provides various options, like:

    o **File menu**: Options to create a new template, open an existing template, save the current template, and import resources from existing AWS resources.

    o **Undo/redo**: Easily revert or reapply changes.

    o **Actions**: Options to validate the template, generate diagrams, and export the template.

Working with stacks

When working with stacks in AWS CloudFormation Designer, you leverage a combination of visual tools and detailed configuration options to efficiently design, deploy, and manage your AWS resources. Here is how you can effectively work with stacks in the CloudFormation Designer.

Creating a stack

The necessary steps to create a stack are as follows:

- **Designing the template**:

    o **Drag and drop interface**: Start by dragging AWS resource types from the **Resource types** tab onto the design canvas. Arrange and connect these resources to reflect the architecture of your application.

    o **Configuring resources**: Use the **Properties** pane to set up resource specific properties, such as instance types for EC2 instances or bucket policies for S3 buckets.

- **Defining Parameters and Conditions**:

  o **Parameters tab**: Define input Parameters to allow customization of stack creation. For instance, you might use Parameters to specify different instance types or regions.

  o **Conditions tab**: Set up Conditions to control the creation of resources based on Parameter values or other criteria, ensuring that your stack is flexible and adaptable to different environments.

- **Specifying resource dependencies**:

  o **DependsOn attribute**: Use the `DependsOn` attribute to specify dependencies between resources. This ensures that resources are created or Deleted in the correct order, avoiding potential issues during stack operations.

Deploying a stack

The necessary steps for deploying a stack are as follows:

- **Validation**:

  o **Validate template**: Before deploying, use the validation feature to check your template for syntax errors and logical issues. This step helps prevent deployment failures due to template errors.

- **Creating and managing the stack**:

  o **Creating stack**: After validation, deploy your template by creating a new stack. During stack creation, you can specify Parameter values and monitor the progress through the AWS Management Console.

  o **Updating stack**: To make changes to your deployed infrastructure, update the stack with a modified template. CloudFormation will handle the updates while maintaining the integrity of your existing resources.

Managing stack lifecycle

Managing the lifecycle of a CloudFormation stack is crucial for ensuring stability, resource optimization, and operational efficiency. Throughout the lifecycle, from stack creation to deletion, there are several key aspects that must be carefully managed to maintain control over resources and to avoid unintended consequences. In this section, we will explore how to set appropriate deletion policies, define stack Outputs for better visibility, and leverage monitoring and troubleshooting tools to effectively manage and resolve issues during the stack's lifecycle. Let us explore each of them:

- **Deletion policy**:

  o **Setting deletion policies**: For each resource, define a DeletionPolicy to control what happens when the stack is Deleted. Options include retaining the resource, deleting it, or taking a snapshot. This policy ensures that critical data is not lost inadvertently.

- **Outputs**:

  o **Defining Outputs**: Use the Outputs tab to specify stack Outputs. Outputs can include important information, such as resource IDs or endpoints, which can be useful for integration with other systems or for providing feedback to users.

- **Monitoring and troubleshooting**:

  o **Stack events and logs**: Monitor stack events and logs to troubleshoot issues during stack creation, update, or deletion. CloudFormation provides detailed logs that can help identify and resolve problems quickly.

By utilizing the CloudFormation Designer's visual interface, along with its robust configuration and management options, you can efficiently create, deploy, and manage your AWS stacks, ensuring a streamlined and error free infrastructure setup.

Visual modelling

Let us explore the use of CloudFormation Designer to efficiently design and deploy a CloudFormation stack using an alternative approach. We will demonstrate this concept with an example of deploying an EC2 instance within a VPC, explained step-by-step:

1. From the **Resource types** tab, drag the **VPC** resource onto the design canvas.

2. Select the VPC resource on the canvas.

3. In the **Properties** pane, rename the VPC to **MyVPC**. After renaming, click the refresh icon in the top-right section of the page to update the canvas with the new name. The visual representation for your reference, is as follows:

Before refresh:

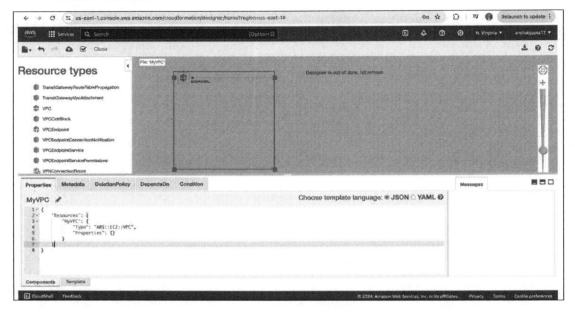

Figure 9.5: VPC resource name change

After refresh:

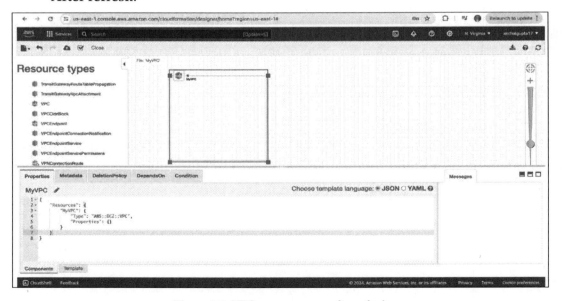

Figure 9.6: VPC resource name after refresh

4. Next, let us add a subnet to the previously defined VPC. Select the **Subnet** resource type and drag it onto the canvas, placing it within the VPC block:

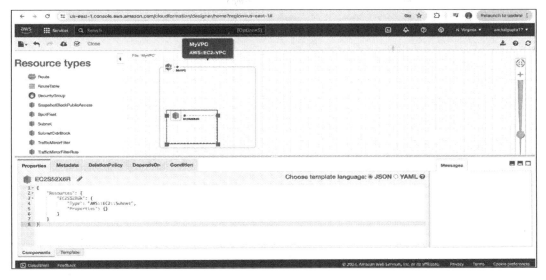

Figure 9.7: Subnet declaration

5. Just like with the VPC, select the Subnet block and rename it to **MySubnet** in the **Properties** section. Then, click the refresh button to update the canvas with the new name:

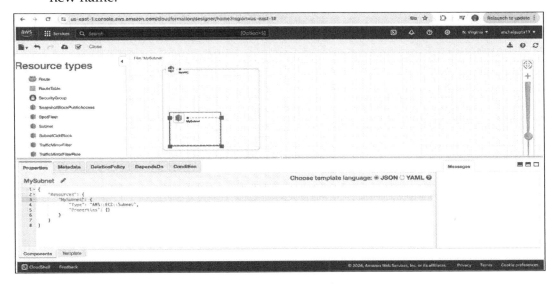

Figure 9.8: Subnet name change

6. Now, select the EC2 instance and drag it onto the canvas within the Subnet block. Like with the VPC and Subnet, rename the EC2 instance to **MyEC2** in the **Properties** section and refresh the page to see the updated name. Refer to the following figure for reference:

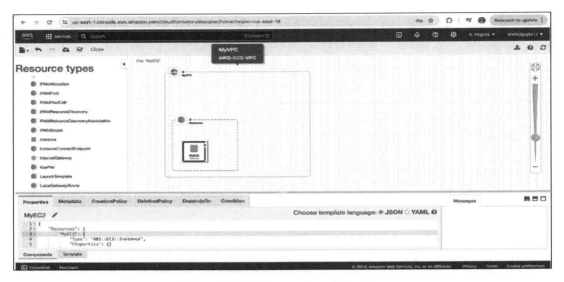

Figure 9.9: EC2 resource type declaration

7. Now, we will add a **SecurityGroup** in the similar fashion. We will drag it and place it within the VPC block. We will name it as **MySG**:

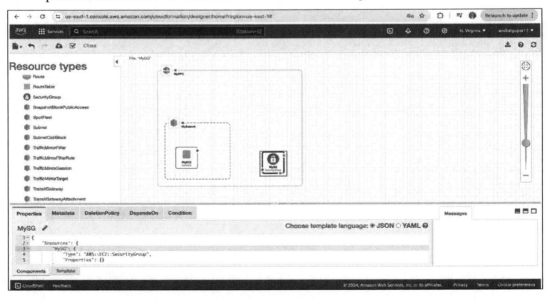

Figure 9.10: SecurityGroup declaration

8. Next, add a routing table within the VPC block. Inside this routing table, add a route. Rename both resources to **MyRoutingTable** and **MyRoute**, respectively in the **Properties** section. Then, click the refresh button to update the canvas with the new names. Refer to the following figure for further clarification:

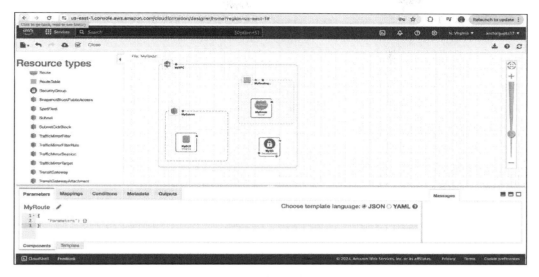

Figure 9.11: Routing table and Route declaration

9.   Next, include an **InternetGateway** to enable communication between the resources within the VPC and the internet. Drag the **InternetGateway** resource onto the canvas, place it outside the VPC block, and rename it to **MyIG**. Then, establish a connection between the **InternetGateway** and the VPC, and between the route and the **InternetGateway** by dragging the connection arrows, which signify the DependsOn attribute, as shown in the following figure. Additionally, ensure connectivity between other components, such as between EC2 and route, and between the routing table and subnet, as depicted in the following figure:

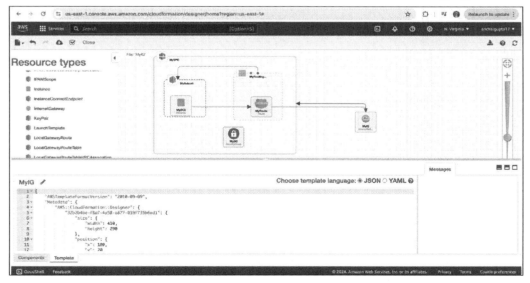

Figure 9.12: Final setup

After completing the setup on the canvas, navigate to the **Template** section. Here, you will find that the template has been automatically generated based on the integrations established between the various resources on the canvas.

> **Note: The setup described is not fully complete; however, it has generated a template skeleton that can be further modified and edited as needed. This approach saves effort by providing a starting point, eliminating the need to write a complete template from scratch.**

Template import and export

AWS CloudFormation Designer provides powerful features for creating, visualizing, and managing AWS CloudFormation templates. Among these features, template import and export functionalities stand out as essential tools for efficient template management. This section will detail how to import and export templates within CloudFormation Designer.

Importing templates

Importing templates into CloudFormation Designer allows users to bring pre-existing templates into the visual canvas for further modification and visualization. This is particularly useful for users who prefer to start with a template skeleton or modify templates generated outside of the Designer. The following steps outline the process:

1. **Access CloudFormation Designer**: Navigate to the AWS Management Console, select the CloudFormation service, and open CloudFormation Designer.

2. **Import a template**:

   a. Click on the template into the Designer canvas. Refer to the following screenshot:

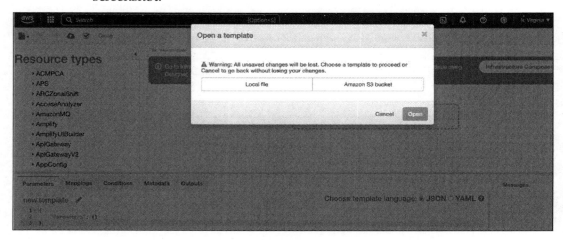

Figure 9.13: Importing Template

3. **Review and edit**: Once the template is imported, it will appear on the canvas with all defined resources and relationships. You can now use the Designer's drag and drop interface to modify resources, adjust configurations, and visualize dependencies.

Exporting templates

Exporting templates from CloudFormation Designer allows users to save their work and share templates with others or use them in different AWS environments. This ensures that the designs created in the Designer can be easily utilized in automated deployments. The following steps explain how to export the templates:

1. **Access CloudFormation Designer**: Open the CloudFormation service from the AWS Management Console and launch CloudFormation Designer.

2. **Design or modify a template**: Create or modify your infrastructure design on the canvas using CloudFormation Designer's tools.

3. **Export the template**:

   a. Click on the "File" menu in the CloudFormation Designer interface.

   b. Select "Save As" to bring up the export dialog.

   c. Choose the format for your template (JSON or YAML) based on your preference or organizational standards.

   d. Specify the location to save the file:

   e. Local File: Click "Download" to save the file directly to your computer.

   f. S3 Bucket: Enter the destination S3 bucket URL to upload the template file directly to your specified S3 bucket.

   g. Click "Save" to complete the export process.

4. **Use the exported template**: The exported template can now be used in AWS CloudFormation to create or update stacks. You can also share this template with team members or incorporate it into version control systems for collaborative development.

Benefits of template import and export

Let us have explore some benefits of template's import and export feature:

- **Efficiency**: Quickly modify and enhance existing templates without starting from scratch.

- **Collaboration**: Share templates easily with team members and integrate them into collaborative workflows.

- **Visualization**: Use the Designer's visual interface to better understand and optimize template configurations and resource relationships.

- **Flexibility**: Seamlessly switch between visual design and code-based modifications, leveraging the strengths of both approaches.

By utilizing the import and export features of AWS CloudFormation Designer, users can streamline their IaC processes, ensuring a more efficient and collaborative approach to managing AWS resources.

Best practices

Let us now discuss some of the best practices to ensure that you make the most of this tool:

- **Plan your architecture beforehand**: Determine what AWS resources (for example, EC2 instances, S3 buckets, RDS databases) you need. Map out how these resources will interact and depend on each other.

- **Sketch a rough design**: Before diving into CloudFormation Designer, create rough sketches or diagrams to visualize your architecture. Tools like *Lucidchart* or *draw.io* can be helpful. Have a list of all resources with their properties and configurations ready.

- **Optimize the design**: Keep the design canvas uncluttered by organizing resources and avoiding overlapping connections. Maintain a consistent layout and alignment for better readability and understanding.

- **Use drag and drop functionality**: Use the drag-and-drop feature to quickly add and position resources on the design canvas.

- **Use built-in validation**: Regularly use the built-in validation feature to check for errors and ensure your template meets CloudFormation requirements.

- **Collaborate with team members**: Share the design with team members for collaboration and feedback.

- **Maintain security best practices**: Ensure resources have appropriate IAM policies attached, following the principle of least privilege.

Conclusion

In summary, this chapter covered the AWS CloudFormation Designer, including its introduction, working with stacks, visual modeling, and template import and export. We also discussed best practices for optimizing efficiency and security. These insights equip you to design, edit, and visualize your infrastructure effectively. In the next chapter, we will explore advanced stack management topics such as stack protection, CloudFormation drift, drift detection and remediation, rollback triggers, and stack notifications, providing you with essential tools for efficient stack management and security.

Multiple choice questions

1. **What is CloudFormation Designer primarily used for?**

    a. Managing IAM policies

    b. Deploying and managing IaC

    c. Analyzing network traffic

    d. Monitoring server performance

2. **How does CloudFormation Designer facilitate visual modeling of AWS resources?**

    a. By providing a drag and drop interface to design and modify templates.

    b. By sending email notifications for resource changes.

    c. By offering real-time chat support for troubleshooting.

    d. By automatically generating code snippets based on user inputs.

3. **What is the benefit of importing and exporting templates in CloudFormation Designer?**

    a. It allows collaboration between multiple teams using different tools.

    b. It automatically optimizes resource allocation for cost savings.

    c. It triggers automated security scans on the templates.

    d. It generates graphical reports of resource usage.

4. **In the CloudFormation Designer, what is the significance of visual modeling in terms of infrastructure management?**

    a. It helps in identifying potential security vulnerabilities

    b. It allows for intuitive visualization of resource dependencies and relationships

    c. It provides suggestions for cost reduction strategies

    d. It automatically optimizes resource allocation based on usage patterns.

Answers

1. a
2. a
3. a
4. b

Join our book's Discord space

Join the book's Discord Workspace for Latest updates, Offers, Tech happenings around the world, New Release and Sessions with the Authors:

https://discord.bpbonline.com

Section III
Stack Management

CHAPTER 10

Understanding Stacks and Management

Introduction

This chapter provides a comprehensive exploration of AWS CloudFormation stacks and their efficient management. We will gain an in-depth understanding of stack management, starting with a comprehensive overview of the concepts and methodologies involved. We will learn how to protect our stacks and safeguard them from unintended changes. We will discover the power of CloudFormation drift and its role in detecting configuration differences. We will dive into practical strategies for drift detection and remediation to ensure our stacks remain in their desired states. Rollback triggers, an essential aspect of stack management, are also covered, allowing us to define precise Conditions for stack rollback, enhancing the resilience and reliability of our infrastructure. We will also learn how to send notifications for our CloudFormation stacks. By the end of this chapter, we will be well equipped to manage AWS CloudFormation stacks effectively and confidently.

Structure

The chapter covers the following topics:

- Introduction to stacks management
- Protecting stacks
- CloudFormation drift
- Detecting and remediating drift

- Rollback triggers
- CloudFormation stack notification

Objectives

The objective of this chapter is to equip you with a comprehensive understanding of AWS CloudFormation stack management. By the end of this chapter, you will understand the importance of protecting your stacks from unintended changes, master the use of CloudFormation drift for detecting configuration differences, and learn practical strategies for drift detection and remediation to maintain stack integrity. Additionally, you will gain skills in configuring rollback triggers to enhance infrastructure resilience and reliability, as well as setting up notifications for your CloudFormation stacks. This foundation will enable you to efficiently manage AWS CloudFormation stacks with confidence and precision.

Introduction to stacks management

Managing AWS CloudFormation stacks effectively is crucial for maintaining a well-structured and reliable cloud infrastructure. A CloudFormation stack is a collection of AWS resources that can be managed as a single unit, defined, and provisioned through CloudFormation templates. This section will explore the essential aspects of stack management, focusing on best practices and strategies to ensure the integrity and resilience of your infrastructure.

Effective stack management is essential for several reasons. They are as follows:

- **Consistency and reproducibility**: Proper stack management ensures that resources are consistently provisioned according to predefined configurations, reducing the risk of human error and maintaining uniformity across deployments.

- **Automation and efficiency**: Automating stack operations minimizes manual intervention, saving time and effort. This is particularly beneficial in large scale environments where managing resources individually would be impractical.

- **Change management and version control**: CloudFormation templates allow for version control, enabling you to track and manage infrastructure changes over time. This facilitates better auditing and rollback capabilities when needed.

Key concepts in stack management

Let us now explore some key concepts essential for effective stack management:

- **Stack creation**: The process begins with defining a new stack using a CloudFormation template. This template includes the specifications for all AWS resources that the stack will provision.

- **Stack updates**: As infrastructure needs evolve, updates to the stack may be necessary. This involves modifying the CloudFormation template and applying changes, with CloudFormation determining and executing the necessary resource modifications.

- **Stack deletion**: When a stack is no longer required, it can be Deleted, which removes all associated resources as defined in the template. This process helps in managing costs and reducing unused resources.

- **Stack protection**: To safeguard stacks from unintended changes, mechanisms such as stack policies and termination protection can be employed. These measures help prevent accidental updates or deletions, ensuring resource stability.

- **Drift detection and remediation**: Drift detection identifies any changes made to stack resources outside of CloudFormation, ensuring that the actual configuration matches the defined template. Remediation involves correcting any detected drift to align resources with their desired states.

- **Rollback triggers**: Rollback triggers define specific Conditions under which a stack should revert to its previous state during an update. This enhances the resilience and reliability of the infrastructure by preventing failed updates from causing disruptions.

Principal strategies for stack management

To effectively manage AWS CloudFormation stacks, it is important to implement strategies that streamline operations and ensure consistency. These strategies help automate processes, maintain version control, and safeguard your infrastructure against unintended changes. Some key strategies to consider are:

- **Use version control for templates**: Storing CloudFormation templates in a version control system (for example, Git) allows for tracking changes and managing different infrastructure versions, ensuring consistent deployments.

- **Automate stack operations**: Leveraging automation tools and scripts to create, update, and Delete stacks enhances consistency and reduces the potential for manual errors, streamlining the management process.

- **Regularly check for drift**: Implementing regular drift detection checks ensures that stacks remain in their intended state. Automating drift detection can further streamline this process and promptly identify discrepancies.

- **Implement stack policies**: Defining and applying stack policies helps control who can update or Delete stacks and what types of changes are permitted, adding an extra layer of security and control.

- **Monitor and notify**: Setting up monitoring and notification systems keeps track of stack changes and issues, ensuring that any problems or updates are immediately flagged for attention.

Protecting stacks

Protecting your AWS CloudFormation stacks is crucial to ensure the stability and integrity of your infrastructure. Here are several methods to safeguard your stacks from unintended changes and deletions:

- **Stack policies**: Stack policies define the actions that are allowed or denied on specific resources during stack updates. By implementing stack policies, you can restrict certain operations, such as preventing the update or deletion of critical resources. This helps in maintaining the desired state of your stack and avoiding accidental changes. Let us understand this concept with the help of an example:

  Example: Suppose you have a stack that manages a critical database and associated resources. By applying a stack policy, you can prevent updates or deletions to the database resource, ensuring that it remains untouched during stack updates. For instance, you can set a policy that denies all update actions to the database resource:

```
1.  {
2.    "Statement": [
3.      {
4.        "Effect": "Deny",
5.        "Action": "Update:*",
6.        "Principal": "*",
7.        "Resource": "LogicalResourceId/DatabaseResource"
8.      }
9.    ]
10. }
```

- **Termination protection**: Enabling termination protection for a stack prevents it from being accidentally Deleted. When termination protection is enabled, any attempt to Delete the stack will fail unless the protection is explicitly disabled. This is especially useful for critical stacks that must not be removed under any circumstances. Let us explore an example to understand this:

  Example: You have a stack managing your production environment, and you want to prevent accidental deletion. By enabling termination protection, you ensure that any Delete request will fail unless termination protection is disabled first. This setting can be configured when creating or updating the stack:

```
1.  aws cloudformation update-termination-protection --stack-
    name MyProductionStack --enable-termination-protection
```

- **IAM policies and roles**: Utilize AWS IAM policies and roles to control who can create, update, or Delete stacks. By granting the least privilege necessary for each user or role, you minimize the risk of unauthorized changes to your stacks. Let us explore an example to understand this:

  Example: You want to restrict update and Delete permissions for a development team while allowing them to create new stacks. By setting up specific IAM policies, you can grant the necessary permissions. For instance, an IAM policy might allow stack creation but deny update and Delete actions:

```
1. {
2.    "Version": "2012-10-17",
3.    "Statement": [
4.      {
5.        "Effect": "Allow",
6.        "Action": [
7.          "cloudformation:CreateStack"
8.        ],
9.        "Resource": "*"
10.     },
11.     {
12.       "Effect": "Deny",
13.       "Action": [
14.         "cloudformation:UpdateStack",
15.         "cloudformation:DeleteStack"
16.       ],
17.       "Resource": "*"
18.     }
19.   ]
20. }
```

- **Change sets**: Before applying updates to a stack, create a Change set to preview the changes. A Change set shows the proposed modifications to your stack, allowing you to review and confirm that the changes are as expected before executing them. This reduces the risk of unintended updates. We will understand this concept in detail in the upcoming chapter.

- **Stack tags**: Use tags to categorize and identify stacks based on their purpose, environment, or other criteria. Tags can help in organizing and managing stacks, as well as applying policies or automation scripts selectively based on tag values. Let us explore an example to understand the same:

  Example: You have several stacks across different environments (for example, development, testing, production) and want to apply specific policies or automation scripts based on the environment. By tagging stacks with an **Environment** key, you can organize and manage them effectively. For example, tagging a stack during creation:

```
1.  aws cloudformation create-stack --stack-
    name MyDevStack --template-body file://template.
    json --tags Key=Environment,Value=Development
```

By implementing these protective measures, you can ensure that your CloudFormation stacks remain secure and stable, reducing the risk of accidental or unauthorized modifications.

CloudFormation drift

CloudFormation drift refers to the state in which the actual configuration of resources in your AWS environment deviates from the expected configuration defined in your CloudFormation templates. This deviation can occur due to manual changes made to resources outside of CloudFormation changes made directly to resources that are managed by CloudFormation, or even due to bugs in your templates. Managing drift is crucial for ensuring the consistency, reliability, and security of your AWS infrastructure.

Drift can lead to significant issues if left unchecked. For instance, unexpected changes might introduce security vulnerabilities, cause application downtime, or lead to resource misconfigurations that can result in increased costs or degraded performance. Identifying and addressing drift promptly is essential to maintain the intended state of your infrastructure. To manage drift effectively, it is important to establish robust governance practices. This includes implementing strict policies around who can make changes to your infrastructure and how those changes should be made. Using AWS IAM to control access and enforce least privilege principles can help minimize unauthorized changes that could lead to drift.

Types of drift

Effective management of drift begins with understanding the following two main types:

- **Resource drift**: Resource drift happens when individual resources within an AWS CloudFormation stack deviate from their defined configurations in the template. This usually results from manual changes made directly to the resources, bypassing CloudFormation. For instance, if the template specifies a particular Amazon RDS instance type, an IAM role policy, or an Amazon **Simple Queue Service** (**SQS**) queue attribute, and an administrator manually alters any of these settings, resource drift occurs. Identifying resource drift is essential because it can introduce inconsistencies and misconfigurations that may jeopardize the operational integrity and security of your AWS infrastructure. Detecting and addressing resource drift ensures that each resource remains in sync with the expected state defined in the CloudFormation template.

- **Stack drift**: Stack drift refers to changes that impact the entire AWS CloudFormation stack, including modifications to stack-wide settings like Parameter values, tags, or alterations to multiple resources within the stack. For example, if a stack is set up to deploy instances within a specific Amazon VPC, and changes are made to that VPC outside of CloudFormation, stack drift occurs. Understanding and resolving stack drift is crucial for maintaining the overall consistency of your infrastructure, as these changes can affect several resources.

Detecting and remediating drift

CloudFormation provides a drift detection feature that compares the current state of your stack resources with the state defined in the CloudFormation template. This can be done either through the AWS Management Console, AWS CLI, or programmatically using AWS **software development kit (SDK)**. When you initiate a drift detection, CloudFormation compares the resource configuration properties, such as attribute values, tags, and more, to identify any variances. To determine if your stack has been drifted, perform the following actions:

Note: We will perform the steps on the AWS CloudFormation console.

1. Log in to the AWS CloudFormation Management Console.
2. **Select the stack**: Navigate to the stack you wish to examine.
3. **Initiate drift detection**:
   a. Click on the Stack Actions dropdown menu from the dashboard.
   b. Select Detect Drift from the options.
4. **Confirm drift detection**:
   a. In the Detect Drift dialog box, click Yes, detect to start the drift detection process.
5. **Review drift status**:
   a. After the detection process completes, check the Drift Status and Last drift check time attribute. These fields are listed in the Overview section of the Stack info pane of the stack details page.
   b. The drift detection operation may take several minutes, depending on the number of resources included in the stack. You can only run a single drift detection operation on a given stack at the same time. CloudFormation continues the drift detection operation even after you dismiss the information bar.
   c. If the status is DRIFTED, it indicates that the stack configuration has been altered outside of CloudFormation. Review the drift detection results for

the stack and its resources. With your stack selected, from the Stack actions menu, select View drift results.

d. CloudFormation lists the overall drift status of the stack, in addition to the last time drift detection was initiated on the stack or any of its individual resources. A stack is considered to have drifted if one or more of its resources have drifted.

e. In the Resource drift status section, CloudFormation lists each stack resource, its drift status, and the last time drift detection was initiated on the resource. The logical ID and physical ID of each resource is displayed to help you identify them. In addition, for resources with a status of MODIFIED, CloudFormation displays resource drift details. You can sort the resources based on their drift status using the Drift status column.

6. **Close the dialog**: Click Close to return to the AWS console.

Remediation

Now let us have a look at the remediation steps that will be executed once drift is detected in our stack:

1. Identify the resources and properties that have drifted from the expected configuration. Click on the Drift status column of the stack to view the detailed report of the drifted resource.

2. Determine whether the detected drift needs to be remediated by updating the CloudFormation template, reverting the manual changes, or making other necessary adjustments.

3. Let us assume that updating the CloudFormation template can remediate the drift in our scenario. In this case:

    a. Click on Stack actions and select Update stack.

    b. Choose the appropriate update method. Modify the existing template or use a new template.

    c. Make the necessary changes to align the stack configuration with the desired state.

4. Follow the guided steps to review and apply the changes. Confirm the update by clicking Update stack to apply the remediation actions.

5. Now, we will verify the remediation. After the update completes, repeat the Detect Drift process to ensure that the drift status is now IN_SYNC.

6. If any drift remains, repeat the necessary remediation steps until the stack is fully aligned.

7. Document the changes made during remediation for future reference and audit purposes.

By following these steps, you can effectively remediate drift and ensure your AWS CloudFormation stacks stay consistent with their defined configurations. In the next section, we will illustrate this process with a detailed example.

Example

In this section, we will walk through a detailed example of setting up a CloudFormation stack, inducing drift, and then remediating it. This will help you understand the entire process from start to finish.

1. **Setting up the CloudFormation stack**:

    a. Log in to the AWS Management Console.

    b. **Navigate to CloudFormation**: In the AWS Management Console, navigate to the CloudFormation service.

    c. Create a New Stack using the following simple template.

    ```
    o   AWSTemplateFormatVersion: '2010-09-09'
    o   Resources:
    o     MyS3Bucket:
    o       Type: AWS::S3::Bucket
    o       Properties:
    o         VersioningConfiguration:
    o           Status: Suspended
    ```

    After the stack is created, you can check its status on the CloudFormation console. The figure for the same is as follows:

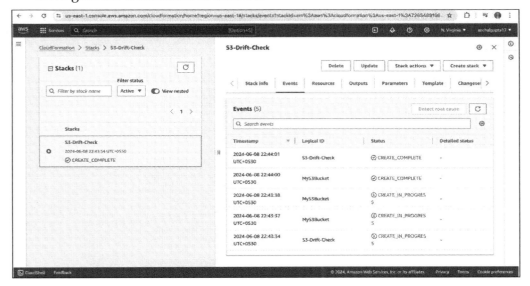

Figure 10.1: S3 stack setup

2. **Inducing drift**:

a. We will try to induce drift manually for the above S3 bucket. Locate the S3 bucket created by CloudFormation.

i. Select the bucket and Delete it manually.

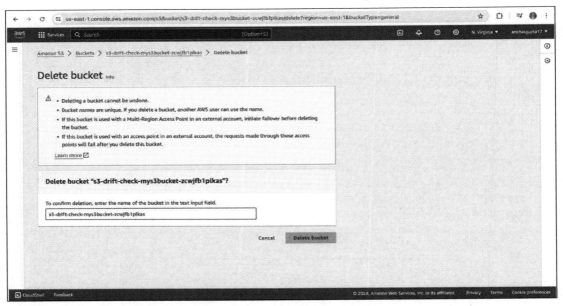

Figure 10.2: S3 bucket deletion

3. **Detecting drift**:

a. Now, once the previously mentioned change is done, we will go back to the CloudFormation console.

b. Select the Stack-S3 stack.

c. Click on **Stack actions** and select the Detect drift. The figure showcasing the console once drift detection is triggered is as follows:

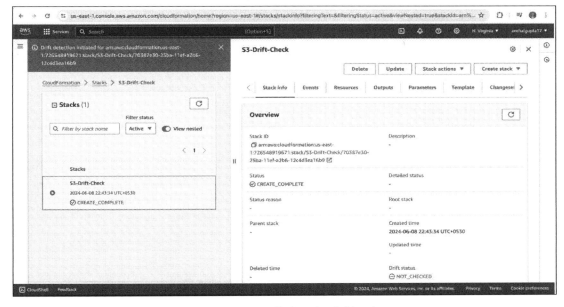

Figure 10.3: Drift detection initiated

Once the process completes check the **Drift status**. It should indicate DRIFTED for **MyS3Bucket**, showing that the bucket is missing. Kindly refer to following figure:

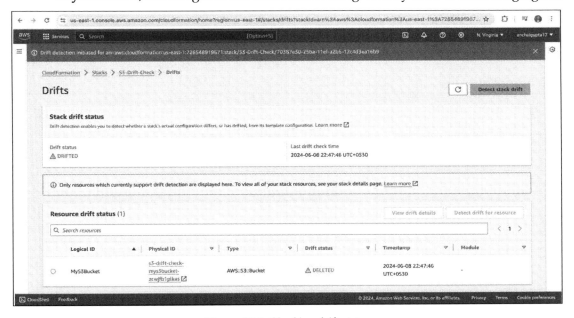

Figure 10.4: Checking drift status

4. **Remediation**:

   a. **CloudFormation drift handling**: CloudFormation can revert drift in certain scenarios. For instance, if a resource is missing, it will be recreated. However, if a property of a resource has been modified, CloudFormation might not detect the change, and it will not be automatically corrected.

   b. **Manual remediation**: If CloudFormation cannot automatically fix the detected drift, you can use the provided information to manually revert the unexpected changes.

In our scenario, we have Deleted the resource, and we will remediate this using the CloudFormation stack update process. To do this, we will modify the template and change the logical ID of the S3 bucket. Currently, the ID is **MyS3Bucket**. We will change it to **MyS3BucketNew**. This modification will prompt CloudFormation to create the necessary changeset and proceed with the bucket creation upon executing the update. This approach will effectively remediate the issue in our environment. The sample structure of the updated template is as follows:

```
o   AWSTemplateFormatVersion: '2010-09-09'
o   Resources:
o     MyS3BucketNew:
o       Type: 'AWS::S3::Bucket'
o       Properties:
o         VersioningConfiguration:
o           Status: Suspended
```

We will now initiate the stack update operation using the template previously provided. Once the stack update is complete, a new S3 bucket will be created, thereby performing the remediation. Please refer to the following figure for details:

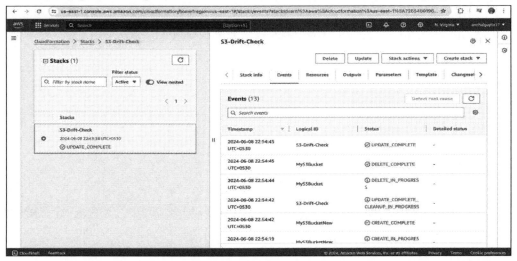

Figure 10.5: Stack update triggered

The following figure shows the S3 bucket set up details:

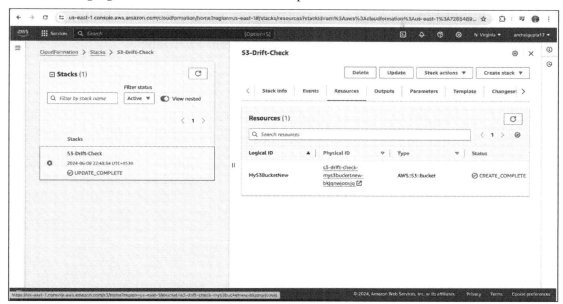

Figure 10.6*: New S3 bucket setup*

Rollback triggers

Rollback triggers in AWS CloudFormation provide a mechanism to monitor and automatically roll back deployments if specific alarms are breached during stack creation or update operations. They enhance the reliability and resilience of your infrastructure by ensuring that changes only proceed if the environment remains healthy. By linking to CloudWatch alarms, they offer proactive monitoring and swift recovery from potential issues, thereby minimizing the risk of deploying unstable configurations and reducing manual intervention. This automated rollback process reinforces system stability, making deployments more predictable and robust.

Key concepts

Let us have a look at the key concepts related to rollback triggers.

- **Purpose**: Rollback triggers are designed to help maintain system stability during stack operations by monitoring specified AWS CloudWatch alarms. If an alarm reaches an ALARM state during stack creation or update, CloudFormation automatically rolls back the stack to its previous state.

- **Benefits**:
  - **Automatic reversion**: Automatically reverts to the last known stable state without manual intervention, reducing downtime and preventing deployment of unstable configurations.

  - **Proactive monitoring**: Ensures that specific operational metrics and thresholds are monitored during critical deployment windows.

  - **Enhanced reliability**: Provides confidence that stack updates or creations will not compromise system health by enforcing operational constraints.

Workings of rollback triggers

Rollback triggers in the AWS CloudFormation function by monitoring specified CloudWatch alarms during the stack operations. These triggers ensure that if any predefined operational thresholds are breached, the stack operation will automatically roll back to maintain stability. Here is a detailed look at the process:

1. **Monitoring duration**: You can set a monitoring period ranging from 0 to 180 minutes. During this period, CloudFormation keeps track of the designated rollback triggers after all necessary resources for the stack creation or update have been deployed. This time frame allows for thorough monitoring to ensure that the new stack configuration does not cause any issues.

2. **Alarm monitoring**: CloudFormation begins monitoring the specified CloudWatch alarms during the stack operation. If any of these alarms transitions to the ALARM state within the monitoring period, the entire stack operation is rolled back to its previous state. For update operations, if no alarms enter the ALARM state by the end of the monitoring period, CloudFormation proceeds to dispose of the old resources as part of the standard cleanup process.

3. **No triggers specified**: Even if no rollback triggers are specified but a monitoring period is set, CloudFormation waits for the specified duration before cleaning up old resources during an update operation. This allows for manual validation and the opportunity to cancel the stack operation if necessary.

4. **Monitoring for 0 minutes**: If the monitoring time is set to 0 minutes, CloudFormation still monitors rollback triggers during the actual stack creation and update. It immediately rolls back the operation if any alarm transitions to ALARM state. In the absence of breaching alarms, CloudFormation begins disposing of old resources as soon as the stack operation is completed.

5. **Handling INSUFFICIENT_DATA**: By default, CloudFormation does not roll back the stack if an alarm enters the INSUFFICIENT_DATA state. To trigger a rollback under this Condition, the CloudWatch alarm settings must be modified to treat missing data as breaching. This configuration is detailed in the Amazon CloudWatch user guide under configuring how CloudWatch alarms treat missing data.

6. **Trigger configuration**: You can specify up to five rollback triggers for a stack. These triggers are defined by the ARNs of the CloudWatch alarms. Supported alarm types include `AWS::CloudWatch::Alarm` and `AWS::CloudWatch::CompositeAlarm`.

7. **Alarm availability and permissions**: If a specified CloudWatch alarm is unavailable during the stack operation, the entire operation fails and rolls back. Proper credentials with the necessary permissions to access CloudWatch resources are required to utilize rollback triggers effectively. Detailed guidelines on these permissions can be found in the Amazon CloudWatch user guide under authentication and access control for Amazon CloudWatch.

This structured approach ensures that your stack operations are closely monitored for potential issues, with automated rollbacks safeguarding the stability and integrity of your cloud infrastructure.

Integrating trigger during stack creation or updating

To incorporate rollback triggers into your stack creation or update process in AWS CloudFormation, follow these steps:

1. **Navigate to rollback configuration**:

    a. While creating or updating a stack, go to the Configure stack options page.

    b. Under Advanced options, expand the Rollback configuration section.

2. **Set monitoring time**:

    a. Input a monitoring duration between 0 and 180 minutes. By default, this value is set to 0.

3. **Add CloudWatch alarms**:

    a. Enter the ARN of the CloudWatch alarm or composite alarm that you wish to designate as a rollback trigger.

    b. Click Add CloudWatch alarm ARN to include it. For instance, a typical ARN for a CloudWatch alarm might look like: `arn:aws:cloudwatch:us-east-1:456878393949:alarm:MyTestAlarmName`.

4. **Finalize configuration**:

    a. Click Next to proceed.

    b. Review your stack's settings and estimated costs on the final page.

5. **Launch the stack**:

    a. After confirming the details, choose Create stack to initiate the stack creation.

CloudFormation stack notification

AWS CloudFormation stack notifications provide a mechanism to track and respond to changes in the state of CloudFormation stacks. These notifications are delivered through Amazon SN), enabling automated monitoring and handling of stack events such as stack creation, update, or deletion.

Key features

Let us have a look at the primary features that make CloudFormation stack notifications an effective tool for tracking and responding to stack events:

- **Automated event tracking**: CloudFormation stack notifications automatically track changes in the state of your CloudFormation stacks, such as stack creation, update, or deletion.

- **Real-time notifications**: Notifications are sent in real-time, allowing immediate awareness and response to stack events.

- **Integration with SNS**: Notifications are integrated with Amazon SNS, enabling a broad range of subscription options, including email, SMS, HTTP/S endpoints, and Lambda functions.

- **Customizable notifications**: Users can subscribe to specific types of events, filtering notifications to only the relevant stack activities.

Use cases

Let us explore some use cases where CloudFormation stack notifications prove particularly beneficial:

- **Monitoring stack deployments**: Receive notifications when stacks are created, updated, or Deleted, providing visibility into deployment processes.

- **Automated responses**: Trigger automated workflows or corrective actions in response to specific stack events using Lambda functions or other automated processes.

- **Audit and compliance**: Maintain records of stack events for auditing purposes, ensuring compliance with organizational policies or regulatory requirements.

- **Alerting and incident management**: Integrate with alerting and incident management systems to ensure timely response to issues arising from stack changes.

Implementation

Let us examine how to implement state change notifications for a CloudFormation stack with an example. We will create a stack to launch an EC2 instance and integrate SNS notifications to alert us of any changes in the stack's status. Here are the steps required to accomplish this:

1. **Setup an SNS topic**: Create an SNS topic for sending notifications, as seen in the following figure:

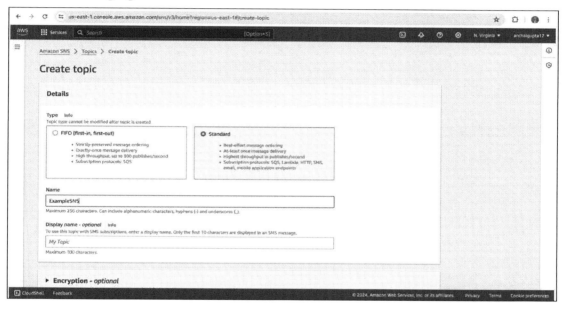

Figure 10.7: SNS topic creation

For this demonstration, we will name the topic **ExampleSNS**. We will choose the **Standard** category, as we only need to send email notifications for any changes in stack status.

2. After the topic is created, the following screen will appear, allowing us to create a subscription. Click the **Create subscription** button, select Email as the protocol, and enter our email address in the **Endpoint** field:

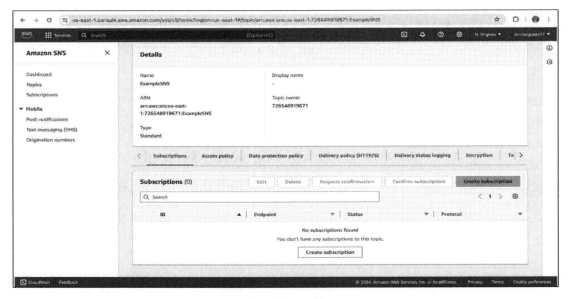

Figure 10.8: Subscription setup

3. After the subscription is created, we need to confirm it via email. We will receive a confirmation email that looks like this:

Figure 10.9: AWS Notification Subscription confirmation mail

4. Once we confirm the subscription, the notification functionality will be ready for use, as shown in the following figure:

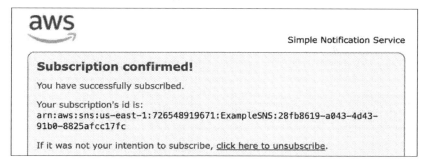

Figure 10.10: Subscription confirmation message

5. Next, we will set up the stack to create an EC2 instance. We will use the following sample template we will use to launch it. We will set up the EC2 instance in the us-east-1 region:

```
o   AWSTemplateFormatVersion: '2010-09-09'
o   Description: Example stack with email notifications
o   Resources:
o     MyInstance:
o       Type: AWS::EC2::Instance
o       Properties:
o         InstanceType: t2.micro
o         ImageId: ami-00beae93a2d981137
```

6. On the CloudFormation console, when we reach the Configure Stack options page during stack setup, there is a section for Notification options. Expand this section and enter the SNS topic ARN that we set up earlier. Please refer to the following figure:

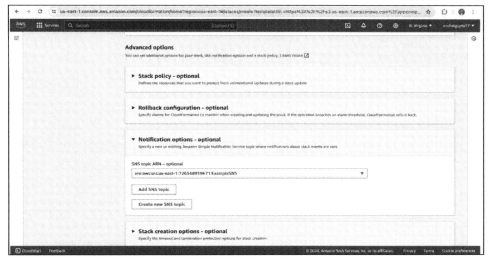

Figure 10.11: Setting SNS topic

7. After configuring the notification options and clicking Submit on the final page, we will start receiving automatic email notifications with the stack status. Some reference figures of these email notifications, including the relevant stack information are as follows:

Figure 10.12: CREATE_IN_PROGRESS notification

Reference figure of email notifications, including the relevant stack information:

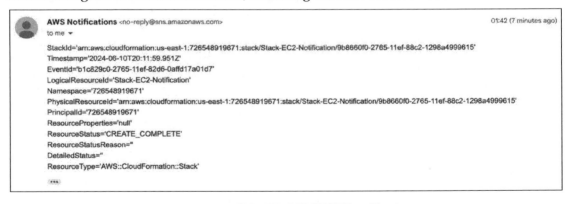

Figure 10.13: CREATE_COMPLETE notification

In the snippet above, we can see that we received a notification for **CREATE_COMPLETE**, indicating that the stack creation was successfully completed. To verify this, we can check the stack status directly in the console:

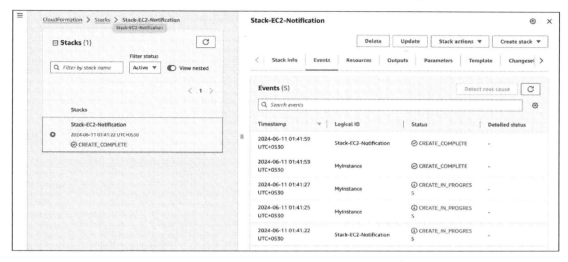

Figure 10.14: *Stack status validation*

This concludes the integration of notification functionality with the CloudFormation service.

Conclusion

In this chapter, we covered a range of crucial topics for effective CloudFormation stack management. We began by understanding stack management fundamentals and explored methods to protect stacks. We examined how to handle configuration changes with drift detection and remediation and discussed rollback triggers for smooth recovery from issues. Additionally, we integrated notifications to monitor and respond to changes in stack states.

In the next chapter, we will explore Nested stacks, learn how to organize resources with them, and handle updates and deletions.

Multiple choice questions

1. **Which of the following is a method to protect a CloudFormation stack from accidental deletion?**

    a. Enabling versioning

    b. Setting stack policies

    c. Enabling termination protection

    d. Using IAM roles

2. **Which feature in CloudFormation is used to detect drift in stacks?**

    a. CloudWatch

    b. Drift detection

    c. CloudTrail

    d. Notification

3. **What must be configured in a CloudFormation template to enable notifications for stack events?**

    a. SNS topic ARN in the NotificationARNs section

    b. IAM Role ARN in the Resources section

    c. EC2 Instance ID in the Parameters section

    d. CloudWatch Alarm in the Outputs section

4. **Which of the following can be used as a rollback trigger?**

    a. SNS Topic

    b. CloudWatch alarm

    c. S3 Bucket

    d. All of the above

5. **How can you restrict updates to certain resources in a CloudFormation stack?**

    a. By applying AWS WAF rules

    b. By creating IAM policies

    c. By using stack policies

    d. By enabling multi-factor authentication

Answers

1. c

2. b

3. a

4. b

5. c

CHAPTER 11
Nested Stacks

Introduction

This chapter serves as a comprehensive guide to Nested stacks in AWS CloudFormation. We will begin by exploring Nested stacks, which enable efficient organization of resources within CloudFormation templates. You will learn how to leverage Nested stacks to structure your infrastructure for enhanced reuse, maintainability, and scalability, along with techniques for updating and deleting them to ensure a streamlined configuration.

By the end of this chapter, you will have gained the insights and tools necessary to design and manage complex AWS deployments with modularity and scalability, utilizing the strengths of Nested stacks.

Structure

The chapter covers the following topics:

- Introducing Nested stacks
- Organizing resources using Nested stacks
- Nested stacks updates and deletion
- Cross stacks versus Nested stacks

Objectives

The objective of this chapter is to provide you with a thorough understanding of Nested stacks and cross stacks in AWS CloudFormation. By the end of this chapter, you will be proficient in organizing your infrastructure using Nested stacks to achieve optimal reuse, maintainability, and scalability. You will also be adept at managing updates and deletions of Nested stacks to keep your configurations well-organized. This knowledge will empower you to design and manage complex AWS deployments with modularity and scalability, leveraging the full potential of nested and cross stacks.

Introducing Nested stacks

Nested stacks are a powerful feature within AWS CloudFormation that allows you to organize and manage complex infrastructure more effectively. By using Nested stacks, you can break down a large CloudFormation template into smaller, more manageable pieces, each encapsulated in its own template file. This approach not only simplifies the management of your infrastructure but also promotes the reuse, maintainability, and scalability of your AWS resources.

Benefits of Nested stacks

The benefits of Nested stacks are:

- **Modularity**: Nested stacks enable a modular design, where each Nested stack represents a distinct component or service of your architecture. This modularity allows for better organization and isolation of different parts of your infrastructure, making your templates easier to understand, maintain, and troubleshoot.

- **Reusability**: By encapsulating common infrastructure patterns into ested stacks, you can reuse these patterns across different projects or environments. This reduces duplication of effort and ensures consistency across your deployments.

- **Simplification**: Nested stacks help in reducing the size and complexity of your main CloudFormation template by delegating the creation of certain resources to sub-templates. This simplifies the main template, making it more readable and easier to manage.

- **Scalability**: As your infrastructure grows, Nested stacks allow you to scale your CloudFormation templates more effectively. You can independently manage and update Nested stacks without having to modify the entire template, facilitating incremental changes and scaling of your architecture.

The workings of Nested stacks

In a Nested stack setup, a parent stack references one or more child stacks through the **AWS::CloudFormation::Stack** resource. Each child stack is defined in its own template, which can be hosted in an Amazon S3 bucket. The parent stack passes parameters to the child stacks and integrates their outputs back into its own template.

Example of a Nested stack:

Consider a scenario where you need to deploy a multi-tier application consisting of a web server, an application server, and a database. Instead of defining all these resources in a single template, you can create separate templates for each tier:

- **Web server stack**: Contains resources for the web server, such as EC2 instances, security groups, and load balancers.

- **Application server stack**: Contains resources for the application server, such as EC2 instances and IAM roles.

- **Database stack**: Contains resources for the database, such as RDS instances and security groups.

These templates are then referenced by a parent stack, which orchestrates the creation of the entire multi-tier application. Here is a simplified example of how a parent stack might reference a Nested stack:

```
o    Resources:
o      WebServerStack:
o        Type: AWS::CloudFormation::Stack
o        Properties:
o          TemplateURL: https://s3.amazonaws.com/my-bucket/web-server-
  stack.yaml
o          Parameters:
o            InstanceType: t2.micro
o            KeyName: my-key
o
o      ApplicationServerStack:
o        Type: AWS::CloudFormation::Stack
o        Properties:
o          TemplateURL: https://s3.amazonaws.com/my-bucket/application-
  server-stack.yaml
o          Parameters:
o            InstanceType: t2.medium
o            KeyName: my-key
o
o      DatabaseStack:
o        Type: AWS::CloudFormation::Stack
o        Properties:
o          TemplateURL: https://s3.amazonaws.com/my-bucket/database-
  stack.yaml
```

```
o        Parameters:
o            DBInstanceType: db.t2.small
o            DBName: mydatabase
```

In this example, the parent stack references child stacks for the web server, application server, and database. Each ested stack can accept parameters from the parent stack and return outputs that the parent stack can use.

Organizing resources using Nested stacks

So far, we have understood that Nested stacks are a vital tool in AWS CloudFormation for managing complex infrastructures by breaking them down into smaller, reusable components. This approach not only enhances the organization of your resources but also promotes a more modular, maintainable, and scalable cloud environment. Here is a detailed guide on how to effectively organize resources using Nested stacks:

Modularizing your infrastructure

Let us explore how to effectively plan the modularization of our infrastructure. Here are the essential steps to follow:

1. **Identify reusable components**: Start by analyzing your infrastructure to identify common patterns or configurations that are used across multiple stacks. These could include network configurations, IAM roles, security groups, or application components like databases and load balancers.

2. **Create dedicated templates**: For each identified component, create a dedicated CloudFormation template. This template should encapsulate all resources, parameters, and outputs necessary for the component to function independently. For example, you might create a separate template for a load balancer setup:

```
o    Resources:
o      LoadBalancer:
o        Type: AWS::ElasticLoadBalancingV2::LoadBalancer
o        Properties:
o          Name: MyLoadBalancer
o          Type: application
o          Subnets:
o            - subnet-12345678
o            - subnet-876543213
```

3. **Reference templates as Nested stacks**: In your main stack, use the **AWS::CloudFormation::Stack** resource to reference these dedicated templates. This approach integrates the Nested stacks into the main stack without duplicating their configurations:

```
o   Resources:
o      LoadBalancerStack:
o         Type: AWS::CloudFormation::Stack
o         Properties:
o            TemplateURL: https://s3.amazonaws.com/my-bucket/load-
   balancer-template.yaml
o            Parameters:
o               InstanceType: t2.micro
o               KeyName: my-key
```

Managing parameters and outputs

Let us delve into how to effectively manage parameters and outputs in Nested stacks. The key considerations to ensure seamless integration and customization of Nested stacks within your CloudFormation templates area are as follows:

- **Passing parameters**: Define parameters in your Nested stack templates that allow customization from the parent stack. This makes the Nested stack flexible and adaptable to different environments or requirements. In the parent stack, pass these parameters to the Nested stack:

```
o   Parameters:
o      InstanceType:
o         Type: String
o      KeyName:
o         Type: String
```

The sample template of the parent stack where these parameters can be passed is as follows:

```
o   Resources:
o      LoadBalancerStack:
o         Type: AWS::CloudFormation::Stack
o         Properties:
o            TemplateURL: https://s3.amazonaws.com/my-bucket/load-
   balancer-template.yaml
o            Parameters:
o               InstanceType: t2.micro
o               KeyName: my-key
```

- **Using outputs**: Utilize outputs in your Nested stack templates to provide essential information back to the parent stack. This enables the parent stack to use the results or resources created by the Nested stack. For example, a Nested stack creating a database might output the database endpoint:

```
o   Outputs:
o     DatabaseEndpoint:
o       Value: !GetAtt DatabaseInstance.Endpoint.Address
o       Export:
o         Name: DatabaseEndpoint
```

The sample template of the parent stack where above defined output value can be passed is as follows:

```
o   Resources:
o     AppServerStack:
o       Type: AWS::CloudFormation::Stack
o       Properties:
o         TemplateURL: https://s3.amazonaws.com/my-bucket/app-
server-template.yaml
o         Parameters:
o           DBEndpoint: !ImportValue DatabaseEndpoint
```

Hierarchical organization

Let us explore how to effectively design the hierarchical structure for parent and child stacks. Here are the critical considerations for establishing this framework:

- **Designing the hierarchy**: Structure your stacks in a hierarchy based on logical groupings or layers of your application. The root stack is the top-level stack that references all other stacks, directly or indirectly. Each Nested stack acts as a building block, creating a clean and organized infrastructure.

- **Levels of nesting**: Consider how many levels of nesting are appropriate for your deployment. While nesting adds modularity, excessive nesting can complicate stack updates and error handling. Generally, limit the depth of nesting to two or three levels for optimal manageability.

- **Parent-child relationships**: Understand the parent-child relationships between stacks. Each Nested stack is a child of its referencing stack, which becomes its parent. This relationship determines the flow of parameters and outputs, ensuring that Nested stacks can communicate and integrate seamlessly.

An example hierarchy for the same is as follows:

- o **Root stack (stack A)**: Main stack that references:

  - ▪ **Stack B (network stack)**: Defines VPC, subnets, and routing.

  - ▪ **Stack C (application stack)**: Contains application servers and scaling policies.

- **Stack D (database stack)**: Nested within stack C, defines database instances and backups.

Example

Let us dive into a detailed example to grasp the concepts of Nested stacks more effectively. This straightforward scenario showcases how to use AWS CloudFormation to create a parent stack that references a child stack to set up an EC2 instance configured with a security group. The necessary steps to achieve the same are as follows:

1. **Create the child stack template**: Create a template for the security group (child stack) and save it as **SG.yaml**. This template defines a basic security group:

```
# SG.yaml
AWSTemplateFormatVersion: '2010-09-09'
Description: Simple Security Group

Resources:
  MySecurityGroup:
    Type: AWS::EC2::SecurityGroup
    Properties:
      GroupDescription: Allow SSH
      SecurityGroupIngress:
        - IpProtocol: tcp
          FromPort: 22
          ToPort: 22
          CidrIp: 0.0.0.0/0

Outputs:
  SecurityGroupId:
    Value: !Ref MySecurityGroup
    Export:
      Name: SecurityGroupId
```

2. **Upload the child stack template to S3 bucket**:

   a. Go to the S3 Management Console.

   b. Upload the **SG.yaml** file to an S3 bucket. In this scenario, we will upload the template in our S3 bucket **myexamplecf**. Please refer to the following figure:

Figure 11.1: S3 bucket with child template object

3. **Create the parent stack template**: Create a template for the EC2 Instance (parent stack) and save it as **ec2-instance.yaml**. We will deploy the stacks in us-east-1 region of AWS. This template references the security group defined in the child stack:

```
# ec2-instance.yaml
AWSTemplateFormatVersion: '2010-09-09'
Description: EC2 Instance with Nested Security Group

Resources:
  SecurityGroupStack:
    Type: AWS::CloudFormation::Stack
    Properties:
      TemplateURL: https://myexamplecf.s3.amazonaws.com/SG.yaml

  MyEC2Instance:
    Type: AWS::EC2::Instance
    Properties:
      InstanceType: t2.micro
      ImageId: ami-01b799c439fd5516a
      SecurityGroupIds:
        - !GetAtt SecurityGroupStack.Outputs.SecurityGroupId
      KeyName: mykey   # Replace with your actual key pair name

Outputs:
```

```
o    InstanceId:
o      Value: !Ref MyEC2Instance
o      Export:
o        Name: InstanceId
```

4. **Deploy the parent stack**:

   a. Go to the CloudFormation Management Console.

   b. Click Create stack and select With new resources (standard).

   c. Choose Upload a template file and upload the **ec2-instance.yaml** file.

   d. Click Next.

   e. Provide a stack name, for example, EC2-Parent.

   f. Provide any additional parameters if needed and click Next.

   g. Review the stack settings and click Create stack.

   h. AWS CloudFormation will create the SecurityGroupStack Nested stack and then use the output from this Nested stack to create the EC2 instance with the specified security group.

5. **Verification**:

   a. **Check security group**: Go to the EC2 Management Console. Under Security Groups, you should see the security group created by the Nested stack.

   b. **Check EC2 instance**: Under Instances, you should see the EC2 instance running with the security group attached.

Refer to the following figure for more details:

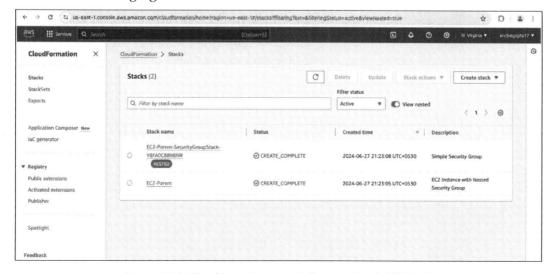

***Figure 11.2**: CloudFormation console for parent and child stack*

In the preceding figure, you can observe that initiating the parent stack also triggers the deployment of the child stack (marked as Nested). Once the child stack is successfully created, it outputs the necessary information for the security group. This output is then used to configure the EC2 instance in the parent stack. The parent stack waits for the child stack to complete before proceeding, ensuring that the security group details are available for the EC2 instance setup.

Nested stacks updates and deletion

Managing updates and deletions in Nested stacks requires a careful consideration to ensure that changes are propagated correctly, and resources are appropriately managed. This section covers best practices and methods for handling updates and deletions of Nested stacks in AWS CloudFormation, helping you maintain a consistent and reliable infrastructure.

Understanding updates in Nested stacks

Updating Nested stacks involves making changes to the child stacks while ensuring that these updates are reflected in the parent stack. Here is how to effectively manage updates:

- **Types of updates**:
  - o **Direct updates to child stacks**: Changes can be made directly to a child stack's template. These changes will automatically propagate to the parent stack the next time it is updated.
  - o **Indirect updates via parent stack**: Updates can also be applied to the parent stack, which in turn will trigger updates to the child stacks based on their definitions and dependencies.
- **Update mechanisms**:
  - o **Stack update operations**: Use AWS CloudFormation's stack update operations to apply changes. When updating the parent stack, AWS CloudFormation compares the new template with the current state of the stack and applies the necessary changes to both the parent and child stacks.
  - o **Change sets**: Before executing updates, use Change sets to preview the changes. This allows you to review the changes that will be made to the stack, including which child stacks will be affected.
- **Propagation of changes**:
  - o **Automatic propagation**: When you update a child stack template and then update the parent stack, changes in the child stack automatically propagate through the parent stack.
  - o **Explicit parameter updates**: If the parent stack uses parameters to pass values to child stacks, ensure that any parameter changes in the parent stack are also reflected in the child stacks.

- **Handling dependencies**:
    - o **Order of updates**: Ensure that updates are made in a sequence that respects the dependencies between stacks. For example, if a child stack depends on resources from another child stack, update the dependent stack last to avoid inconsistencies.

    - o **Atomic operations**: AWS CloudFormation attempts to update all resources as a single atomic operation. If any part of the update fails, it will roll back the entire operation, including all Nested stacks.

Deleting Nested stacks

Deletion of Nested stacks adheres to a structured process to ensure resources are removed systematically, preventing the creation of orphaned resources. Here are some key considerations to follow when deleting Nested stacks:

- **Deletion process**:
    - o **Triggering deletion**: Deleting a parent stack automatically triggers the deletion of all its nested child stacks. AWS CloudFormation handles this recursively, ensuring each child stack is deleted before the parent stack.

    - o **Stack termination protection**: Enable stack termination protection on critical stacks to prevent accidental deletion. This protection applies to both parent and child stacks.

- **Deletion policy**:
    - o **Retention of resources**: Use deletion policies to control what happens to resources when a stack is deleted. You can set policies like Retain, Delete, or Snapshot for specific resources.

    - o **Nested stack deletion policies**: Specify deletion policies for Nested stacks to define whether they should be deleted or retained when the parent stack is deleted. For example, you might want to retain a database while deleting other infrastructure.

- **Handling dependencies**:
    - o **Cascading deletions**: Ensure that the deletion of the parent stack does not leave orphaned resources. AWS CloudFormation handles cascading deletions, ensuring that child stacks are properly deleted before the parent stack is removed.

    - o **Clean-up operations**: After deletion, verify that all intended resources have been properly removed and that no unintended resources remain. This helps maintain a clean infrastructure environment.

Practical considerations

Let us explore some important considerations for both updating and deleting Nested stacks:

- **Monitoring and logging**:

  o **Stack events**: Monitor stack events in the AWS CloudFormation console to track the progress of updates and deletions. Stack events provide insights into each step of the process and help identify issues.

  o **CloudWatch logs**: Use Amazon CloudWatch Logs to capture detailed logs for AWS CloudFormation operations. This can be useful for troubleshooting and understanding the behavior of Nested stacks during updates and deletions.

- **Error handling and rollbacks**:

  o **Rollback triggers**: Configure rollback triggers to specify conditions under which AWS CloudFormation should roll back the update. This provides an additional layer of protection against failed updates.

  o **Manual rollbacks**: If an update fails and automatic rollback is not configured, manually initiate a rollback to the previous stable state. This can help recover from failed updates or partial deletions.

- **Best practices**:

  o **Use version control**: Keep templates under version control to track changes and maintain a history of updates. This facilitates easier rollbacks and troubleshooting.

  o **Test changes**: Test updates in a staging environment before applying them to production. This helps identify potential issues and ensures that updates will not negatively impact the production environment.

  o **Document dependencies**: Maintain clear documentation of the dependencies between Nested stacks to ensure that updates and deletions are handled correctly.

Note: Effectively managing updates and deletions in Nested stacks is crucial for maintaining a stable and reliable AWS infrastructure. By following best practices, leveraging AWS CloudFormation features like Change sets (will be covered in the next chapter), and monitoring operations, you can ensure that Nested stacks are updated and deleted smoothly without disrupting the overall infrastructure. Understanding the interplay between parent and child stacks allows for more modular and scalable deployments, making it easier to manage complex cloud environments.

Cross stacks versus Nested stacks

In AWS CloudFormation, the choice between cross stacks and Nested stacks is crucial for achieving optimal infrastructure management, scalability, and modularity. This section explores the key distinctions, advantages, and practical use cases of each approach, providing a comprehensive understanding to help you make informed architectural decisions. Some of the key differentiators are outlined:

- **Fundamental concept**:
    - Nested stacks are sub-stacks embedded within a parent stack using the `AWS::CloudFormation::Stack` resource. This creates a hierarchical structure where child stacks are directly managed by the parent stack. Nested stacks are advantageous for organizing complex infrastructures into smaller, more manageable units, while still maintaining a unified deployment process.

    - Cross stacks involve separate, independent stacks that communicate and share resources through exports and imports. By using the `Fn::ImportValue` function, one stack can reference outputs defined by another stack. This method promotes a modular architecture where resources can be reused across different stacks without direct hierarchical dependencies.

- **Hierarchical versus modular architecture**:
    - Nested stacks establish a clear hierarchy, with a parent stack controlling and managing the lifecycle of its child stacks. This structure allows for centralized updates, making it easier to manage dependencies and propagate changes. However, it also means that child stacks are tightly coupled to the parent stack, leading to a more rigid architecture.

    - Cross stacks operate independently, allowing for the decoupling of stack management. This independence means that stacks can be updated or deleted without directly affecting each other, promoting a flexible and modular architecture. This approach is especially useful when different stacks share common resources, as it allows for easier resource reuse and management.

- **Update and deletion dynamics**:
    - Updating Nested stacks involves propagating changes from the parent stack to its child stacks. AWS CloudFormation ensures consistency by applying changes throughout the hierarchy, but this can also lead to complex dependencies and potential issues if changes are not carefully managed. Deletion of Nested stacks is straightforward, as removing the parent stack automatically deletes all associated child stacks, ensuring no orphaned resources are left behind.

      o   Cross stacks allow for independent updates, meaning changes to one stack do not directly impact others. This isolation reduces the risk of unintended consequences during updates. However, careful sequencing is required during deletion to prevent dependency issues. Consumer stacks should be deleted before producer stacks to avoid missing resource references.

- **Use cases and practical applications**: Nested stacks are particularly beneficial in the following scenarios:

  - **Hierarchical deployments**: Ideal for scenarios where components have a parent-child relationship, such as multi-tier applications with dependencies between tiers.

  - **Centralized control**: Suitable when centralized management of stack updates and dependencies is needed.

  - **Complex architectures**: Useful for managing large, intricate infrastructures where hierarchical organization simplifies deployment and maintenance.

- **Cross stacks are beneficial in the following scenarios**:

  - **Shared resources**: Perfect for scenarios where multiple stacks need access to common resources, such as VPCs, IAM roles, or security groups.

  - **Independent lifecycles**: Suitable when different parts of the infrastructure have distinct updates and maintenance schedules.

  - **Modular development**: Beneficial for promoting modular development, where different teams manage separate components of the infrastructure.

Summary

Choosing between cross stacks and Nested stacks depends on the specific needs and complexities of your AWS infrastructure. Nested stacks offer a structured, hierarchical approach suitable for centralized management and complex dependencies. They are beneficial when a unified deployment process is essential. In contrast, cross stacks provide flexibility and modularity, enabling independent updates and resource reuse without direct hierarchical dependencies. This approach is ideal for infrastructures requiring shared resources and separate lifecycles.

By understanding the strengths and use cases of each method, you can design AWS CloudFormation stacks that align with your architectural goals, fostering efficient management, scalability, and maintainability. Whether you opt for the hierarchical organization of Nested stacks or the modular flexibility of cross stacks, each approach offers unique advantages that can enhance your infrastructure's robustness and adaptability.

Conclusion

In conclusion, this chapter has provided a comprehensive overview of the use of nested and cross stacks in AWS CloudFormation. We examined how Nested stacks facilitate the organization of complex infrastructures into hierarchical units, enhancing modularity and manageability. The chapter also addressed the nuances of updating and deleting Nested stacks, emphasizing the need for careful lifecycle management to ensure consistency and avoid disruptions. Additionally, we compared Nested stacks with cross stacks, highlighting how both enable flexible, independent stacks management and resource sharing.

In the next chapter, we will explore AWS CloudFormation StackSets and Change sets, starting with an overview of StackSets and their role in multi-account, multi-region deployments. We will cover creating, updating, detecting drifts, and deleting StackSets, along with how to override parameters for specific deployments. Additionally, we will introduce Change sets, highlighting their use for safely previewing and managing stack changes. This will equip you with advanced strategies for large-scale infrastructure management.

Multiple choice questions

1. **What is the primary advantage of using Nested stacks in AWS CloudFormation?**

    a. Reduces the number of templates required to manage resources.

    b. Centralizes logging and monitoring of AWS resources.

    c. Organizes complex infrastructures into smaller, manageable units.

    d. Enhances the security of AWS resources.

2. **In AWS CloudFormation, how is a Nested stack created within a parent stack?**

    a. By using the AWS::CloudFormation::NestedStack resource.

    b. By directly referencing the stack in the parent stack's outputs.

    c. By using the AWS::CloudFormation::Stack resource.

    d. By embedding the child stack's template within the parent stack's template.

3. **What happens when a parent stack that contains Nested stacks is deleted?**

    a. Only the parent stack is deleted, leaving the Nested stacks intact.

    b. The Nested stacks must be manually deleted first.

    c. The parent stack and all Nested stacks are automatically deleted.

    d. The Nested stacks are converted into independent stacks.

Answers

1. c
2. c
3. c

Join our book's Discord space

Join the book's Discord Workspace for Latest updates, Offers, Tech happenings around the world, New Release and Sessions with the Authors:

https://discord.bpbonline.com

CHAPTER 12
Understanding StackSets and Change Sets

Introduction

This chapter serves as an in-depth guide to AWS CloudFormation StackSets and Change sets. We will start by exploring StackSets, a powerful feature for deploying and managing stacks across multiple AWS accounts and regions. You will learn the essentials of creating and updating StackSets, detecting drift, and deleting them effectively, along with strategies for overriding Parameters to tailor deployments. Additionally, we will introduce Change sets, exploring their crucial role in previewing and managing stack updates. By the end of this chapter, you will be equipped with the knowledge and practical skills to leverage StackSets and Change sets for sophisticated, large-scale CloudFormation deployments, ensuring efficient and controlled infrastructure management.

Structure

The chapter covers the following topics:

- Introduction to StackSets
- Creating and updating StackSets
- Stack override Parameters
- Deleting StackSets

- Introduction to Change sets
- Using Change sets

Objectives

The goal of this chapter is to provide you with the essential skills and knowledge for leveraging AWS CloudFormation StackSets and Change sets effectively. You will gain proficiency in deploying and managing stacks across multiple AWS accounts and regions using StackSets, including creating, updating, and deleting them, as well as detecting and addressing drift. Additionally, you will learn to customize stack Parameters during deployments and harness the power of Change sets to preview and control updates. By mastering these tools, you will be able to implement robust and scalable infrastructure solutions, ensuring precise and efficient large-scale Cloud management.

Introduction to StackSets

AWS CloudFormation StackSets is a powerful feature that allows you to deploy and manage CloudFormation stacks across multiple AWS accounts and regions from a single template. This capability streamlines the management of resources in a large-scale environment, enabling centralized control and consistency across diverse deployments.

StackSets extends the functionality of individual CloudFormation stacks by facilitating the replication and management of stacks in multiple target accounts and regions. This is particularly beneficial for organizations with complex, multi-account architectures or geographically distributed applications. By using StackSets, you can ensure that your infrastructure is uniformly deployed and maintained, regardless of where it resides.

The following figure shows the official AWS documentation demonstrating how StackSets operates:

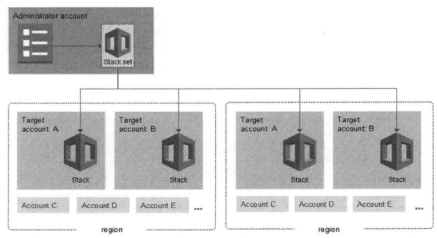

Figure 12.1: *StackSets architecture example*

This preceding figure illustrates the architecture of AWS CloudFormation StackSets, showcasing how a StackSet can deploy and manage stacks across multiple accounts and regions from a central administrator account.

Here is a breakdown of *Figure 12.1:*

- **Administrator account**:
  - o **Role**: Acts as the central management point for the StackSet.
  - o **Components**: Contains the StackSet, which defines the template and Parameters for the stack deployments.

- **Target accounts**:
  - o **Accounts**: Represents multiple AWS accounts (A, B, C, D, E) where stacks will be deployed.
  - o **Stacks**: Each target account receives stacks based on the StackSet defined in the administrator account.

- **Regions**:
  - o **Function**: Represents different geographical AWS Regions where the stacks are deployed.
  - o **Contents**: Each region contains stacks within the target accounts.

Now, let us have a look at the key concepts illustrated in *Figure 12.1:*

- **Centralized stack management**: The administrator account manages the StackSet, which is a single point of configuration for deploying stacks across various target accounts and regions.

- **Cross-account deployment**: The image shows that stacks are deployed to different target accounts (A, B, C, D, E) using the StackSet from the administrator account. This highlights the capability of StackSets to operate across multiple AWS accounts.

- **Cross-region deployment**: Stacks are deployed in different regions, as indicated by the two columns labeled region. This demonstrates the ability of StackSets to manage deployments in multiple AWS Regions, ensuring global reach and redundancy.

- **Uniform deployment**: Each target account across various regions receives stacks based on the same StackSet configuration. This ensures consistency and uniformity in the deployment of infrastructure resources.

- **Scalability and efficiency**: By deploying stacks from a central StackSet to multiple accounts and regions, StackSets streamline the process, reducing manual effort and potential errors associated with managing numerous individual stack deployments.

StackSets concepts

AWS CloudFormation StackSets provide a framework for deploying CloudFormation stacks across multiple AWS accounts and regions from a single template. This capability is essential for organizations that need to manage large-scale infrastructure deployments with consistency and efficiency. To effectively use StackSets, it is crucial to understand the following core concepts:

- **Deployment targets**:
  - o **Administrator account**: This is the AWS account from which you create and manage the StackSet. It holds the StackSet configuration and initiates deployments to the target accounts and regions.

  - o **Target accounts**: These are AWS accounts where stacks are deployed. The target accounts receive the stacks based on the StackSet defined in the administrator account. Target accounts can be part of different AWS organizations or standalone accounts. Before you can use a StackSet to create stacks in a target account, set up a trust relationship between the administrator and target accounts.

  - o **Regions**: StackSets allow deployments across multiple AWS Regions. This is critical for ensuring geographical redundancy, disaster recovery, and proximity to end users. Each region receives a consistent stack deployment from the StackSet, maintaining uniform infrastructure across locations.

- **Deployment models**:
  - o **Service-managed permissions**: This model allows AWS CloudFormation to manage permissions. It is suitable for organizations using AWS Organizations, as it simplifies permissions management by automatically configuring roles required for StackSet operations across accounts.

  - o **Self-managed permissions**: In this model, you manually manage the IAM roles and permissions required for StackSet operations. It provides more control and flexibility over access configurations but requires careful setup to ensure proper permissions across target accounts.

- **Operations on StackSets**:
  - o **Creating StackSets**: To create a StackSet, you specify a template and deployment Parameters. The StackSet is configured with details about the target accounts and regions and, optionally, the deployment strategy (for example, deployment order, failure tolerance).

  - o **Updating StackSets**: Updates to a StackSet can include changes to the template, Parameters, or deployment targets. Updates are propagated to all stacks associated with the StackSet, ensuring that changes are consistently applied across all deployments.

- o **Deleting StackSets**: When you Delete a StackSet, AWS CloudFormation Deletes all associated stacks in the target accounts and regions. This operation needs to be handled carefully to avoid accidental deletion of critical resources.

- **Drift detection**: Drift refers to a situation where the actual state of resources differs from their expected configuration as defined in the CloudFormation template. StackSets provide drift detection to identify and report these discrepancies across all target stacks. This helps maintain consistency and compliance with the defined infrastructure state.

- **Stack instance and StackSet instance**:

  - o **Stack instance**: A stack instance represents a single deployment of a stack in a specific account and region. The combination of each target account and region creates a stack instance based on the StackSet configuration. A stack instance can exist independently even if the corresponding stack has not been successfully created. In such cases, the stack instance will display the failure reason for the stack creation attempt. Each stack instance is uniquely associated with a single StackSet.

  - o **StackSet instance**: The StackSet instance is the collective term for all stack instances created from a single StackSet across various accounts and regions. It provides a holistic view of the deployment status and configuration across the entire StackSet.

  - o **Parameter overrides**: StackSets allow you to override template Parameters for specific accounts or regions. This flexibility enables customized deployments to meet varying requirements across different environments without altering the base template.

- **Use cases**:

  - o **Multi-account resource management**: Centralize the deployment of shared resources like logging, monitoring, and security configurations across multiple accounts.

  - o **Global application deployment**: Deploy application infrastructure across multiple regions to ensure availability and performance for global user bases.

  - o **Compliance and policy enforcement**: Implement consistent security policies and compliance configurations across all accounts and regions using a unified StackSet.

Note: Each of these concepts will be comprehensively covered in the upcoming sections, providing detailed explanations and practical insights to ensure a thorough understanding.

Creating and updating StackSets

AWS CloudFormation StackSets offer a powerful solution for deploying and managing stacks across multiple AWS accounts and regions. This section provides a detailed exploration of how to create and update StackSets, highlighting essential concepts, practical steps, and best practices for effective use.

Creating StackSets

Before we dive into the process of creating StackSets, it is essential to understand the prerequisites that need to be in place. Let us review the following requirements to ensure a smooth and effective StackSet creation:

- **Administrator account setup**: Identify the AWS account that will serve as the administrator for the StackSet. This account will manage the StackSet and initiate deployments.

- **Permissions**: Configure the necessary IAM roles and permissions. For service-managed permissions, ensure that the roles are automatically set up using AWS organizations. For self-managed permissions, manually create and assign IAM roles in both the administrator and target accounts.

- **CloudFormation template**: Prepare the CloudFormation template that defines the resources and configurations you intend to deploy. This template will serve as the blueprint for the StackSet.

To better understand the process, let us examine an example from the official AWS documentation. This example provides a sample CloudFormation template for setting up the StackSet administration role and StackSet execution role. You can find these templates on the following page:

https://docs.aws.amazon.com/AWSCloudFormation/latest/UserGuide/stacksets-prereqs-self-managed.html

Following is the sample permission policy which we will be configuring for this setup:

```
1. {
2.   "Version": "2012-10-17",
3.   "Statement": [
4.     {
5.       "Action": [
6.         "sts:AssumeRole"
7.       ],
8.       "Resource": [
9.         "arn:aws:iam::*:role/AWSCloudFormationStackSetExecutionRole"
10.      ],
11.      "Effect": "Allow"
```

```
12.    }
13.   ]
14. }
```

Here is the URL for a CloudFormation template that can be used to directly create the specified policy. You can create the stack by using the template available at: **https://s3.amazonaws.com/cloudformation-stackset-sample-templates-us-east-1/ AWSCloudFormationStackSetAdministrationRole.yml**

The following figure showcases the stack creation for the previously mentioned role:

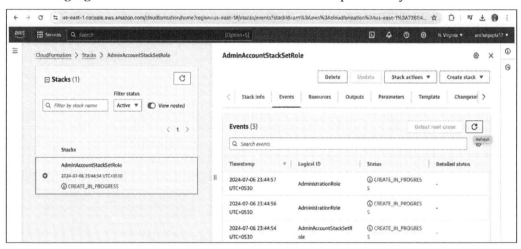

Figure 12.2: Admin account role setup (part one)

The following figure showcases part two of stack creation:

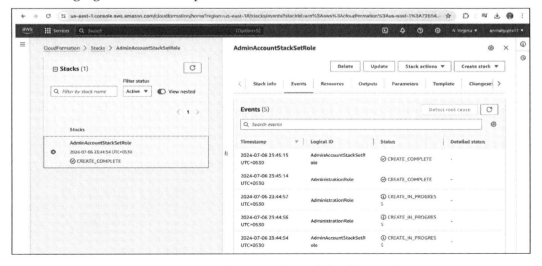

Figure 12.3: Role setup stack completion (Part two)

Now, we will also create a service role that will trust the administrator account. This can be achieved by creating the stack from the following sample template URL:

https://s3.amazonaws.com/cloudformation-stackset-sample-templates-us-east-1/ AWSCloudFormationStackSetExecutionRole.yml

During the deployment of the stack, you will be prompted to provide the account ID of the administrator account, which must have a trust relationship with your target account. The service role in the target account needs permissions to execute the operations specified in your CloudFormation template. This includes comprehensive CloudFormation permissions to create, update, Delete, and describe stacks in the target account.

> **Note: In this example, the administrator and target accounts are the same. To demonstrate how StackSets operate, the deployment will occur in a different region within the same account. This setup will help us understand the StackSets concept in a controlled environment.**

Next, we will set up the role using the provided stack URL. The following figure shows the steps involved in this process:

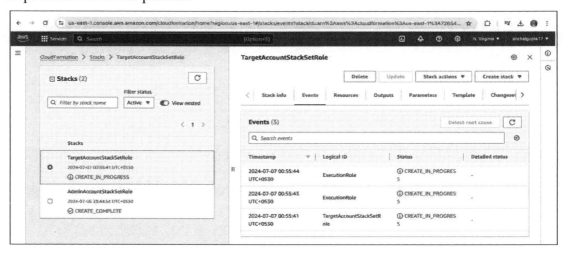

Figure 12.4: Target account role setup

After the stack is complete, you can verify the creation of the new role by checking the **Resources** section of the template. Kindly refer to the following figure:

Figure 12.5: Target account role detail

We are now ready to establish our initial StackSet. We will use the following details to demonstrate this concept:

- **Administrator account ID**: 726548919671
- **Administrator region**: us-east-1 that is, N.Virginia
- **Target account ID**: 726548919671
- **Target region**: eu-west-1, that is, Ireland

We will now return to the AWS CloudFormation console page in the administrator account. Once there, we will locate the StackSets option in the left panel of the page, as shown in the following figure:

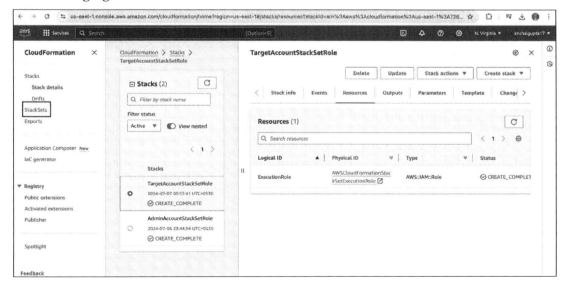

Figure 12.6: *StackSets option on CloudFormation console*

We will click on the **StackSets** option, and then a new window will open where we can see our **StackSets** detail. As of now, we do not have any StackSets created in our account. Kindly refer to the following figure:

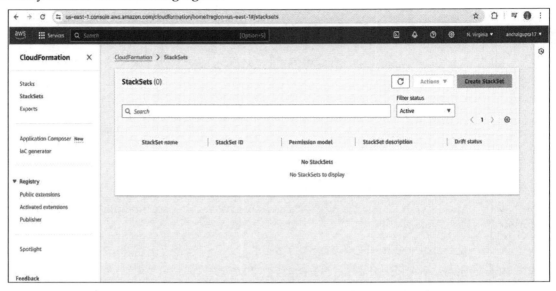

Figure 12.7: StackSets console page

We are ready to create our first StackSet from the administrator account and region. We will click on the **Create StackSet** option, which will take us to the next page where we can define the necessary details for setting up the StackSet. Please refer to the following figure:

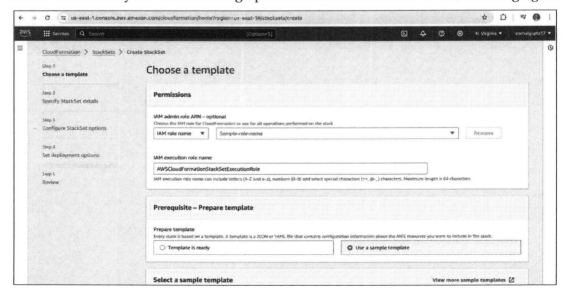

Figure 12.8: StackSet setup page

Here, we need to select the template that will be deployed as a StackSet in the administrator account. Before proceeding, we must choose the required role that we previously created as part of the prerequisites.

Next, we will select the template for setting up the StackSet. For simplicity, we will choose the Use a sample template option. AWS provides several sample templates that can be used for deploying StackSets. After clicking on this option, a dropdown list will be displayed from which we can select a template. For this particular example, we will select the first option Enable AWS CloudTrail. Kindly refer the following figure for the same:

Note: By default, CloudTrail is not enabled in any AWS Region. This template will handle the deployment necessary to enable the CloudTrail service in the target region.

Figure 12.9: Selection of sample template

After selecting the desired template, we will proceed by clicking the Next button. This will direct us to the following page where we will input details such as the StackSet name, description, and any required Parameters (such as those for CloudTrail) needed for the template deployment:

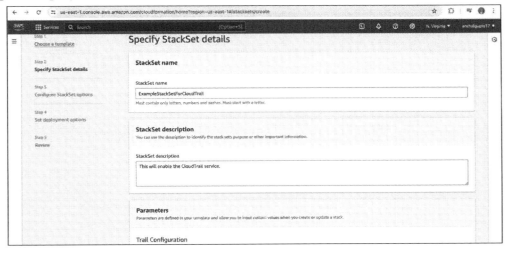

Figure 12.10: StackSet detail input

Under the **Parameters** section, we can select the necessary option as per our requirement. For this deployment we will go with the options, shown in the following figure:

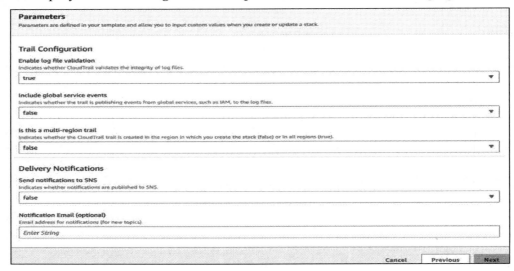

Figure 12.11: *Parameters selection for CloudTrail setup*

Once we are done with our choices, we will click on the **Next** button. This will direct us to the following page where we will select the Execution configuration option. This option describes whether StackSets performs non-conflicting operations concurrently and queues conflicting operations. We can leave it with the default option, that is, Inactive:

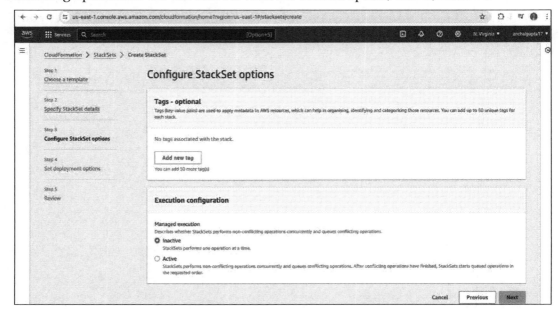

Figure 12.12: *Configure StackSet options*

We will then click on the **Next** button. This will navigate us to the page where we need to set the deployment options. Kindly refer to the following figure:

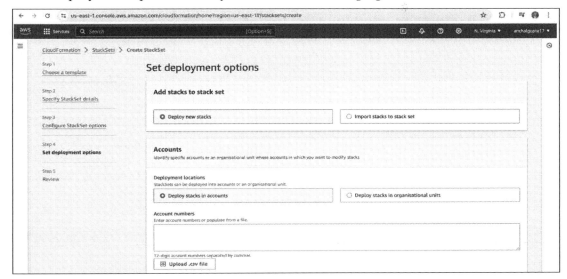

Figure 12.13: Set deployment options (part one)

For additional details, refer to the following figure:

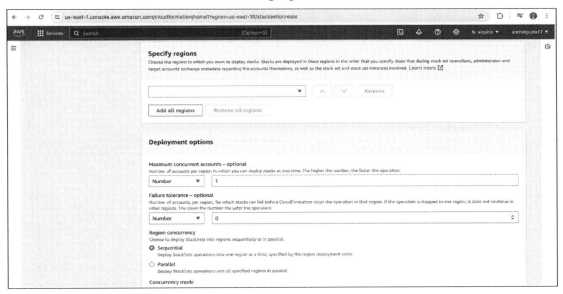

Figure 12.14: Set deployment options (part two)

This is an important section where we need to define certain attributes which will define how the StackSet deployment will actually happen.

A list of options which we will input here to proceed further is as follows:

- **Add stacks to StackSet**: Here we need to define if we are deploying a new stack or we are importing stacks to StackSet. In our scenario, we will go with the default option, that is, **Deploy new stacks**.

- **Accounts**: Here we need to input the target account ID number. Since we have same account ID for both administrator and target account, we can enter the same account number, that is, 726548919671.

- **Specify regions**: We need to specify the target deployment region. In our scenario, we are deploying to the eu-west-1 region, which will be selected from the dropdown list.

- **Deployment options**: Here, we need to input multiple information. Please refer to the following figure:

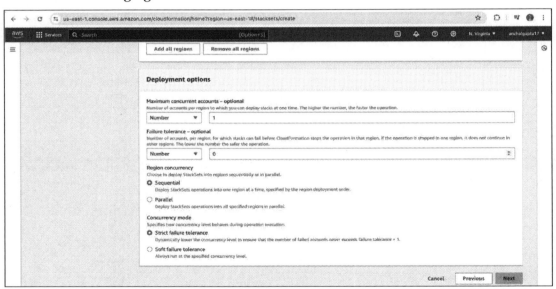

Figure 12.15: Define deployment options

- o **Maximum concurrent accounts**: This defines the number of accounts per region to which you can deploy stack at one time. We will go with the default option, that is, **1** since are deploying in in one region only.

- o **Failure tolerance**: This defines the number of accounts per region for which stacks can fail before the CloudFormation stops the operation in that region. If the operation is stopped in one region, it does not continue in other regions. We will go with the default value **0**.

- o **Region concurrency**: Here, choose to deploy StackSets into regions sequentially or in parallel. We will go with the default option.

o   **Concurrency mode**: This defines how the concurrency level behaves during operation execution. We will go with the default option.

After configuring the options, click on the **Next** button to review the selected information from the previous steps. Once reviewed, click on the **Submit** button. This will navigate you to the page where you can check the status of the StackSet setup.

Kindly refer to the following figures:

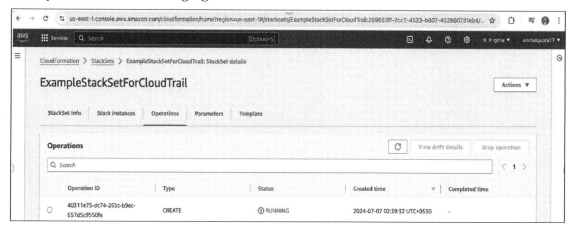

Figure 12.16: StackSet Creation in progress (part one)

Kindly refer to the following figures for more detail:

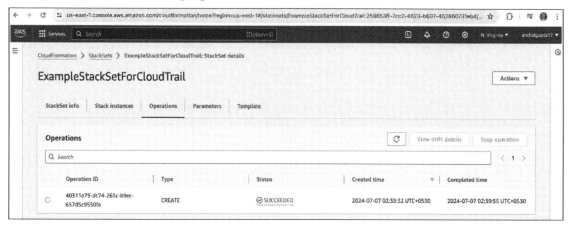

Figure 12.17: StackSet creation successful (part two)

The preceding figures captures the StackSet deployment status in the administrator region. Once the status changes from **RUNNING** to **SUCCEEDED**, you can check the stack status in the target account region. In the following figure, the stack status in the target account region is shown as **CREATE_COMPLETE**, indicating a successful StackSet deployment.

To further validate, navigate to the CloudTrail service page to confirm that CloudTrail was successfully enabled in the target account's region. Please refer to the following figure:

Figure 12.18: Stack status in target account region (part one)

For additional details, please refer to the following figure:

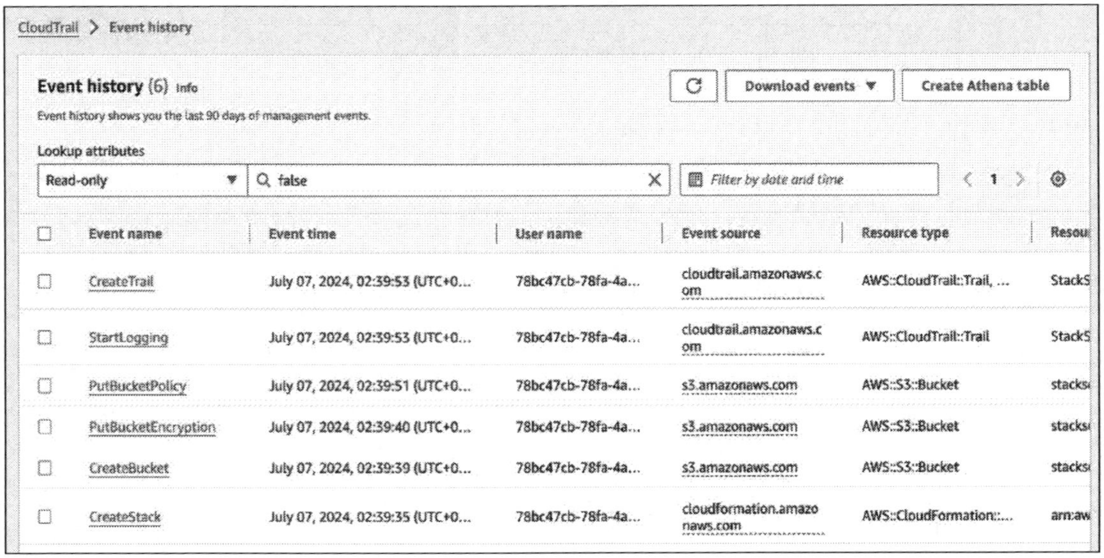

Figure 12.19: CloudTrail console in target account region (part two)

This concludes the StackSet creation process, successfully enabling CloudTrail in the target region.

Updating StackSets

Updating a CloudFormation StackSet enables you to apply changes to stack instances across multiple AWS accounts and regions. Continuing with the previous example, we will update a StackSet to configure AWS CloudTrail in the EU region from the us-east-1 region. This ensures consistent logging and monitoring settings across various regions. The following steps will help in achieving the StackSets update area:

1. Modify the CloudFormation template or update the Parameters in existing template. Under both scenarios, we are trying to update the existing stack with some new attributes. For this example, since we are using the sample template provided by AWS, so we will try to change the Parameters to update the StackSets.

2. Initiate the StackSet update from the AWS Management Console. To do the same, choose StackSets option from the navigation pane. On the **StackSets** page, select the StackSet that we created previously. With the StackSet selected, choose **Edit StackSets details** from the **Actions** menu, as shown in the following figure:

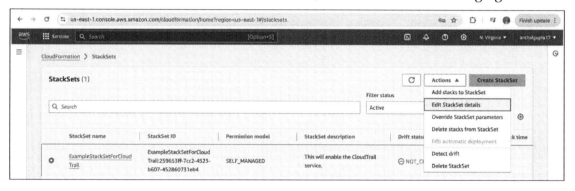

Figure 12.20: StackSets update

3. On the Choose a template page, choose whether you want to update the current template, specify an S3 URL to another template, or upload a new template to AWS CloudFormation. For this scenario, we will continue with using the current template option. Choose Use current template, and then choose Next.

4. On the Specify StackSet details page, modify one of the Parameter values. In this example, set the Parameter value for **Enable log file validation** from **true** to **false**. Then, click **Next**. Kindly refer to the following figure for the same:

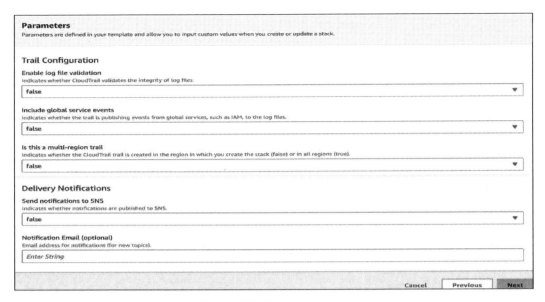

Figure 12.21: Parameter update

5. Next, we will specify the deployment options just like we did while creating the StackSet for the first time. We will mention the target account number in the dialog box and will choose the desired region from the drop-down list. Please refer to the following figure:

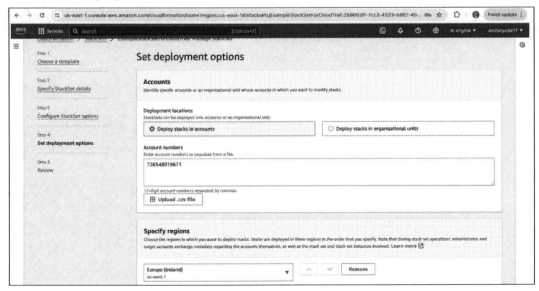

Figure 12.22: Set deployment options

6. We will leave the other options with the default values and then choose **Next**.

7. Once we are done, we will get navigated to the review page where we just need to review the configurations which we did in earlier steps. Once everything looks fine, we will click on **Submit**.

8. On the StackSets console page, we can check the status of StackSet update. Refer to the following figures for more detail:

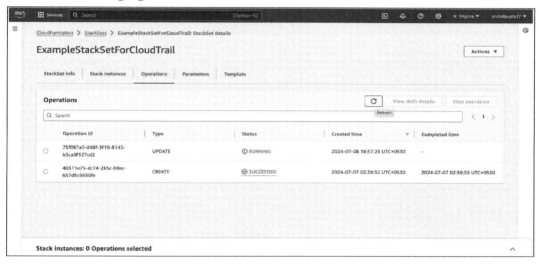

Figure 12.23: StackSets update in progress (part one)

Refer to the following figure for more details on the status of StackSet:

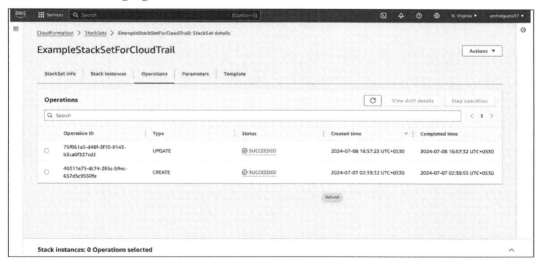

Figure 12.24: StackSets update successful (part one)

9. For further validation, we will check the status of stack in eu-west-1 region (target region). Kindly refer to the following figure:

Figure 12.25: *Stack update in target region*

This completes the StackSets update process, successfully applying the new configuration across all target regions and ensuring that CloudTrail is consistently set up for enhanced logging and monitoring.

StackSets drift

Drift detection in AWS CloudFormation StackSets identifies differences between the actual configurations of stack resources in your target accounts and regions and the expected configurations defined in your CloudFormation template. Drift occurs when the configuration of a stack instance deviates from the StackSet template. Detecting and resolving drift ensures that all stack instances remain consistent with the defined architecture, maintaining compliance and operational integrity.

Detecting and resolving StackSets drift

Let us take a detailed look at the step-by-step process for detecting and resolving StackSets drift. The necessary steps are as follows:

1. **Initiating drift detection**:
   o Go to the StackSets page and choose the StackSet you want to perform drift detection on.
   o From the **Actions** menu, click on **Detect drifts**. An information bar will appear, indicating that drift detection has started for the selected StackSet.

2. **Monitor drift detection progress (optional)**:
   o Click on the StackSet name to open the StackSet details page.
   o Go to the Operations tab, select the ongoing drift detection operation, and then click View drift details. CloudFormation will display the operation details dialog box.

3. **Wait for completion**:

    o Allow CloudFormation to complete the drift detection process. The duration depends on the number of stack instances and resources involved.

    o Once finished, the Drift status and Last drift check time will be updated on the Overview tab of the StackSet details page.

4. **Review drift detection results**: Switch to the Stack instances tab to view the results. The Stack name column shows each stack's name, while the Drift status column indicates if the stack has drifted (that is, if any resources have deviated from the template).

5. **Detailed drift detection review for specific instances**:

    o On the Operations tab, select the drift operation you are interested in. A split panel will show the status and reason for the selected operation, including the drift status for stack instances.

    o Choose the specific stack instance you want to examine and click View resource drifts.

    o On the Resource Drifts page, you will see a table listing each resource, its drift status, and the last time drift detection was performed. Logical IDs and physical IDs of resources are provided for easier identification. You can sort resources by their drift status using the Drift status column.

6. **View detailed drift information for a modified resource**: Select the resource and click View drift details. The drift detail page will display, listing the differences, expected and current property values of the resource.

Stopping drift detection on a StackSet

Drift detection on a StackSet can sometimes be a lengthy process. If you need to halt a drift detection operation that is currently in progress, perform the following steps:

1. **Navigate to StackSets**: Open the AWS CloudFormation console and navigate to the StackSets page. There, select the name of the StackSet which you want to stop the drift detection operation.

2. **View StackSet details**: CloudFormation will display the details page for the selected StackSet.

3. **Access operation tab**: On the StackSet details page, go to the Operations tab. Locate and select the ongoing drift detection operation.

4. **Stop the operation**: Click on Stop operation to halt the drift detection process. By following these steps, you can effectively stop a running drift detection operation on a StackSet through the AWS Management Console.

Stack override Parameters

StackSet override Parameters are specific values that you set for individual stack instances within a StackSet. These overrides enable you to tailor the deployment of resources to meet the unique requirements of different accounts or regions while still using a single StackSet template. AWS CloudFormation StackSets allow you to manage stacks across multiple AWS accounts and regions. StackSet override Parameters provide flexibility by enabling you to customize stack configurations for individual stack instances, rather than applying the same Parameters to all instances. This is particularly useful when different environments or regions require unique settings.

Benefits of using override Parameters

Let us explore some of the benefits of using override Parameters in our templates:

- **Flexibility**: Customize configurations for specific accounts or regions.
- **Consistency**: Maintain a single CloudFormation template while applying unique settings where needed.
- **Efficiency**: Simplify management by avoiding the need to create separate StackSets for different configurations.

Overriding Parameters on stack instances

Customizing stack configurations with override Parameters allows you to tailor deployments for specific accounts or regions while using a single StackSet template. Perform the following steps to override Parameters on stack instances:

1. Ensure your CloudFormation template includes Parameters that you want to override. Parameters should be defined in a way that they can be customized for different stack instances. For instance, in the sample template of AWS, which we used previously for enabling Cloud Trail, the set of Parameters that can be override can be seen in the following figure:

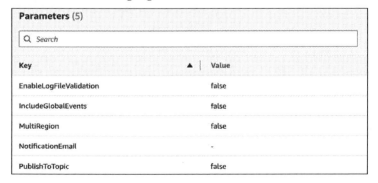

Figure 12.26: Parameters

2. From the navigation pane, select **StackSets**. On the **StackSets** page, choose the StackSet that we created earlier for the CloudTrail enablement. With the StackSet selected, choose **Override StackSet parameters** from the **Actions** menu:

Figure 12.27: StackSet selection for override Parameters

3. On the **Set deployment options** page, specify the accounts and regions for the stack instances whose Parameters you want to override. AWS CloudFormation will deploy stacks in the designated accounts within the first region, then proceed to the next, and so forth, as long as the deployment failures in a region do not exceed a specified failure tolerance. This step is similar to the one we performed while creating the StackSet. For this specific example, we will just provide the account number and region:

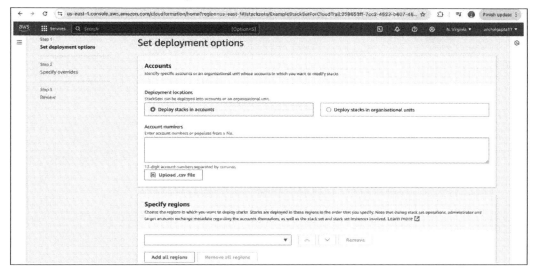

Figure 12.28: Set deployment options

4. On the next page, we will select the Parameters which we need to override. For instance, we will select the Parameters **MultiRegion** and **IncludeGlobalEvents** for overriding. Post this, we will select the **Override StackSet value** option from the dropdown list. Kindly refer to the following figure:

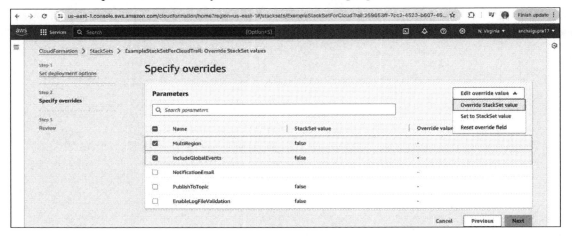

Figure 12.29: Parameters selection for override

5. You will then see a screen for overriding the Parameter values. Select the desired values and click Save Changes. After this, the new values will appear in the **Override value** column, allowing you to verify that the correct choices have been made. Click on **Next**:

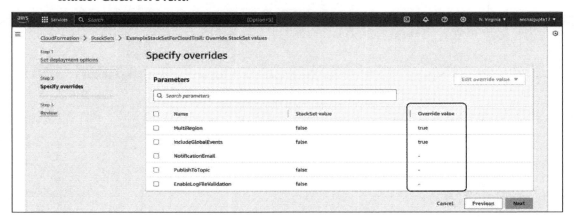

Figure 12.30: Override parameters validation

6. Next, we will get the review page where we need to review all the configurations which we have done in the earlier steps. Once everything looks good, we can simply choose Submit. AWS CloudFormation then starts updating your stack instances. View the progress and status of the stack instances in the StackSet details page.

Note: It is important not to confuse StackSet updates with Parameter overrides for StackSets. While Parameter overrides are part of the StackSet update process, they are not the only aspect. StackSet updates can include changes to the CloudFormation template, modifications to tags or permissions, and the addition or removal of stack instances. Parameter overrides specifically allow customization of Parameter values for individual stack instances, tailoring configurations to specific requirements. Remember that StackSet updates encompass a broader range of changes beyond just Parameter updates.

Deleting StackSets

Deleting a StackSet in AWS CloudFormation involves removing the StackSet and its associated stack instances from all target accounts and regions. This section will guide you through the process of deleting a StackSet, using the example of an AWS CloudTrail configuration in the EU region, managed from the us-east-1 region.

Steps to Delete a StackSet

Let us now have a look at the steps required to Delete a StackSet and related instances:

1. Navigate to the **StackSets** from the navigation pane.

2. On the **StackSets** page, choose the StackSet that we created previously. We will then, go the **Actions** tab, where we will find two options: **Delete StackSet** and **Delete stacks from StackSet**, as shown in the following figure:

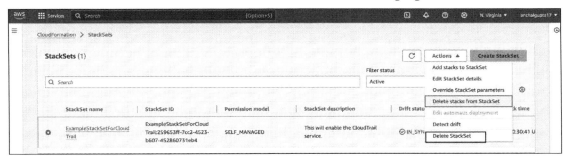

Figure 12.31: StackSet deletion

Before we proceed further, let us try to understand the key difference between both options. The terms **Delete StackSet** and **Delete stacks from StackSet** refer to different actions within AWS CloudFormation when managing StackSets and their stack instances. The options mean:

a. **Delete StackSet:** Deleting a StackSet means removing the entire StackSet configuration, including its definition and all associated stack instances across all specified AWS accounts and regions.

b. **Delete stacks from StackSet**: Deleting stacks from a StackSet involves removing specific stack instances that were created from a particular StackSet template in specified AWS accounts and regions.

We will cover both the options to understand how it works.

a. If we select the **Delete stacks from StackSet** option, it will ask to fill the target account number, regions and deployment options. Once we input all required information, we will choose **Next**. The next page will be the review page just like we saw previously. Once we click on **Submit**, it will start deleting the stack instance. This allows us to Delete only the selected stack instances from different target account and regions keeping few of them intact. Please note that this will not Delete the StackSet.

> **Note: For this discussion, we just have one stack instance within the StackSet but in practical scenarios, we will always have multiple stack instances being managed from the single StackSet.**

b. If we select the **Delete StackSet** option, it will Delete the StackSet. To Delete a StackSet, you must first Delete all stack instances in the StackSet. So, we need to be careful before we proceed with this option.

3. If we need to Delete the StackSet and associated stack instances, we will first go with **Delete stacks from StackSet**. Once all stack instances are Deleted, we will again select the **Delete** StackSet option. and Once we select it, it will ask us to confirm the action. We will again choose **Delete**. This will initiate the deletion of StackSet. Kindly refer to the following figure:

Figure 12.32: Delete StackSet

4. StackSet will get Deleted and now the StackSets console will not show any information for the previously deployed StackSet. This concludes the StackSet deletion process.

Introduction to Change sets

Change sets in AWS CloudFormation provide a powerful mechanism to preview the potential impact of changes to your CloudFormation stacks before applying them. This feature allows you to understand and review the changes that will be made, helping to prevent unintentional disruptions or misconfigurations in your AWS resources.

Knowing Change set

A Change set is a summary of proposed changes to a CloudFormation stack. When you create a Change set, AWS CloudFormation compares your current stack configuration to the new template or Parameter values you specify. It then generates a detailed list of changes, including the resources that will be added, modified, or Deleted.

Benefits of using Change sets

The benefits of using Change sets are:

- **Risk mitigation**: By reviewing the changes before applying them, you can identify and mitigate potential issues that might arise from the update.

- **Transparency**: Change sets provide clear visibility into what exactly will be changed, which helps in planning and coordination among team members.

- **Control**: You can approve or cancel changes after reviewing the Change set, giving you greater control over your stack updates.

Using Change sets

This section demonstrates how to create and execute a Change set using an example of updating an S3 bucket configuration.

Pre-requisites:

Before creating and executing a Change set, ensure the following:

- **Existing stack**: A CloudFormation stack must already exist. In this example, the stack provisions an S3 bucket with versioning disabled. The template structure for the same is as follows:

  - ```
    AWSTemplateFormatVersion: '2010-09-09'
    ```
  - ```
    Description: Initial template to create an
    S3 bucket with versioning disabled
    ```
  -
  - ```
    Resources:
    ```
  - ```
      MyS3Bucket:
    ```

```
o        Type: 'AWS::S3::Bucket'
o        Properties:
o          BucketName: 'my-demo-bucket'
o          VersioningConfiguration:
o            Status: 'Suspended'
```

We will create a stack using the preceding template and name it **S3-Versioning-Stack**. Kindly refer to the *Figure 12.33*.

- **AWS CLI or AWS Management Console**: You need access to the AWS CLI or AWS Management Console to create and manage Change sets.

Updated CloudFormation template

We want to update the stack to enable versioning on the S3 bucket. Here is the updated template:

```
o  AWSTemplateFormatVersion: '2010-09-09'
o  Description: Updated template to enable versioning on the S3 bucket
o
o  Resources:
o    MyS3Bucket:
o      Type: 'AWS::S3::Bucket'
o      Properties:
o        BucketName: 'my-demo-bucket'
o        VersioningConfiguration:
o          Status: 'Enabled'
```

Here, we have modified the versioning setting from **Suspended** to **Enabled**. Next, we will review how Change sets reflect this change. Based on the Change sets preview, we will decide whether to proceed with executing the Change sets.

Creating and executing a Change set

Now, let us explore the steps to create a Change set for updating the stack through the following steps:

1. **Open the AWS CloudFormation console**: Navigate to the AWS CloudFormation console at AWS CloudFormation console.

2. **Select the stack**: In the console, select the stack you want to update, in this case, **S3-Versioning-Stack**.

3. **Create a ChangeSet**:

   a. From the **Stack actions** options, select **Create ChangeSet for the current stack**.

   b. Upload the updated template with versioning enabled or edit it in Application Composer.

    c. Next, provide a name and description for the ChangeSet:

        i. Name: **EnableVersioningChangeSet**

        ii. Description: **ChangeSet to enable versioning on MyS3Bucket**

    d. Click on **Next** to review the configuration. After confirming the details, click on Submit.

    e. Refer to the following figure:

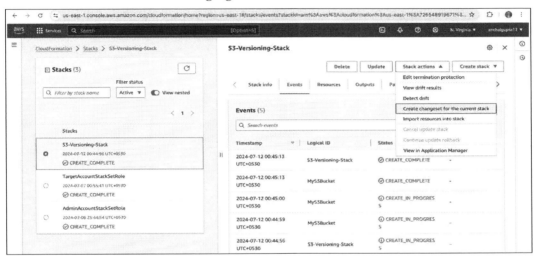

Figure 12.33: Change set creation

For additional details, please refer to the following figure:

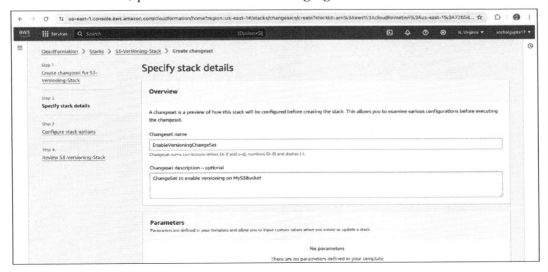

Figure 12.34: Change set detail

4. **Review the ChangeSet**:

   a. AWS CloudFormation generates the ChangeSet and provides a summary of the proposed changes.

   b. Review the details to ensure the changes are as expected, such as changing **VersioningConfiguration** from **Suspended** to **Enabled**.

5. **Execute the ChangeSet**:

   a. If the proposed changes are satisfactory, select Execute ChangeSet to apply the changes to the stack.

   b. If modifications are needed, adjust the template, and create a new ChangeSet.

6. **Monitor the update**:

   a. After executing the ChangeSet, monitor the stack update process.

   b. Check the stack events and status updates in the AWS CloudFormation console to ensure the changes are applied correctly.

Conclusion

Throughout this chapter, we embarked on a detailed exploration of AWS CloudFormation StackSets and Change sets. We gained a thorough understanding of how StackSets facilitate resource management across multiple AWS accounts and regions. Our journey covered the creation, update, and deletion of StackSets, as well as the importance of drift detection for maintaining configuration compliance. We also explored how to customize stack instances with Parameter overrides and the significance of Change sets in previewing and applying updates. With this comprehensive knowledge, we are now well-prepared to leverage StackSets and Change sets effectively in our CloudFormation workflows, ensuring an efficient infrastructure management.

In the next chapter, we will dive into the world of Continuous delivery with respect to CloudFormation. We will cover the basics of AWS CodePipeline, learn how to implement CloudFormation Continuous delivery with CodePipeline, and explore a practical use case deployment. These topics will equip us with the skills to automate and streamline our deployment processes.

Multiple choice questions

1. **Which AWS service is primarily used to create and manage StackSets?**

   a. AWS Lambda

   b. AWS EC2

   c. AWS CloudFormation

   d. AWS RDS

2. **StackSets allow you to create, update, or Delete stacks across multiple?**

    a. Regions and Accounts

    b. VPC's

    c. AZ

    d. EC2 instances

3. **Can you Delete a StackSet if it has associated stacks?**

    a. Yes

    b. No

    c. Only if the stacks are in the same region.

    d. Only if the stacks are in the same account.

4. **What is the purpose of override Parameters in StackSets?**

    a. To change template files.

    b. To specify different Parameter values for different stack instances.

    c. To override AWS IAM roles.

    d. To monitor stack resources.

5. **How do Change sets improve stack management?**

    a. By reducing costs.

    b. By providing a way to review changes before execution.

    c. By increasing resource limits.

    d. By automating stack creation.

Answers

1. c

2. a

3. b

4. b

5. b

Join our book's Discord space

Join the book's Discord Workspace for Latest updates, Offers, Tech happenings around the world, New Release and Sessions with the Authors:

https://discord.bpbonline.com

Section IV
Continuous Delivery and Best Practices

CHAPTER 13
CloudFormation Continuous delivery

Introduction

In this chapter, we will explore the world of CloudFormation **continuous delivery** (**CD**), covering several key areas. We start with an introduction to CD and we will move on to the fundamentals of AWS CodePipeline. Next, we will examine how to integrate CloudFormation into the CD workflow using AWS CodePipeline. To illustrate these concepts, a real-world use case that demonstrates the practical application of CloudFormation within a CD framework will be presented.

Structure

The chapter covers the following topics:

- Introduction to continuous delivery
- AWS CodePipeline basics
- CloudFormation Continuous delivery with CodePipeline
- Use case deployment

Objectives

The goal of this chapter is to equip you with the foundational knowledge and skills necessary for implementing CloudFormation CD using AWS CodePipeline. You will gain an understanding of CD principles and learn the basics of AWS CodePipeline. Additionally, you will discover how to seamlessly integrate CloudFormation into a CD workflow with AWS CodePipeline. Finally, you will see a practical deployment example, which will illustrate the end-to-end process of deploying CloudFormation templates within a CD framework. By mastering these concepts, you will be able to create and manage automated, repeatable, and reliable infrastructure deployments.

Introduction to Continuous delivery

CD is a software engineering approach in which teams produce software in short cycles, ensuring that the software can be reliably released at any time. It aims to build, test, and release software faster and more frequently. This approach reduces the cost, time, and risk of delivering changes, allowing for more incremental updates to applications in production.

At the heart of CD is the automation of all steps from code commit to deployment, enabling teams to ship code more frequently and with higher confidence. The CD pipeline automates the software delivery process, including building, testing, and deploying code. It ensures that software can be released to production at any time by automating the release process. This automation not only speeds up the release cycle but also reduces human error, making the deployment process more reliable.

Origins and evolution

The concept of CD emerged from agile development methodologies, which emphasized iterative progress, collaboration, and adaptability. As software systems became more complex and the demand for faster release cycles grew, traditional manual deployment processes became bottlenecks. These processes were often error prone and time consuming, leading to delays, reduced quality, and increased operational costs.

The rise of CD was a response to these challenges. By automating the software delivery pipeline, CD aims to minimize manual interventions, standardize the deployment process, and ensure that the software is always in a releasable state. This automation not only accelerates the release cycle but also enhances the overall quality and stability of the software.

Key principles of Continuous delivery

CD is grounded in several key principles that guide its implementation. Let us explore few of them:

- **Automated build and deployment**: Automation is at the core of CD. All steps, from code commit to deployment, are automated. This includes building the application, running tests, and deploying to various environments. Automation reduces the potential for human error, ensures consistency, and speeds up the entire process.

- **Version control of all artifacts**: All components of the software, including code, configuration files, and deployment scripts, are versioned and stored in a version control system. This ensures that every change is tracked and that previous versions can be easily retrieved if needed. It also allows for a clear audit trail of all modifications made to the system.

- **Continuous integration (CI)**: CI is a prerequisite for CD. In CI, developers integrate code into a shared repository frequently, and each integration is verified by an automated build and test process. This practice helps detect issues early, prevents integration problems, and keeps the codebase in a healthy state.

- **Test automation**: Automated testing is essential in CD to ensure the reliability and stability of the software. A comprehensive suite of automated tests, including unit tests, integration tests, and end-to-end tests, is executed at various stages of the pipeline. This testing ensures that code changes do not introduce new bugs and that the software behaves as expected.

- **Frequent and small deployments**: CD encourages small, incremental changes that are easier to test, review, and deploy. This approach reduces the risk associated with large, complex deployments and allows for quicker feedback and issue resolution.

- **Continuous monitoring and feedback**: Monitoring is critical to CD. By continuously monitoring the application and infrastructure, teams can detect issues in real time and respond swiftly. Monitoring also provides valuable feedback on the performance and usage of the software, which can inform future improvements.

AWS CodePipeline basics

AWS CodePipeline is a fully managed continuous integration and CD service that automates the build, test, and deployment phases of your software release process. It enables developers and DevOps teams to model, visualize, and automate the steps needed to release software changes, ensuring the rapid and efficient delivery of high-quality applications. You can use AWS CodePipeline through the AWS CLI or a user-friendly UI within the AWS Console. The following figure, referenced from the official AWS documentation for CodePipeline, illustrates an example release process using CodePipeline:

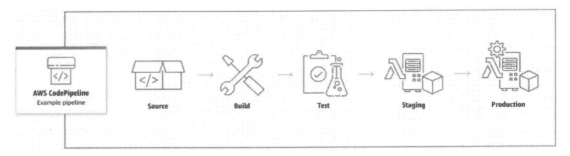

Figure 13.1: AWS CodePipeline stages

Let us now understand the different stages shown in the preceding figure:

- **Source**: The starting point where the source code is stored. This could be in a version control system like AWS CodeCommit (now deprecated), GitHub, S3 bucket or Bitbucket. It is represented by a cloud icon.

- **Build**: The stage where the source code is compiled and built using a build tool like AWS CodeBuild. This stage ensures that the code is correctly compiled and ready for testing. It is represented by a wrench icon.

- **Test**: Automated tests are run on the built code to ensure it works correctly and meets quality standards. This stage helps catch any bugs or issues before the code is deployed further. It is represented by a test tube icon.

- **Staging**: The code is deployed to a staging environment, which is a replica of the production environment. This allows for further testing and validation to ensure the code works as expected in a live-like setting. It is represented by a server icon.

- **Production**: The final stage where the code is deployed to the live production environment, making it available to end users. This stage is represented by a gear icon, symbolizing the application being fully operational.

This is a very common scenario. We can add more stages to the preceding figure according to our requirements. Let us explore the additional stages that can be integrated into the pipeline structure:

- **Code quality checks**: This stage involves running static code analysis tools to ensure that the code adheres to coding standards and is free from common vulnerabilities. Tools like SonarQube can be integrated to perform these checks.

- **Security testing**: Incorporate security testing to identify and address potential security vulnerabilities in the code. This can include **dynamic application security testing (DAST)** and **static application security testing (SAST)**.

- **Integration testing**: After unit tests, you can add a stage for integration testing where multiple components of the application are tested together to ensure they work correctly as a whole.

- **User Acceptance testing (UAT)**: In this stage, the application is tested in an environment that mimics the production environment, and real users test the application to validate its functionality and performance.

- **Performance testing**: Adding a performance testing stage helps ensure that the application meets performance requirements under expected load Conditions. Tools like Apache JMeter or Gatling can be used for this purpose.

- **Approval gates**: Implement manual approval gates at critical points in the pipeline. This ensures that stakeholders review and approve changes before they move to the next stage or are deployed to production.

- **Canary deployment**: This stage involves deploying the new version of the application to a small subset of users to monitor its performance and gather feedback before a full-scale deployment.

- **Rollback mechanisms**: Integrate stages that enable quick rollback to a previous version in case of deployment failure or critical issues in the new release.

The following figure shows one more sample pipeline structure (referenced from the official AWS documentation) with some more stages:

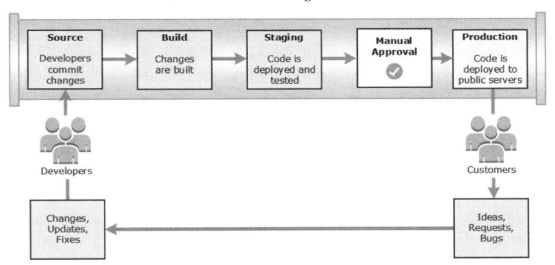

Figure 13.2: *AWS CodePipeline example*

This image represents a simplified **continuous integration/continuous deployment (CI/CD)** pipeline, which is a method used in software development to automate the process of deploying code changes. Here is a step-by-step explanation of the process depicted in *Figure 13.2*:

- **Source**: This is the first step in the pipeline. Developers make changes to the code and commit these changes to the source code repository.

- **Build**: The committed code changes are then built. This step involves compiling the code, running unit tests, and packaging the application.

- **Staging**: The built code is deployed to a staging environment. This environment is used for further testing, ensuring that the changes work as expected and do not introduce any new issues.

- **Manual approval**: Before the code is deployed to production, a manual approval step is included. This ensures that a human reviews the changes and approves them for production deployment.

- **Production**: Once approved, the code is deployed to the production environment, where it becomes available to end users (customers).

- **Feedback loop**:

  o End users interact with the deployed application in the production environment.

  o Customers provide feedback, which can include ideas for new features, requests for changes, or bug reports.

  o This feedback is sent back to the developers, who use it to make further changes, updates, and fixes, starting the cycle again.

The entire process forms a continuous loop where customer feedback informs ongoing development, ensuring that the application evolves in response to user needs and issues are promptly addressed.

> Note: This section covers the basics of AWS CodePipeline, providing a foundational understanding of how it can be used for continuous delivery. It illustrates the key stages involved, from committing changes to deploying code in production. While this gives a solid overview of CodePipeline's role in the CI/CD process, we will not dive deeper into CodePipeline as it is out of the scope of this book. However, in the next section, we will explore how CodePipeline can be integrated with AWS CloudFormation to facilitate continuous delivery, enabling automated and consistent deployment of infrastructure and applications.

CloudFormation Continuous delivery with CodePipeline

Until now we learned that AWS CodePipeline is a fully managed CI/CD service that helps you automate your release pipelines for fast and reliable application and infrastructure updates. It orchestrates the various stages involved in the software release process, from code changes to deployment, ensuring a smooth and efficient flow. By integrating CodePipeline with AWS CloudFormation, you can automate the deployment of your infrastructure as code, ensuring that your applications and environments are always in sync with your latest code changes. This powerful combination not only reduces the potential for human error but also accelerates the deployment process, enabling rapid iterations and improvements. This section will explore how to set up a CD pipeline using CodePipeline and CloudFormation, providing you with the tools and knowledge to streamline your deployment workflow and maintain consistency across your infrastructure.

Setting up the pipeline

Let us quickly review the different stages that can be integrated for the CD of a CloudFormation stack. Before we begin, it is essential to have a CloudFormation template ready.

Pre-requisite: Start by defining your infrastructure as code using a CloudFormation template. This YAML or JSON file describes the AWS resources you want to provision, such as EC2 instances, S3 buckets, IAM roles, and more. Ensure that your template is version controlled in a repository like GitHub or Bitbucket. It is important to validate your template to avoid syntax errors and ensure it meets your infrastructure requirements. Tools like the AWS CloudFormation Designer can help in visualizing and designing your stack.

Once the template is ready, we can proceed with configuring CodePipeline. While the detailed configuration will be covered in the next topic, let us look at the various stages that can be integrated for CloudFormation CD. Here are some essential stages that will form our CodePipeline structure:

- **Source stage**: The first stage in CodePipeline is the source stage, where your code repository is specified. CodePipeline will automatically detect changes in your repository and trigger the pipeline. You can integrate with S3, GitHub, Bitbucket or other supported version control systems.

- **Build stage**: Although it is not always necessary for infrastructure changes, you might include a build stage if you need to validate your CloudFormation templates or run tests. AWS CodeBuild can be used to perform these tasks, ensuring your templates are syntactically correct and compliant with your standards before deployment.

- **Deploy stage**: The deploy stage is where CodePipeline integrates with CloudFormation. You configure this stage to deploy your CloudFormation stack based on the template stored in your repository. When the pipeline reaches this stage, CodePipeline uses the AWS CloudFormation service to create or update the stack, provisioning the specified resources.

- **Manual approval stage**: Optionally, you can include a manual approval stage before the deploy stage. This allows a team member to review and approve the changes before they are applied to your production environment, adding an extra layer of oversight.

- **Production deployment**: In the final stage, your infrastructure changes are deployed to your production environment. CloudFormation handles the provisioning, updating, or deleting of resources as specified in your template, ensuring that your infrastructure matches the desired state.

These stages help automate the process of deploying and managing your AWS infrastructure, ensuring a consistent and reliable delivery pipeline.

Use case deployment

To illustrate the practical application of CD with CodePipeline and CloudFormation, let us consider a straightforward example where we deploy an EC2 instance using a CloudFormation template, with a CI/CD pipeline orchestrated through AWS CodePipeline. The goal is to automate the deployment of this infrastructure using AWS CodePipeline and AWS CloudFormation.

Steps to implement

Let us explore the steps required to implement continuous deployment using CodePipeline and CloudFormation:

1. **Define the CloudFormation template**: Create a CloudFormation template that outlines the essential components for setting up an EC2 instance. Following is a sample template we will use for this scenario. We are using default Parameter values suitable for our test environment, but these values can be adjusted according to your specific AWS account and region requirements:

   - AWSTemplateFormatVersion: '2010-09-09'
   - Description: Template to Create an
     EC2 instance in a VPC in us-east-1a region
   -
   - Parameters:
   -   ImageId:
   -     Type: String
   -     Description: 'Amazon Linux 2 AMI for us-east-1a region'
   -     Default: 'ami-0ae8f15ae66fe8cda'
   -   VpcId:
   -     Type: String
   -     Description: VPC id
   -     Default: vpc-03966c78
   -   PublicSubnetId:
   -     Type: String
   -     Description: Subnet in which to launch an EC2

- Default: subnet-af0d1ae4
- AvailabilityZone:
- Type: String
- Description: Availability Zone into which instance will launch
- Default: us-east-1a
- InstanceType:
- Type: String
- Description: Choosing t2 micro to start with free tier
- Default: t2.micro
- SSHKeyName:
- Description: SSH Keypair to login to the instance
- Type: AWS::EC2::KeyPair::KeyName
- Default: newkey
-
- Resources:
- DemoInstance:
- Type: 'AWS::EC2::Instance'
- Properties:
- ImageId: !Ref ImageId
- InstanceType: !Ref InstanceType
- AvailabilityZone: !Ref AvailabilityZone
- KeyName: !Ref SSHKeyName
- NetworkInterfaces:
- - DeviceIndex: '0'
- AssociatePublicIpAddress: true
- DeleteOnTermination: true
- SubnetId: !Ref PublicSubnetId
- GroupSet:
-   - !Ref DemoSecurityGroup
-
- DemoSecurityGroup:
- Type: 'AWS::EC2::SecurityGroup'
- Properties:
- VpcId: !Ref VpcId
- GroupDescription: SG to allow SSH access via port 22
- SecurityGroupIngress:
-   - IpProtocol: tcp

```
                        FromPort: 22
                        ToPort: 22
                        CidrIp: '0.0.0.0/0'
            Tags:
              - Key: Name
                Value: DemoStack

  Outputs:
    DemoInstanceId:
      Description: Instance Id
      Value: !Ref DemoInstance
```

The preceding template will let you create a **t2.micro** EC2 instance in a subnet inside a pre-created VPC. There are few pointers which we need to keep in mind:

- We will be using the S3 bucket as the source stage in our pipeline. So, to achieve the same, we need to zip the CloudFormation template file and upload it to the S3 bucket. For this example, we will name the template file **ec2-setup.yaml** and its zipped version **ec2-setup.yaml.zip**. We will upload this zip file to an S3 bucket named **cft-template-deployment**. By storing the template in an S3 bucket, CodePipeline can easily access and use it during the deployment process. Following is a supporting screenshot to demonstrate the upload process:

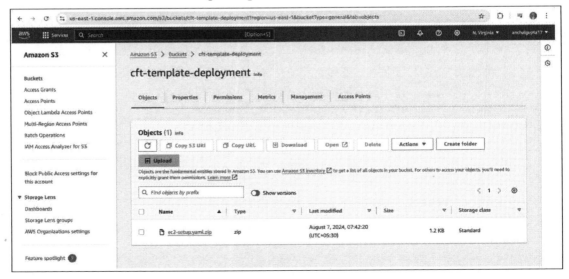

Figure 13.3: *Template uploaded to S3 bucket*

2. **Create a service role for CodePipeline**: Next, we will create a service role for CodePipeline to access the S3 bucket and deploy the CloudFormation template. To do this, navigate to the IAM console, select **Roles**, and click on **Create role**. You can refer to the following figure for more understanding on this:

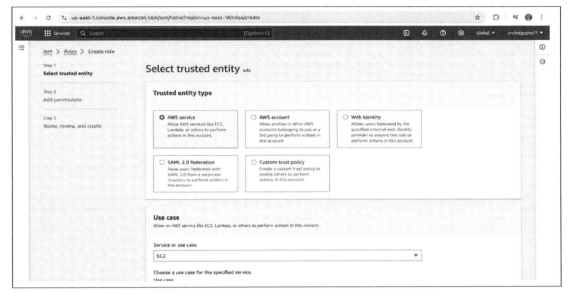

Figure 13.4: Role creation

3. We will select **AWS service** as the trusted entity. For the specific service or use case option, we will initially select **EC2** since there is no direct option for CodePipeline. We will modify it later to be used by CodePipeline. We will click on **Next** where we will get the option to add permissions policies. We will not add any permissions yet. Post this, we will again click on **Next**.

4. We will provide the relevant **Role name** here and will add the required description. Post this we will click on **Create role**. Please refer to the following figure:

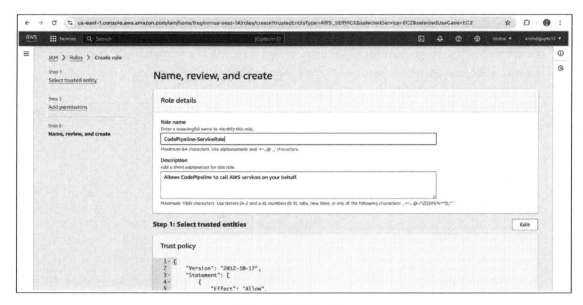

Figure 13.5: Role setup

5. Now we will again go back to the **Roles** and search for the newly created role **CodePipeline-ServiceRole**. We will now edit the role.

6. We will add the following inline customized policy in this role and will save it:

```
{
    "Statement": [
        {
            "Action": [
                "s3:GetObject",
                "s3:GetObjectVersion",
                "s3:GetBucketVersioning",
"s3:PutObject"
            ],
            "Resource": "arn:aws:s3:::codepipeline*",
            "Effect": "Allow"
        },
        {
            "Action": [
                "codedeploy:CreateDeployment",
                "codedeploy:GetApplicationRevision",
                "codedeploy:GetDeployment",
                "codedeploy:GetDeploymentConfig",
                "codedeploy:RegisterApplicationRevision"
```

```
        ],
        "Resource": "*",
        "Effect": "Allow"
    },
    {
        "Action": [
            "ec2:*",
            "cloudwatch:*",
            "s3:*",
            "sns:*",
            "cloudformation:*",
            "sqs:*",
            "sqs:*",
            "ecs:*",
            "iam:PassRole"
        ],
        "Resource": "*",
        "Effect": "Allow"
    },
    {
        "Action": [
            "lambda:InvokeFunction",
            "lambda:ListFunctions"
        ],
        "Resource": "*",
        "Effect": "Allow"
    },
    {
        "Action": [
            "cloudformation:CreateStack",
            "cloudformation:DeleteStack",
            "cloudformation:DescribeStacks",
            "cloudformation:UpdateStack",
            "cloudformation:CreateChangeSet",
            "cloudformation:DeleteChangeSet",
            "cloudformation:DescribeChangeSet",
            "cloudformation:ExecuteChangeSet",
            "cloudformation:SetStackPolicy",
            "cloudformation:ValidateTemplate",
            "iam:PassRole"
```

```
o                    ],
o                    "Resource": "*",
o                    "Effect": "Allow"
o                },
o                {
o                    "Action": [
o                        "codebuild:BatchGetBuilds",
o                        "codebuild:StartBuild"
o                    ],
o                    "Resource": "*",
o                    "Effect": "Allow"
o                }
o            ],
o            "Version": "2012-10-17"
o        }
```

7. Next, we will edit the trust relationship to change the trusted entity from EC2 to CodePipeline. This modification will complete the creation of the custom CodePipeline service role. Kindly refer to the following screenshot:

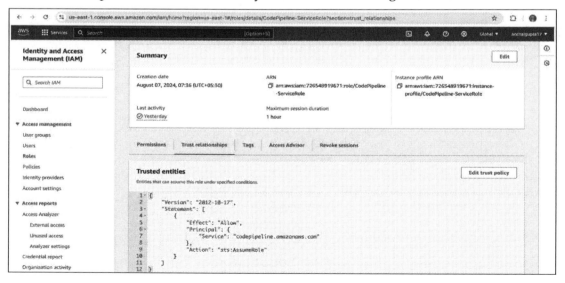

Figure 13.6: Trust relationship changes

8. **Create a service role for CloudFormation**: Next, we will set up a service role to allow CloudFormation to access the S3 bucket and deploy the template for configuring the EC2 instance in a VPC. To do this, go to the IAM console, choose **Roles**, and click **Create role**, as we did before. Then, follow the guidelines outlined to complete the role creation:

a. Select the service as **CloudFormation** and click **Next**.

b. On the next page, select the Permission Policies for AmazonEC2FullAccess and S3FullAccess. Click Next.

c. Provide the desired **Role name** along with the **Description**. Click on **Create role**.

Kindly refer to the following screenshots for preceding steps:

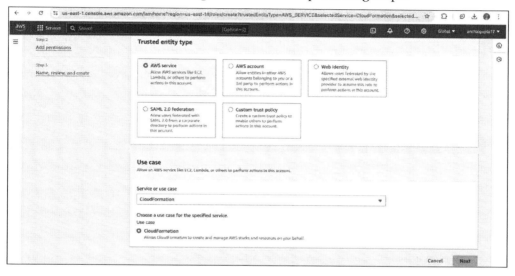

Figure 13.7: CloudFormation role setup (part one)

See the following figure for the next step:

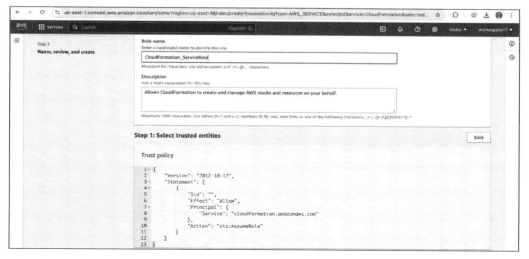

Figure 13.8: CloudFormation role setup (part two)

For further details, refer to the following figure:

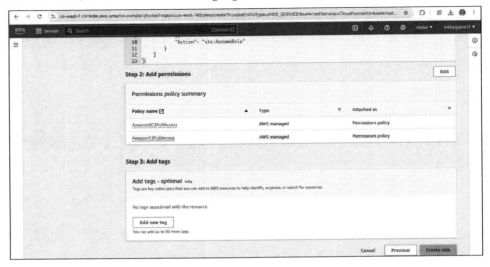

Figure 13.9: *CloudFormation role setup (part three)*

9. **Setup CodePipeline to deploy stack**: This is the last step where we will setup the CI/CD pipeline using AWS CodePipeline. To achieve this, follow the guidelines outlined:

   a. Navigate to the CodePipeline console and click on Create Pipeline. Enter **DemoCodePipeline-CFT-deployment** as the pipeline name. From the dropdown menu, select the role named **CodePipeline-ServiceRole**, which we created earlier.

   b. Click **Next**. Kindly refer to the following screenshot:

Figure 13.10: *Pipeline setup*

c. In the next step, select the **Source provider**. Since we are using an S3 bucket in this scenario, choose the S3 bucket option (**Amazon S3**) from the dropdown list. After selecting it, you will need to provide the **Bucket** name and **S3 object key**. Enter the required details, as shown in the following figure:

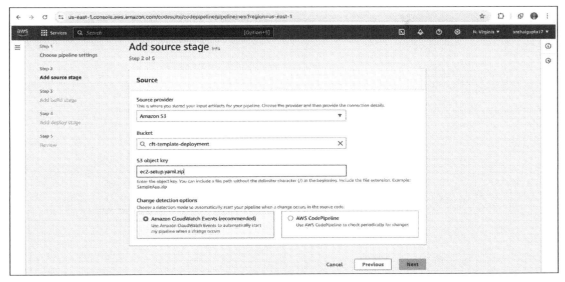

Figure 13.11: Add source stage

d. We will choose the default detection option, which is **Amazon CloudWatch Events**. Click on **Next**.

e. Skip the next build stage since we will not be building any code.

f. In the next step, we will provide the **Deploy provider** information. Here, we will select **AWS CloudFormation** from the drop-down menu. Refer to the following figures to fill in other necessary information:

Figure 13.12: Add deploy stage (part one)

For additional details, refer to the following figure:

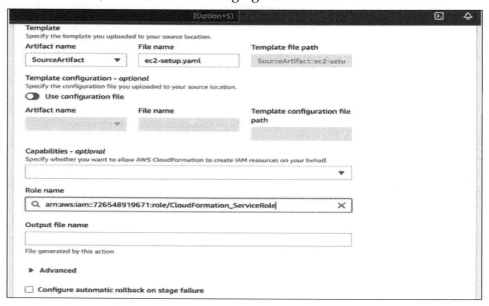

Figure 13.13: Add deploy stage (part two)

g. Click **Next** to proceed to the Review page, where you can review the configuration you have set up in the previous steps for the pipeline. Once done, we will click on Create pipeline.

h. This will trigger the two stage deployment pipeline. In stage one, it will read the CloudFormation template from the S3 bucket which we have specified.

i. In stage two it will deploy the EC2 instance as defined in the template. Kindly refer to the following figure for the same:

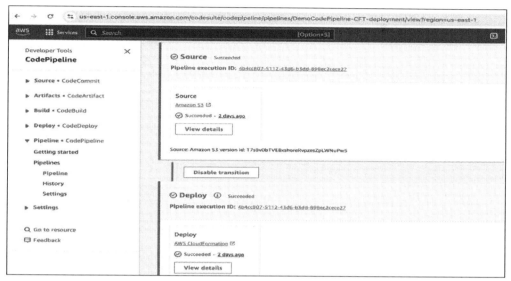

Figure 13.14: *Pipeline status*

j. Next, go to the CloudFormation console to verify that the stack has been deployed automatically. We will go to the **Events** to check the status. Refer to the following figure:

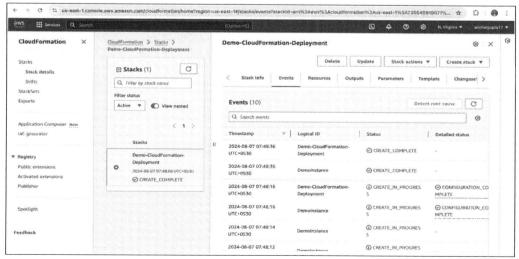

Figure 13.15: *Stack status check*

k. To further validate, we will navigate to the EC2 console page to check the status of EC2 instance:

Figure 13.16: EC2 instance validation

l. This concludes the CloudFormation CD process. Similarly, you can apply the concepts demonstrated in this example to design and execute similar pipelines for various CloudFormation stack deployment scenarios.

Conclusion

In this chapter, we explored the principles of CD and its integration with AWS services. We introduced AWS CodePipeline and its role in automating deployments, followed by how it integrates with CloudFormation to automate infrastructure provisioning. We also covered creating and deploying CloudFormation templates through CodePipeline, demonstrating a seamless workflow. To reinforce these concepts, we applied them to a real-world use case, showcasing practical CD implementation. With this foundation, we are now prepared to build effective CD pipelines using AWS tools. In the next chapter, we will focus on CloudFormation best practices, disaster recovery strategies, and template samples for various scenarios.

Multiple choice questions

1. **What is the primary goal of CD?**

   a. To automate code review processes.

   b. To deploy code only after manual approval

   c. To ensure that software can be released to production at any time

   d. To create infrastructure as code

2. **Which AWS service is primarily used to automate the steps required to release software?**

   a. AWS Codebuild

   b. AWS CodePipeline

    c. AWS CodeDeploy

    d. AWS CloudFormation

3. **How does CloudFormation integrate with CodePipeline for continuous delivery?**

    a. By building and testing the application code

    b. By monitoring the application performance in real-time

    c. By automating the deployment of infrastructure changes

    d. By storing application code in an S3 bucket

4. **Which of the following is a typical use case for deploying with AWS CodePipeline and CloudFormation?**

    a. Manual patching of production servers

    b. Automatic scaling of EC2 instances

    c. Automated deployment of a multi-tier web application

    d. Storing data backups in Amazon Glacier

5. **Which stage in AWS CodePipeline is responsible for deploying resources defined in a CloudFormation template?**

    a. Build stage

    b. Source stage

    c. Deploy stage

    d. Test stage

Answers

1. c

2. b

3. c

4. c

5. c

Join our book's Discord space

Join the book's Discord Workspace for Latest updates, Offers, Tech happenings around the world, New Release and Sessions with the Authors:

https://discord.bpbonline.com

CHAPTER 14

Best Practices and Sample Templates

Introduction

In this chapter, we will dive into the critical domain of CloudFormation best practices, offering a thorough examination to ensure that your IaC adheres to industry standards. Key considerations around disaster recovery are also explored, providing insights into safeguarding your deployments. Furthermore, we examine a range of pre-tested template samples designed for diverse use cases, all aimed at helping you optimize AWS CloudFormation deployments. This chapter serves as a practical guide to ensure robust, reliable, and efficient Cloud infrastructure management.

Structure

The chapter covers the following topics:

- CloudFormation best practices overview
- Disaster recovery
- Template samples for different use cases

Objectives

The goal of this chapter is to equip you with the foundational knowledge and skills necessary to implement CloudFormation best practices. You will gain an understanding of industry standards for IaC and learn essential strategies for disaster recovery in the context of AWS CloudFormation. Additionally, you will explore a range of pre-tested CloudFormation templates tailored to various use cases. Finally, you will see how to optimize your CloudFormation deployments, ensuring they are efficient, reliable, and aligned with best practices. By mastering these concepts, you will be able to create and maintain a robust, scalable, and well-architected Cloud infrastructure.

CloudFormation best practices overview

AWS CloudFormation is a powerful tool that allows you to define and manage your Cloud IaC. However, using CloudFormation effectively requires adherence to best practices that ensure your deployments are scalable, secure, and maintainable. This section outlines some of the most important best practices to follow when working with AWS CloudFormation, like:

- **Template organization and modularity**: A well-organized template is easier to manage, update, and debug. By breaking down larger templates into smaller, reusable components, you can improve clarity and maintainability. This approach allows for the separation of different resource types or logical sections of your infrastructure, making it easier to track changes and update specific parts. Following are some of the key tips for template organization:

   o Use Nested stacks for better resource grouping and reusability.

   o Follow a naming convention for Resources and Parameters to ensure consistency.

   o Store Parameters, Mappings, and Outputs in a logical order to improve readability.

- **Version control for templates**: Storing your CloudFormation templates in a **version control system** (**VCS**) like Git is essential for tracking changes and maintaining history. Version control allows you to revert to previous states, collaborate with teams, and ensure that your IaC evolves in a controlled and traceable manner. Let us have a look on the benefits of version control:

   o Enables collaboration and peer review.

   o Provides a history of changes, making it easier to troubleshoot issues.

   o Allows rollbacks in case of deployment failures.

- **Use Parameterization and Outputs**: Parameterization allows you to create dynamic templates that can be reused across different environments (for example, development, staging, and production). By externalizing values like AMI IDs, instance types, or VPC IDs, you can avoid hardcoding and promote template reuse.

Outputs are equally important, as they provide a way to export key values from one stack to another, improving integration between different parts of your infrastructure.

Some key benefits of using parameters and outputs are:

o Use Parameter constraints to validate input values.

o Limit the number of Parameters by using Mappings and conditions when possible.

o Export critical values such as VPC IDs, security group IDs, and resource ARN's for cross-stack references.

• **Implement resource policies and permissions**: Security is a fundamental aspect of any Cloud infrastructure, and CloudFormation is no exception. Ensuring that only authorized users can deploy, update, or delete resources is vital for maintaining the integrity of your infrastructure. Following are some of the key pointers:

o Use IAM roles with the least privilege access when deploying stacks.

o Define Resource policies to control who can interact with specific resources.

o Implement stack policies to protect critical resources from unintended updates.

• **Test and validate templates**: Before deploying a CloudFormation template in a production environment, it is crucial to validate and test it. AWS provides tools like the **aws cloudformation validate-template** command, which can catch syntactical errors before deployment. Additionally, performing test deployments in a staging environment allows you to identify and fix potential issues without impacting production. Some testing strategies are:

o Validate templates using the AWS CLI or management console before deployment.

o Use automated testing tools like AWS configuration and AWS CloudFormation Guard to ensure compliance with organizational policies.

o Implement integration tests to ensure resource dependencies and configurations work as expected.

• **Implement Change sets**: Change sets allow you to preview the modifications a template will make before applying them. This is especially useful for avoiding unintended updates, as CloudFormation will show you what resources will be created, modified, or deleted. Let us explore some of the benefits of using Change sets:

- o   Provides visibility into the impact of changes before they are applied.
- o   Allows teams to review proposed modifications in a collaborative environment.
- o   Reduces the risk of unintended downtime or resource disruption.

- **Monitor and roll back failures**: Monitoring your CloudFormation stacks is essential for detecting issues early and minimizing the impact of deployment failures. AWS CloudFormation provides built-in stack monitoring and rollback functionality, which automatically reverts any changes if a failure occurs during the deployment process. Following are some of the key pointers:
  - o   Enable stack rollback on failure to automatically revert changes when an error occurs.
  - o   Use AWS CloudWatch logs and events to track the status of your stack and monitor for anomalies.
  - o   Implement automated alerts to notify your team of any stack failures.

- **Optimize for cost and performance**: Infrastructure costs can quickly escalate if not properly managed, so it is crucial to optimize your CloudFormation stacks for both cost and performance. Ensure that you are provisioning resources efficiently and that unnecessary resources are not being deployed.

Some strategies for cost optimization are:

- o   Use AWS Trusted Advisor to identify cost saving opportunities.
- o   Implement auto-scaling for dynamic resource management.
- o   Regularly review and terminate unused resources.

Some strategies for the performance optimization are:

- o   Use CloudFormation stack policies to prevent unnecessary updates.
- o   Provision resources with the appropriate sizing and scaling strategies.
- o   Ensure that templates are well-architected to support high availability and fault tolerance.

Note: Adhering to CloudFormation best practices is essential for building secure, scalable, and maintainable Cloud infrastructure. By organizing templates, enforcing version control, testing, securing resources, and optimizing for performance and cost, you can ensure that your CloudFormation deployments align with industry standards and are resilient in the face of challenges. Following these guidelines will not only help you avoid common pitfalls but also enable your team to build Cloud environments that are robust, reliable, and efficient.

Disaster recovery

Disaster recovery (DR) is a critical component of any cloud infrastructure strategy, ensuring that your systems can quickly recover from unexpected failures such as data loss, hardware malfunctions, or cyber-attacks. AWS CloudFormation, as a service for managing IaC, plays a crucial role in implementing DR plans by automating the restoration and redeployment of resources in the event of a disaster.

In this section, we will look at the best practices and strategies for incorporating disaster recovery into your AWS CloudFormation deployments. We will focus on key areas such as backup and restore, failover mechanisms, and multi-region redundancy:

- **Backup and restore strategies**: Backup and restore are fundamental aspects of DR. AWS CloudFormation can be leveraged to automate backups of essential infrastructure components and their configurations, making it easier to restore the environment if needed.

  The best practices for backup and restore with CloudFormation are:

  - **Automate snapshots and backups**: Use AWS services like Amazon RDS, Amazon **Elastic Block Storage (EBS)**, and Amazon S3 to automate regular backups of critical data. CloudFormation can manage and automate the creation of these backups as a part of the stack lifecycle, ensuring that you always have recent data available for restoration.

  - **Store CloudFormation templates in version control**: Maintain all your CloudFormation templates in a VCS such as Git to ensure that you have a historical record of infrastructure changes. This makes it easier to revert to previous versions or restore environments to a known good state.

  - **Use stack outputs for quick restoration**: Use CloudFormation's Outputs feature to export key information such as database identifiers, VPC IDs, or security group ARNs. These outputs can be used to quickly recreate resources in case of a disaster.

- **Failover and high availability**: Failover mechanisms are important to minimize downtime and ensure high availability during a disaster. CloudFormation can help automate the setup of failover environments by deploying redundant infrastructure across multiple AWS AZs or regions.

  Best practices for failover with CloudFormation are:

  - **Deploy Multi-AZ architectures**: Use CloudFormation to design and deploy infrastructure that spans multiple AZs. Services like Amazon RDS, ELB, and Auto Scaling groups can be configured to distribute workloads across AZs, ensuring that your applications remain available even if one zone fails.

o **Implement Route 53 for failover**: AWS Route 53 DNS service can be configured with failover routing policies. You can use CloudFormation to automate the setup of Route 53 health checks and failover policies that route traffic to a backup environment in the event of a failure in the primary region.

o **Create standby stacks in secondary regions**: Deploy standby stacks in secondary AWS Regions that can be activated in case of a regional failure. This allows you to quickly shift traffic and workloads to another region without manual intervention.

- **Multi-region redundancy**: A critical aspect of disaster recovery is protecting against the failure of an entire AWS Region. CloudFormation supports multi-region deployments, allowing you to create infrastructure in multiple AWS Regions and distribute critical workloads across different geographic locations. This approach is vital for businesses with stringent uptime requirements.

Best practices for multi-region redundancy are:

o **Deploy duplicate stacks in multiple regions**: Use CloudFormation to automate the creation of identical infrastructure stacks in multiple AWS Regions. This ensures that in the event of a regional outage, you can fail over to the secondary region with minimal disruption.

o **S3 cross-region replication**: Configure Amazon S3 buckets for cross-region replication using CloudFormation. This ensures that any data stored in S3 is automatically copied to another region, providing geographic redundancy for your critical data.

o **Use CloudFormation StackSets**: AWS CloudFormation StackSets allows you to create, update, or delete stacks across multiple accounts and regions with a single operation. This makes it easier to manage multi-region deployments and ensure that your disaster recovery environments remain in sync with your primary infrastructure.

- **Automated rollbacks and failover testing**: Testing and validation are key components of a robust disaster recovery strategy. AWS CloudFormation provides tools to automate the rollback of failed deployments and the testing of failover scenarios, ensuring that your DR plan works as expected when disaster strikes.

Best practices for rollback and testing with CloudFormation are:

o **Enable automatic rollbacks**: When deploying CloudFormation stacks, enable automatic rollback on failure to ensure that if a deployment fails, CloudFormation will revert to the previous stable state. This prevents half-configured infrastructure from causing outages or additional failures.

    ○ **Test DR plans regularly**: Periodically test your failover and disaster recovery processes by simulating outages or region failures. Use CloudFormation to redeploy stacks in secondary regions and verify that failover mechanisms work as intended.

    ○ **Blue-green deployments for DR testing:** Implement blue-green deployment strategies with CloudFormation, where you create identical environments (blue and green) and switch between them for testing or recovery purposes. This approach allows you to test DR processes without impacting production workloads.

- **Monitoring and alerting**: Monitoring your disaster recovery environment is essential to ensure that your failover systems are working correctly and that any issues are detected early. AWS CloudFormation integrates with AWS CloudWatch to provide monitoring and alerting for stack events, making it easier to track the health of your infrastructure.

Best practices for monitoring and alerting:

    ○ **Set up CloudWatch alarms**: You can use CloudWatch alarms to monitor key metrics, such as CPU utilization, memory usage, or network traffic in your DR environment. CloudFormation can automate the creation of these alarms as part of your stack.

    ○ **Enable AWS configuration for compliance monitoring**: AWS configuration can monitor your resources for compliance with predefined rules, ensuring that your DR environment remains properly configured over time.

    ○ **Using AWS SNS for notifications**: Set up AWS SNS notifications to alert your team whenever a stack failure happens or when a failover is triggered. This ensures that your team is aware of any issues and can take action.

- Security considerations in DR: Security is key when recovering from a disaster, as downtime can expose your infrastructure to vulnerabilities or data breaches. Ensuring that security policies are enforced during and after disaster recovery is crucial.

Some best practices for security in DR are:

    ○ **IAM role and policy replication**: Ensure that IAM roles and policies are replicated across regions as part of your DR strategy. Use CloudFormation templates to ensure consistent permissions and avoid security gaps during failover.

    ○ **Encrypt data at rest and in transit**: Configure encryption for all data stored in AWS services, including S3, RDS, and EBS. CloudFormation can enforce these encryption policies, ensuring that sensitive data remains secure during backup, failover, and recovery.

o **Secure cross-region replication**: Make sure that any data replicated across regions—such as S3 buckets, DynamoDB tables, or RDS databases—is encrypted and transmitted securely. AWS **Key Management Service (KMS)** keys can be used for cross-region replication, managed via CloudFormation.

- **Data durability and backup**: Beyond automating infrastructure, data durability is important for a comprehensive DR strategy. While AWS provides durable storage options, CloudFormation can help manage data redundancy and backups.

Some best practices for data durability and backups are:

o **Leverage RDS read replicas**: Create Amazon RDS read replicas in different regions using CloudFormation to ensure that your database remains available in case of a regional failure. These replicas can be promoted to standalone instances in case of primary database failure.

o **Amazon DynamoDB global tables**: For highly available, globally distributed databases, consider using DynamoDB global tables. You can automate the provisioning of these tables using CloudFormation, ensuring low latency reads and writes across multiple regions.

o **Automate backup and retention policies**: Use CloudFormation to enforce backup and retention policies for data stored in RDS, DynamoDB, and other AWS services. For example, you can define automated snapshots and specify retention durations for EBS volumes and RDS databases.

- **Compliance and auditing**: For many industries, maintaining compliance with standards, such as HIPAA, GDPR, or PCI-DSS during DR, is crucial. CloudFormation can enforce compliance rules and provide auditability across your infrastructure.

Some best practices for compliance and auditing are:

o **AWS configuration rules for compliance**: Use AWS configuration in conjunction with CloudFormation to monitor compliance with your organization's security and governance policies. CloudFormation can automatically deploy configuration rules that track resource changes and validate them against compliance requirements.

o **Auditing changes with CloudTrail**: AWS CloudTrail can be configured to log all changes to your CloudFormation stacks, providing an audit trail for compliance purposes. This ensures that any changes made during disaster recovery are documented and can be reviewed during audits.

o **Define and enforce tagging policies**: Use CloudFormation to enforce a consistent tagging strategy across your infrastructure, ensuring that all resources are properly categorized for compliance, cost allocation, and security.

Note: Incorporating DR into your AWS CloudFormation strategy ensures that your infrastructure is resilient, secure, and prepared for unexpected failures. By leveraging automated deployments, multi-region redundancy, failover mechanisms, data protection strategies, and cost-efficient solutions, you can create a robust disaster recovery plan that minimizes downtime and ensures business continuity. By following these enhanced best practices, your organization will be able to recover quickly and efficiently in the face of any disaster, all while maintaining security, compliance, and operational readiness.

Template samples for different use cases

In this section, we will explore a variety of sample templates designed for different use cases, showcasing how CloudFormation can be utilized to deploy a wide range of AWS services for common infrastructure requirements. A few examples of these use cases are:

- **Basic VPC setup template**: A VPC is the foundation of any AWS network architecture. Setting up a basic VPC with subnets, route tables, and gateways is one of the most common use cases. The sample template for a basic VPC setup is as follows:

  - AWSTemplateFormatVersion: 2010-09-09
  -
  - Resources:
  - # VPC
  - NetworkVPC:
  -   Type: AWS::EC2::VPC
  -   Properties:
  -     CidrBlock: 10.1.0.0/16
  -     EnableDnsSupport: true
  -     EnableDnsHostnames: true
  -     Tags:
  -       - Key: Name
  -         Value: !Join ['',
    [!Ref "AWS::StackName", "-NetworkVPC"]]
  -
  -   # Internet Gateway
  -   NetInternetGateway:
  -   Type: AWS::EC2::InternetGateway
  -
  -   GatewayAttachment:
  -     Type: AWS::EC2::VPCGatewayAttachment
  -     Properties:

```yaml
    VpcId: !Ref NetworkVPC
    InternetGatewayId: !Ref NetInternetGateway

  # Public Subnet
  PubSubnetA:
    Type: AWS::EC2::Subnet
    Properties:
      VpcId: !Ref NetworkVPC
      CidrBlock: 10.1.10.0/24
      AvailabilityZone: !Select [0, !GetAZs '']
      Tags:
        - Key: Name
          Value: !Sub ${AWS::StackName}-PubSubnet-A

  # Private Subnet
  PrivSubnetA:
    Type: AWS::EC2::Subnet
    Properties:
      VpcId: !Ref NetworkVPC
      CidrBlock: 10.1.50.0/24
      AvailabilityZone: !Select [0, !GetAZs '']
      Tags:
        - Key: Name
          Value: !Sub ${AWS::StackName}-PrivSubnet-A

  # Public Route Table and Route
  PublicRoute:
    Type: AWS::EC2::RouteTable
    Properties:
      VpcId: !Ref NetworkVPC
      Tags:
        - Key: Name
          Value: PublicRoute

  PublicRouteRule:
    Type: AWS::EC2::Route
    DependsOn: GatewayAttachment
    Properties:
      RouteTableId: !Ref PublicRoute
```

```yaml
        DestinationCidrBlock: 0.0.0.0/0
        GatewayId: !Ref NetInternetGateway

    # Private Route Table and Route
    PrivateRoute:
      Type: AWS::EC2::RouteTable
      Properties:
        VpcId: !Ref NetworkVPC
        Tags:
          - Key: Name
            Value: PrivateRoute

    PrivateRouteRule:
      Type: AWS::EC2::Route
      DependsOn: NetworkNATGateway
      Properties:
        RouteTableId: !Ref PrivateRoute
        DestinationCidrBlock: 0.0.0.0/0
        NatGatewayId: !Ref NetworkNATGateway

    # Subnet Route Table Associations
    PubSubnetARouteAssoc:
      Type: AWS::EC2::SubnetRouteTableAssociation
      Properties:
        SubnetId: !Ref PubSubnetA
        RouteTableId: !Ref PublicRoute

    PrivSubnetARouteAssoc:
      Type: AWS::EC2::SubnetRouteTableAssociation
      Properties:
        SubnetId: !Ref PrivSubnetA
        RouteTableId: !Ref PrivateRoute

    # NAT Gateway and Elastic IP
    ElasticIP:
      Type: AWS::EC2::EIP
      Properties:
        Domain: VPC
```

```
• NetworkNATGateway:
•     Type: AWS::EC2::NatGateway
•     DependsOn: ElasticIP
•     Properties:
•         AllocationId: !GetAtt ElasticIP.AllocationId
•         SubnetId: !Ref PubSubnetA
•         Tags:
•             - Key: Name
•               Value: !Sub NAT-${AWS::StackName}
```

This AWS CloudFormation template defines the creation of a basic networking infrastructure in AWS by deploying a VPC with both public and private subnets across a AZ. It also configures an **internet gateway (IGW)** for outbound internet access from public subnets and a **network address translation (NAT)** gateway for egress traffic from private subnets. This is a typical architecture for securely running Cloud applications that require internet connectivity while keeping critical resources isolated.

- **EC2 instance with Apache web server**: The EC2 instance with Apache web server use case involves deploying an EC2 instance configured to serve web traffic using the Apache HTTP Server. This setup is ideal for hosting simple websites or web applications. The CloudFormation template can automate the installation and configuration of Apache on the instance, enabling it to handle HTTP requests. This use case is suitable for static websites, basic web hosting, or serving front-end components in a larger application architecture. Following is the sample template for the basic setup:

```
• AWSTemplateFormatVersion: 2010-09-09
•
• # This CloudFormation template will setup an EC2 instance with
•   apache server installed on it. The default region is us-east-1.
•
• Resources:
•   EC2Apache:
•     Type: AWS::EC2::Instance
•     Properties:
•       ImageId: ami-0ae8f15ae66fe8cda
•       InstanceType: t2.micro
•       Tags:
•         - Key: Env
•           Value: Test
•         - Key: Name
•           Value: Web Server
```

```
        •               UserData: !Base64
        •                 Fn::Sub: |
        •                   #!/bin/sh
        •                   yum update -y
        •                   yum install httpd.x86_64 -y
        •                   systemctl start httpd.service
        •                   systemctl enable httpd.service
        •                   echo «Hello World» > /var/www/html/index.html
        •               SecurityGroups:
        •                 - !Ref SecGrp
        •               KeyName: apache
        •
        •       SecGrp:
        •         Type: AWS::EC2::SecurityGroup
        •         Properties:
        •           GroupName: EC2 Group
        •           GroupDescription: EC2 Group
        •           SecurityGroupIngress:
        •             - IpProtocol: tcp
        •               CidrIp: 0.0.0.0/0
        •               FromPort: 22
        •               ToPort: 22
        •             - IpProtocol: tcp
        •               CidrIp: 0.0.0.0/0
        •               FromPort: 80
        •               ToPort: 80
        •             - IpProtocol: tcp
        •               CidrIp: 0.0.0.0/0
        •               FromPort: 443
        •               ToPort: 443
```

This CloudFormation template sets up an EC2 instance with an Apache web server pre-installed. It provisions a **t2.micro** instance using a specified AMI and installs Apache through the **UserData** script. The template also configures the Apache web server to start automatically and serves a simple **Hello World** page. Additionally, it creates a security group to allow inbound SSH (port 22), HTTP (port 80), and HTTPS (port 443) traffic, making the web server accessible over the internet. This setup is ideal for quickly deploying a basic web server for development or testing purposes.

- **Simple S3 bucket setup with encryption and versioning**: The S3 bucket use case involves creating an S3 bucket configured to store data with optional encryption and versioning. This setup is ideal for securely managing data, including backups, logs, or application assets. The CloudFormation template automates the bucket creation, enabling default encryption with AES-256 and object versioning to track data changes. This use case is suitable for long-term data storage, data recovery, or managing file versions in a scalable environment. Following is the sample template for the basic setup:

```yaml
AWSTemplateFormatVersion: '2010-09-09'
Parameters:

  BucketName:
    Type: String
    Description: Specify the S3 Bucket.
    AllowedPattern: "^([a-z0-9]{1}[a-z0-9-]{1,61}[a-z0-9]{1})$"
    ConstraintDescription: "Bucket names must be between 3
and 63 characters, start and end with a letter or number."

  Encryption:
    Type: String
    Description: Enable default encryption for the S3 bucket.
    AllowedValues:
      - "true"
      - "false"
    Default: "true"

  Versioning:
    Type: String
    Description: Enable or suspend versioning
for objects in the S3 bucket.
    AllowedValues:
      - "Enabled"
      - "Suspended"
    Default: "Suspended"

Resources:

  S3Bucket:
    Type: AWS::S3::Bucket
    Properties:
      BucketName: !Ref BucketName
      VersioningConfiguration:
```

```
    •           Status: !Ref Versioning
    •         BucketEncryption:
    •           !If
    •             - IsEncrypted
    •             - ServerSideEncryptionConfiguration:
    •                 - ServerSideEncryptionByDefault:
    •                     SSEAlgorithm: AES256
    •             - !Ref "AWS::NoValue"
    •
    •   Conditions:
    •     IsEncrypted: !Equals [!Ref Encryption, "true"]
    •
    •   Outputs:
    •
    •     BucketURL:
    •       Description: "URL for accessing the S3 bucket"
    •       Value: !Join ['', ["https://", !GetAtt S3Bucket.
    •   DomainName]]
    •
    •     BucketARN:
    •       Description: "ARN of the S3 bucket"
    •       Value: !GetAtt S3Bucket.Arn
```

This template allows you to provision an S3 bucket with custom parameters for bucket name, versioning, and encryption settings. The user can choose whether to enable encryption using AES-256 and manage object versioning for better data control. The bucket's URL and ARN are provided upon creation for easy reference and integration with other AWS.

- **Amazon RDS setup**: This use case involves deploying an Amazon RDS instance configured with the MySQL engine. The template automates the creation of a database instance, allowing users to define critical parameters, such as the database name, master username, and password. This setup is ideal for hosting relational databases in the Cloud, providing a managed MySQL environment with minimal manual configuration. Following is the template for the same:

```
  •   AWSTemplateFormatVersion: '2010-09-09'
  •
  •   Parameters:
  •     myDbName:
  •       Type: String
  •       Description: "The name of the database."
```

```
    myDbUser:
      Type: String
      Description: "The master username for the database."
    myDbPass:
      Type: String
      NoEcho: true
      MinLength: 8
      MaxLength: 41
      Description: "The master user password for the database.
Must be between 8 and 41 characters."

  Resources:
    SQLDemoDbInstance:
      Type: AWS::RDS::DBInstance
      Properties:
        DBName: !Ref myDbName
        MasterUsername: !Ref myDbUser
        MasterUserPassword: !Ref myDbPass
        Engine: MySQL
        DBInstanceClass: db.t3.micro
        StorageType: gp2
        PubliclyAccessible: true
        AllocatedStorage: "20"
        DBInstanceIdentifier: !Sub
"SQLDemoDbInstance-${AWS::Region}"
        MultiAZ: false
        BackupRetentionPeriod: 7
        AvailabilityZone: !Select [1, !GetAZs ""]

  Outputs:
    DBInstanceEndpoint:
      Description: "RDS MySQL Database Endpoint"
      Value: !GetAtt SQLDemoDbInstance.Endpoint.Address
```

The CloudFormation template provisions an RDS MySQL instance using the **db.t3.micro** instance class, which is suitable for small-scale applications or development environments. Key features of the template include user defined database credentials, automatic backup retention for seven days, and the option to make the database publicly accessible. The template also supports custom database naming, storage configuration with 20 GB of general-purpose (**gp2**) storage, and multi-AZ deployment options (though set to **false** by default). The resulting RDS instance is provided with an output for its endpoint, making it easy to integrate into applications.

- **Deploy a serverless static website using AWS CloudFront and S3 bucket**: This use case includes the deployment of a static website using Amazon S3 for storage and Amazon CloudFront for content distribution. It integrates seamlessly with Route 53 for DNS management, allowing users to host a static website with their custom domain and secure the site with an **Secure Sockets Layer (SSL)** certificate. This setup ensures fast global content delivery, security via HTTPS, and error handling with a custom error page. Following is the template for the same in us-east-1 region:

  - AWSTemplateFormatVersion: 2010-09-09
  - Description: Static website hosting with S3 and CloudFront with a custom domain.
  - Parameters:
    - Cert:
    - Description: SSL Certificate ARN
    - Type: String
    - HostedZoneResourceID:
    - Description: Hosted Zone ID
    - Type: String
    - DomainName:
    - Description: Website Domain Name
    - Type: String
    - ErrorPagePath:
    - Description: Directory error path
    - Type: String
    - Default: /error.html
    - IndexDocument:
    - Description: Directory index path
    - Type: String
    - Default: /index.html
    -
  - Resources:
    - S3Bucket:
    - Type: "AWS::S3::Bucket"
    - Properties:
      - BucketName: !Sub ${DomainName}-cloudfront
    - CloudFrontOriginAccessIdentity:

```yaml
      Type: "AWS::CloudFront::CloudFrontOriginAccessIdentity"
    Properties:
      CloudFrontOriginAccessIdentityConfig:
        Comment: !Ref S3Bucket
  ReadPolicy:
    Type: "AWS::S3::BucketPolicy"
    Properties:
      Bucket: !Ref S3Bucket
      PolicyDocument:
        Statement:
          - Action: "s3:GetObject"
            Effect: Allow
            Resource:
              - !Sub "${S3Bucket.Arn}"
              - !Sub "${S3Bucket.Arn}/*"
            Principal:
              CanonicalUser: !GetAtt
  CloudFrontOriginAccessIdentity.S3CanonicalUserId
  CloudFrontDistribution:
    Type: "AWS::CloudFront::Distribution"
    Properties:
      DistributionConfig:
        Aliases:
          - !Ref DomainName
        ViewerCertificate:
          AcmCertificateArn: !Ref Cert
          SslSupportMethod: sni-only
        CustomErrorResponses:
          - ErrorCode: 403
            ResponseCode: 404
            ResponsePagePath: !Ref ErrorPagePath
        DefaultCacheBehavior:
          AllowedMethods:
            - GET
            - HEAD
            - OPTIONS
          CachedMethods:
            - GET
```

```
                        - HEAD
                        - OPTIONS
                    Compress: true
                    DefaultTTL: 3600
                    ForwardedValues:
                        Cookies:
                            Forward: none
                        QueryString: false
                    MaxTTL: 86400
                    MinTTL: 120
                    TargetOriginId: s3origin
                    ViewerProtocolPolicy: redirect-to-https
                DefaultRootObject: "index.html"
                Enabled: true
                HttpVersion: http2
                Origins:
                    - DomainName: !GetAtt S3Bucket.DomainName
                      Id: s3origin
                      S3OriginConfig:
                          OriginAccessIdentity: !Sub >-
                              origin-access-
      identity/cloudfront/${CloudFrontOriginAccessIdentity}
                PriceClass: PriceClass_All
    User:
        Type: "AWS::IAM::User"
        Properties:
            Policies:
                - PolicyName: !Sub "publish-to-${S3Bucket}"
                  PolicyDocument:
                      Statement:
                          - Action: "s3:*"
                            Effect: Allow
                            Resource:
                                - !Sub "${S3Bucket.Arn}"
                                - !Sub "${S3Bucket.Arn}/*"
    DNSRecord:
        Type: AWS::Route53::RecordSet
        Properties:
```

- HostedZoneId: !Ref HostedZoneResourceID
- Comment: DNS name for cloud front
- Name: !Ref DomainName
- Type: A
- AliasTarget:
- HostedZoneId: Z2FDTNDATAQYW2
- DNSName: !GetAtt CloudFrontDistribution. DomainName
- DependsOn: CloudFrontDistribution
-
- Outputs:
- BucketName:
- Description: S3 Bucket Name
- Value: !Ref S3Bucket
- URL:
- Description: Website URL
- Value: !Ref DNSRecord

The template provides an S3 bucket to store website files, a CloudFront distribution for caching and distributing content globally, and a Route 53 DNS record for associating a custom domain with the CloudFront distribution. An IAM user is also created to enable secure publishing of content to the S3 bucket. The CloudFront distribution is secured with an SSL certificate, and the template enforces HTTPS for all website traffic. It supports custom error pages and an index document, making it ideal for hosting static websites with a professional domain and enhanced security.

- **SNS topic with email subscription**: This use case involves setting up an Amazon SNS topic that automatically sends notifications via email whenever a specific event occurs, making it ideal for alerting and communication purposes in Cloud infrastructure. Following is the sample template for the same:
  - AWSTemplateFormatVersion: '2010-09-09'
  - Description: SNS Topic with an email subscription for notifications.
  -
  - Parameters:
  - EmailAddress:
  - Type: String
  - Description: Email address to receive notifications
  -
  - Resources:

- MySNSTopic:
- Type: AWS::SNS::Topic
- Properties:
- DisplayName: "MyNotificationTopic"
-
- MySubscription:
- Type: AWS::SNS::Subscription
- Properties:
- TopicArn: !Ref MySNSTopic
- Protocol: email
- Endpoint: !Ref EmailAddress

This template creates an SNS topic and an email subscription, allowing users to receive notifications when events are published on the topic. It simplifies the process of setting up automated alerts for monitoring, security, or operational events by sending email notifications to the specified address whenever the topic is triggered.

- **SQS queue with dead-letter queue**: This use case can create an SQS queue with a **dead-letter queue (DLQ)**. The dead-letter queue is used to capture messages that fail to be processed after a defined number of attempts, ensuring that unprocessable messages do not get lost and can be reviewed and retried later. This setup is ideal for improving fault tolerance and managing message failures in distributed systems. Following is the template for the same:
  - AWSTemplateFormatVersion: '2010-09-09'
  - Description: SQS Queue with a Dead Letter Queue (DLQ).
  -
  - Resources:
  - MyQueue:
  - Type: AWS::SQS::Queue
  - Properties:
  - QueueName: MyQueue
  - RedrivePolicy:
  - deadLetterTargetArn: !GetAtt MyDeadLetterQueue.Arn
  - maxReceiveCount: 5
  -
  - MyDeadLetterQueue:
  - Type: AWS::SQS::Queue
  - Properties:
  - QueueName: MyDeadLetterQueue

This CloudFormation template sets up an Amazon SQS queue along with a DLQ to handle messages that fail to process successfully. The primary queue is configured with a redrive policy that routes messages to the DLQ after a specified number of failed processing attempts (in this case, five). The DLQ allows for better error handling and ensures that failed messages can be retained for further inspection or reprocessing, making it a robust solution for fault-tolerant message queuing systems.

- **Amazon Kinesis Data Stream setup**: This use case performs the setup of Amazon Kinesis, a powerful service that allows developers to collect, process, and analyze real-time data streams at a massive scale. With Amazon Kinesis Data Streams, organizations can build applications that process or analyze streaming data for use cases, such as log and event data collection, real-time analytics, and continuous monitoring. Automating the setup of Kinesis Data Streams using AWS CloudFormation ensures that the deployment is consistent, repeatable, and easily manageable, fitting seamlessly into IaC workflows. The sample template for the same is as follows:

```
AWSTemplateFormatVersion: '2010-09-09'
Description: CloudFormation template to create an
Amazon Kinesis Data Stream

Resources:
  KinesisDataStream:
    Type: AWS::Kinesis::Stream
    Properties:
      Name: MyKinesisDataStream
      ShardCount: 1  # Number of shards,
adjust as per requirements

  KinesisStreamIAMRole:
    Type: AWS::IAM::Role
    Properties:
      RoleName: KinesisStreamRole
      AssumeRolePolicyDocument:
        Version: '2012-10-17'
        Statement:
          - Effect: Allow
            Principal:
              Service:
                - kinesis.amazonaws.com
            Action: sts:AssumeRole
```

```
•          Policies:
•            - PolicyName: KinesisStreamPolicy
•              PolicyDocument:
•                Version: '2012-10-17'
•                Statement:
•                  - Effect: Allow
•                    Action:
•                      - kinesis:DescribeStream
•                      - kinesis:GetRecords
•                      - kinesis:GetShardIterator
•                      - kinesis:PutRecord
•                      - kinesis:PutRecords
•                    Resource:
•                      !GetAtt KinesisDataStream.Arn
•
•  Outputs:
•    KinesisStreamName:
•      Description: Name of the Kinesis Data Stream
•      Value: !Ref KinesisDataStream
•
•    KinesisStreamArn:
•      Description: ARN of the Kinesis Data Stream
•      Value: !GetAtt KinesisDataStream.Arn
```

The preceding CloudFormation template is designed to automate the creation and configuration of an Amazon Kinesis Data Stream. The template provisions a Kinesis Data Stream with a customizable number of shards, enabling applications to ingest, store, and process large volumes of real-time data. In addition to the stream itself, the template also sets up an IAM role with the necessary permissions to interact with the stream. This role allows actions like adding data to the stream and reading records, which are essential for stream processing tasks. By using this template, teams can quickly establish a robust Kinesis data pipeline, simplifying real-time data handling for a wide variety of applications, such as log aggregation, event-driven architecture, and real-time data analysis.

- **Deploying a simple AWS Lambda function**: This use case demonstrates how to deploy a simple AWS Lambda function using CloudFormation. AWS Lambda is a serverless compute service that allows you to run code without provisioning or managing servers. In this example, we deploy a Lambda function that returns a **Hello, World!** message using Node.js runtime, showcasing the simplicity and efficiency of serverless architecture. The sample template for the same is as follows:

```yaml
AWSTemplateFormatVersion: '2010-09-09'
Description: CloudFormation template to create a simple
AWS Lambda function that returns "Hello, World!".

Resources:
  MyLambdaFunction:
    Type: AWS::Lambda::Function
    Properties:
      FunctionName: SimpleHelloWorldFunction
      Handler: index.handler
      Role: !GetAtt LambdaExecutionRole.Arn
      Runtime: nodejs18.x
      Code:
        ZipFile: |
          exports.handler = async (event) => {
            const response = {
              statusCode: 200,
              body: JSON.stringify(<Hello, World!>),
            };
            return response;
          };

  LambdaExecutionRole:
    Type: AWS::IAM::Role
    Properties:
      AssumeRolePolicyDocument:
        Version: '2012-10-17'
        Statement:
          - Effect: Allow
            Principal:
              Service: lambda.amazonaws.com
            Action: 'sts:AssumeRole'
      Policies:
        - PolicyName: LambdaBasicExecution
          PolicyDocument:
            Version: '2012-10-17'
            Statement:
              - Effect: Allow
                Action:
```

```
              -  'logs:CreateLogGroup'
              -  'logs:CreateLogStream'
              -  'logs:PutLogEvents'
             Resource: 'arn:aws:logs:*:*:*'

  Outputs:
    LambdaFunctionName:
      Description: "The name of the Lambda function"
      Value: !Ref MyLambdaFunction

    LambdaFunctionARN:
      Description: "The ARN of the Lambda function"
      Value: !GetAtt MyLambdaFunction.Arn
```

The CloudFormation template provisions a basic Lambda function with the Node. js 18.x runtime. The function is granted the necessary permissions through an IAM role to write logs to Amazon CloudWatch. The Lambda function's code is embedded directly in the template, and it returns a **Hello, World!** message upon invocation. This use case is perfect for understanding how to set up a Lambda function with minimal configuration and demonstrates the fundamental concepts of serverless functions within AWS.

Conclusion

In conclusion, this chapter has covered key topics essential to effectively managing AWS infrastructure using CloudFormation. We started with an overview of CloudFormation best practices, focusing on strategies to ensure that your templates are secure, scalable, and aligned with industry standards. Next, we explored DR, discussing how CloudFormation can automate recovery processes and ensure high availability and resilience in case of failure. Finally, we examined template samples for different use cases, providing practical examples that demonstrate how CloudFormation can be leveraged across various scenarios to simplify infrastructure deployment and management.

Multiple choice questions

1. **What is one of the key best practices when writing CloudFormation templates?**

    a. Avoid using comments in the template.

    b. Hard-code resource names and IDs.

    c. Use parameters for flexible configurations.

    d. Always use the same instance type for all resources.

2. **Which of the following is a recommended practice for improving template readability and maintainability?**

   a. Avoid using conditions.

   b. Break large templates into multiple smaller templates.

   c. Use single line comments.

   d. Use complex logical operators in all templates.

3. **In disaster recovery best practices, which CloudFormation feature is often utilized to automate failover processes?**

   a. Cross-stack references.

   b. Stack updates.

   c. Backup policies.

   d. StackSets

4. **Which of the following is a key advantage of using CloudFormation templates for different use cases?**

   a. It requires manual intervention for every resource creation.

   b. It allows you to provision and manage resources consistently and repeatedly.

   c. It does not support rollback if the stack creation fails.

   d. It can only be used for creating EC2 instances.

Answers

1. c
2. b
3. d
4. b

Join our book's Discord space

Join the book's Discord Workspace for Latest updates, Offers, Tech happenings around the world, New Release and Sessions with the Authors:

https://discord.bpbonline.com

Index

Printed in Great Britain
by Amazon

55995067R00220